Darwin's Noublelden
— p. 229

9-19, 32-68, 123-50

The Ruling Race

THE
RULING RACE

*A History of American
Slaveholders*

by JAMES OAKES

Vintage Books
A Division of Random House
New York

Library of Congress Cataloging in Publication Data
Oakes, James.
The ruling race.
Bibliography: p.
Includes index.
1. Slaveholders—Southern States.
2. Slavery—Southern States.
3. Southern States—Social conditions.
I. Title.
[E441.O18 1983]   975   83-3472
ISBN 0-394-71639-6 (pbk.)

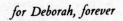

for Deborah, forever

Contents

Introduction

IN RECENT YEARS the history of slavery has been illuminated by a succession of often brilliant studies of Afro-American life and culture. Much work remains to be done; yet, paradoxically, we now know more about the daily experience of the typical slave than we do about the typical slaveholder, not to mention the non-slaveholding white. As I surveyed the literature on the slaveholders, I found virtually no description of what the average slaveholder thought about each day, what his religious principles were, and what they meant to his life. I did not know how a slaveholder became a slaveholder, nor did I fully understand what slavery meant to an aspiring young master. I was not even sure what a typical slaveholder was. Finally, I had almost no idea how any of these—the slaveholders' religion, politics, view of slavery, typicality—changed over time. It was in part in recognition of this paradox that I undertook this study.

There were about 400,000 slaveholders in the South in 1860. In setting out the facts of their history, I have been guided by two priorities: First, I have tried to establish an accurate portrait of the entire slaveholding class, and to demonstrate that the slaveholders were a more diverse group than has generally been appreciated. Second, I have tried to elicit larger patterns of political, ideological, economic, and demographic development without doing violence to the evidence of diversity within the slaveholding class.

In this attempt to fill these voids in the historiography of slaveholders, a few major themes have developed and are implicit throughout the study. The first concerns typicality: Every historian of the Old South knows that while the majority of slaves lived on units with more than twenty bondsmen, the majority of slaveholders owned five slaves or fewer. Thus, the "typical" slaveholder did not necessarily own the "typical" slave. Most historians have used this fact to justify their emphasis on large plantations. Yet the case could be made that since almost half the slaves also lived on units with twenty bondsmen or fewer, equal attention should be paid to the smaller slaveholders. In terms of sheer numbers, small slaveholders over-whelmingly dominate the history of their class.

But historical significance is not determined by numbers alone, and in assigning priorities I have not adhered to any single standard. Planters—if defined as those with twenty slaves or more—were important because they owned so large a proportion of the slave work force, because they have come to play so significant a role in the potent mythology of the antebellum South, and because historians have made them important. Still, there were others—hundreds of thousands of others—who owned slaves but who never entered the planter class. Among slaveholders they were the vast majority, and in large part this is their history.

Coming to terms with the question of typicality—recognizing the preponderance of smaller slaveholders—led me to a second series of questions that form another theme of this study. What was the nature of power in an agricultural society where the greatest wealth was garnered from a work force that played no part in the normal political processes; where, despite concentration, wealth was too diffused to organize effectively; where the owner of five hundred slaves rarely had more legal and political rights than the owner of a single slave, or even a non-slaveholding farmer; where the "ruling class" of slaveholding families frequently amounted to between a third and a half of the state's white population? If the slaveholders, particularly the planters, were disproportionately powerful in the politics and economics of the Old South, what was the nature of that power? How did they exercise it, and how did they justify it?

The answer to these last questions drew me to the third, and perhaps prevailing theme. How did the slaveholding class, which was molded by the same forces that shaped the nation, which fought

America's wars and helped inspire its Revolution, a class which boasted of its patriotism, its devotion to freedom, its adherence to the major tenets of liberalism—how did such a class justify its continuing commitment to slavery and remain so steadfast in that commitment that it willingly separated from the Union it had helped to create? In short, how could the slaveholders' ideology prove so malleable as to reinforce simultaneously their devotion to black slavery and to democratic freedom? It is here, in the triumph of the slaveholders' liberalism, that the legacy of slavery becomes a truly American dilemma.

In suggesting these themes, I have relied heavily on the work of those historians who have preceded me, and, inevitably, I have differed with some of them. I agree with those who locate the origins of southern slavery in the labor shortage of the New World colonies and with those who stress the capitalist nature of the slave system in the Old South. Whatever their disagreements, this theme unifies the work of such diverse scholars as Oscar Handlin, Winthrop Jordan, Peter Wood, Edmund Morgan, Stanley Elkins, Kenneth Stampp, and Herbert Aptheker. I have learned a great deal from all of them, more so than my notes may indicate.

And, although I disagree with many of his conclusions, I have also learned much from Eugene Genovese. Throughout this work I have adopted his definition of "paternalism," for I believe it is historically accurate and conceptually sophisticated. Genovese explicitly discards the popular equation of paternalism with benevolence in favor of a more complex understanding of the term. Thus, "paternalism" suggests a social order which is stable, hierarchical, indeed consciously elitist, and therefore fundamentally antithetical to liberalism. A paternalist assumes an inherent inequality of men: some are born to rule, others to obey. A liberal espouses a far different social fiction: "All men are created equal." A paternalist stresses the organic unity born of each individual's acceptance of his or her place in a stable, stratified social order. A liberal stresses individualism, social mobility, and economic fluidity within a society which promotes equal opportunity. Whereas paternalism takes as its model the extended, patriarchal household, modern Western societies have moved more and more toward the private, nuclear family. Liberal and paternalistic societies are alike, however, in displaying (though of course in different ways) tendencies toward both cruelty and kindness, both benevolence and oppression, and therefore Genovese's argument that paternalism can explain the diversity of treatment within a slave system is well founded.

With these alternative visions of a social order come divergent political and economic implications: paternalism is the ideological legacy of a feudal political system with no fully developed market economy; liberalism developed alongside political democracy and free-market commercialism. The two systems are thus intrinsically antagonistic, and this antagonism will be heightened when a paternalistic social order finds itself virtually isolated in an increasingly liberal world. These appear to be Genovese's assumptions; they are mine also.

Indeed, it is the very clarification of definitions stemming from Genovese's work that throws our disagreements into sharp relief. I see paternalism giving way to liberalism throughout colonial, revolutionary, and pre-Civil War America. Genovese finds a reversal of centuries of historical development in the wake of America's withdrawal from the Atlantic slave trade in 1808, after which the South retreated rapidly into a highly sophisticated paternalistic social order such as the New World had never before known. Genovese argues that slaveholders were temperamentally hostile to the political democracy in which they operated. He sees them as increasingly self-conscious and unified, and he cites as evidence an "advanced fraction" of "thoughtful" planters who represented this tendency. For myself, I have found *some* slaveholders who articulated a paternalistic world view with increasing stridency as the Civil War approached; *some* slaveholders who were overtly and increasingly hostile to democracy; and *one* who went so far as to repudiate free trade. Granted that such a "fraction" existed, however, I see no reason to call it "advanced." What emerges from Genovese's work is a monolithic image of the Old South in which the "advanced fraction" is casually and regularly equated with the entire planter class, and ultimately with slaveholders in general. By contrast, I have found major divisions within a diverse slaveholding class, along with a general tendency away from paternalism and toward an acceptance of liberal democracy and free-

market commercialism. And I have found little reason for the slaveholders to have resisted this tendency.

Implicitly equating capitalism with free labor, Genovese argues
that slavery was a pre-capitalist form of social organization whose
"logical outcome" was a paternalistic world view. And it was the
slaveholders' paternalism, as he sees it, that created a constant tension
between the slaveholders and the capitalist world market in which
they conducted their business. But Genovese does not explore the
nature of this tension, nor does he examine in any detail its manifestations *within* the Old South. Karl Marx argued, for example, that
"negro labour in the Southern States of the American Union preserved something of a patriarchal character, so long as production was
chiefly directed to immediate local consumption. But in proportion,
as the export of cotton became of vital interest to these states, the
over-working of the negro . . . became a factor in a calculated and
calculating system. It was no longer a question of obtaining from him
a certain quantity of useful products. It was now a question of
production of surplus-labour itself." At one point Genovese comes
close to agreeing with Marx: "Once slavery passes from its mild,
patriarchal stage, the laborer is regarded less and less as a human being
and more and more as a beast of burden. . . . The existence of slavery
lays the basis for such a development, especially where markets are
opened and institutional barriers to commercialization removed."
But Genovese never applies this insight to his own analysis of antebellum slavery, and indeed argues something like the opposite: that
paternalism flourished in direct proportion to the expansion of the
cotton economy. In so arguing, he ignores—almost completely—the
profound impact of the market economy on the nature of slavery,
and it is this issue on which our disagreement is deepest.*

EACH OF THE QUESTIONS I raised, each theme they provoked, is
answered and discussed only partially in the pages that follow. I have

---

*Quotations from Karl Marx, *Capital: A Critique of Political Economy*, ed. Frederick Engels, trans.
Samuel Moore and Edward Aveling (New York, 1967), I, 236; Eugene D. Genovese, *The Political
Economy of Slavery* (New York, 1965), 80.

been determined to concentrate on major developments, and have thus omitted whole chapters that might justifiably have been included, but which were thematically tangential. There is no unified discussion of familial and childrearing patterns among slaveholders separate from the larger contexts of socialization, psychological development, and patterns of upward mobility. Similarly, the role of women is not discussed independently at length. I have left to more knowledgeable scholars the task of delineating the economic realities of slavery and have focused instead on the actions masters took on the basis of their perception of those realities. I had originally intended to include a comparative essay on northern and southern elites, but it has also fallen victim to thematic unity.

The slaves' view of and influence upon the masters has been edited down to the form it takes in Chapter 6, and for several reasons. To begin with, I could not hope to surpass the important work on slave culture that has already been published, and I believe it would be inappropriate, if not gratuitous, merely to summarize and reiterate it in these pages. This is not a history of the slaves. Nor is it a history of the master-slave relationship, for that too has been the subject of much study. Virtually every recent historian of slave life argues that Afro-American culture provided the means by which bondsmen successfully resisted the dehumanizing tendencies of the slave regime. I have tried to complement these studies by showing how the often unstated assumptions and daily behavior of the slaveholders contributed to the dehumanization to which Afro-Americans were forced to adapt. In law and custom, in ideology and practice, the masters did their best to ignore or sidestep the inescapable humanity of their slaves. In so doing they created irreconcilable contradictions within their own world, contradictions that were only heightened by the masters' unwillingness and inability to alter their behavior. Through it all they continued to view slaves primarily as property.

Their letters and diaries reveal how oblivious masters were to the complexities of Afro-American life. Historians of slave culture have relied on non-traditional sources precisely because masters persisted in seeing their bondsmen as disembodied abstractions even when they knew better. I fully subscribe to C. Vann Woodward's justly famous dictum that blacks and whites have continually shaped each other's destiny in the South; I do not believe that such influence depended upon close personal relationships, much less mutual understanding. Every law that defined slaves as property, every racist treatise declaring blacks inferior, every southern white man's dream of upward mobility, rested on the presence of large numbers of blacks, but not on an understanding or familiarity with them.

If this is not a history of slaves, neither is it a history of non-slaveholding whites. We know so little about these people that it would be wrong to assume that they shared the assumptions and goals of the slaveholders simply because they were free and white. There is some evidence that as the Civil War approached, important divisions between slaveholders and non-slaveholders, between market and subsistence cultures, generated class tensions that came to the surface of southern white society during the sectional crisis.

This is not, therefore, a history of the Old South. In the absence of an extended analysis of slave and non-slaveholding cultures, my conclusions cannot be read as an effort to address the question of whether the antebellum North and South were "different" or "the same." Even if the slaveholders alone are used as a frame of reference, the obvious answer to the question is that in some ways the North and South were similar and in some ways they were different. I believe that the history of the slaveholders shares much with the overall history of the United States; it does not follow that I believe the North and South were essentially similar in 1860. Nor do I think that cultural differences explain wars any better than cultural similarities. It is surely one of the lessons of Western history that common aims and aspirations are as likely to provoke hostilities as antithetical values, and that similarities and differences are often hard to distinguish.

SOME PASSAGES in the book have been conceived not merely as analytical narrative but as methodological suggestions with historiographical implications. I have been struck particularly by historians' unquestioning use of the hundreds of collections of slaveholders'

papers. One scholar has recently referred to them as an "embarrassment of riches." But if historians examined the representativeness of
the manuscripts with a fraction of the energy they expend questioning the validity of "black" sources, I believe a useful and long-
overdue revision of the received wisdom would follow. For these
collections, despite their large number, are overwhelmingly biased in
favor of the wealthiest, most stable, most highly educated slaveholding families. They are geographically skewed in favor of the Atlantic
coast states and the wealthy strip of land stretching from southern
Louisiana up the shores of the Mississippi River. Yet this geographical bias can hardly be attributed to the older age of the areas represented, since the manuscript collections thin out dramatically for the
years before 1820, leaving a residual bias toward the last thirty or
forty years of slavery's two-hundred-year history. There are relatively few collections for the heavily populated slave state of Georgia,
while manuscripts for North Carolina slaveholders are unrepresentatively abundant.

Inevitably, the biases of the manuscripts have found their way
into the history books. We think of the Old South as a society
imbued with a strong sense of "family," but we draw that conclusion
on the basis of collections saved by families that were unusually
concerned with the preservation of their own legacies. We read the
papers of the wealthiest elite and conclude that the society was
singularly aristocratic. And there are ideological biases as well. I am
convinced, for example, that any reasonable survey of the available
manuscript collections would, if we assume their representativeness,
yield the untenable conclusion that the majority of slaveholders were
philosophically opposed to secession in late 1860.

This is not to say that slaveholders' letters and diaries ought not
to be read. They are invaluable, indeed indispensable, sources; I have
relied upon them heavily. But they must be used with more circum-
spection than has often been the case. They reveal a good deal about
plantation slavery, less about slaveholders in general. They must be
read for what they omit as well as for what they present, for what
they criticize as much as for what they advocate. Most important,
they must be read within the context of other sources—legal, political, demographic. Their biases can be overcome in the same ways that

historians have worked around the biases of hostile travelers' accounts and slave autobiographies.

THE STRUCTURE of the narrative requires a brief comment. Part I and the Epilogue are largely chronological and serve as introductory and concluding statements on the origin and demise of the slaveholding class. Parts II and III are primarily thematic, and though I believe they follow logically from Part I and justify the conclusion, they may leave the impression that the history of the slaveholding class was more static than I think it was. To avoid this impression, I have tried to incorporate historical developments into the thematic discussions that form the core of this study. My analysis of the historical development of the slaveholders' religious practices is basically chronological, for example, but it falls within the context of a discussion of the psychological impact of slave ownership.

RESEARCH AND WRITING, because they are so deeply personal, are notoriously antisocial activities. I am therefore grateful that this project has served over the years to introduce me to a host of individuals whose advice, encouragement, and friendship I am happy to acknowledge. In his or her own way, each of them has drawn me a little further from the exile of the libraries and archives and helped me understand the privilege of membership in a community of scholars.

But those faceless institutions of the academy must not be forgotten, for this book could not have been written without them. Pride of place belongs to the University of California at Berkeley, which has consistently defied its own enormousness by respecting and encouraging my individual intellectual needs. Its Department of History provided me with two Heller Fund travel stipends at the beginning and end of my research. The university's Max Farrand Traveling Fellowship allowed me two years of uninterrupted work from 1978 to 1980. The Departments of History and Economics provided computer funds, and the staff of Berkeley's Quantitative Anthropology

Laboratory saw to it that the money was well spent. The staffs and archivists at the libraries listed in the Bibliography were consistently helpful and unobtrusive.

Several years ago, while an undergraduate at Baruch College, I took Selma Berrol's introductory survey course in United States history. She taught the class with such skill that my interest in the subject has long since become a preoccupation. Her comments on the manuscript, and her continuing friendship, are greatly appreciated. David Watt has been at various times my student, research assistant, and critic; he has also been a good friend, and for that I am most grateful. Shearer Davis Bowman and I have been arguing about each other's work for years, always with high seriousness and good humor. I hope he has learned as much from me as I have from him. Joel Williamson befriended me shortly after I got to Chapel Hill to begin my research. He urged me to organize my first thoughts for presentation to his seminar, offered useful comments, and read a draft of Chapter 1. He has since become one of my most valued friends. Henry F. May and Paula Fass helped me clarify my thoughts through their careful readings of an earlier version of Chapter 4. Richard Sutch was exceptionally generous with his funds and his expertise as he guided me through the microfilm reels of the U.S. Census returns for 1850. Among the others who have read the manuscript, I have come to appreciate Reid Mitchell's keen intelligence and close friendship; E. Wayne Carp's careful scrutiny and lively skepticism; and the insightful comments of Beth Burch, Paul William Burch, Robert Cohen, James Grossman, Rita Roberts, and Paula Shields. Ashbel Green, my editor at Knopf, made various helpful suggestions. My parents, Joan and Frank Oakes, capped their years of support and encouragement with a careful and intelligent reading of an early draft.

I owe major intellectual debts to four more readers, all of whose comments have improved the manuscript, but whose influence extends much further. Leon F. Litwack's seminar inspired me to pursue social history, and his friendship and encouragement have been unfailing ever since. Charles G. Sellers first challenged me to think about the anomaly of slavery in a free society; his scholarship challenges me still. I am convinced that James H. Kettner is a human dynamo—his extraordinarily close readings of successive drafts, his relentless assaults on my illogic, and his quiet, consistent dedication as both teacher and friend have left me with a debt I can do no more than acknowledge. Finally, I offer to Kenneth M. Stampp my deepest respect and appreciation. His unparalleled standards of excellence, his devotion to his students and his craft, and his integrity as a scholar have provided me with a model for which I am profoundly grateful. He has done his best to restrain my interpretive excesses, but neither he nor any of those I have mentioned should be held responsible for the errors that have survived their scrutiny.

My wife, Deborah Bohr, has ensured that some of my most outrageous sentences will never burden my readers. But editorial skill does not begin to explain my appreciation. By her friendship and her love, Deborah made these years of research and writing the happiest of my life. With gratitude and affection, I dedicate this book to her.

Berkeley, California   JAMES OAKES
August, 1981

PART I

The
Colonial
Legacy

Chapter 1

~

Revolutionary Slaveholders

IN 1701, John Saffin, an aging Boston merchant and slaveholder, lifted his pen in anger and produced one of the first sustained defenses of slavery ever published in the American colonies. Offended by the Massachusetts Superior Court's refusal to deny his slave's petition for freedom, Saffin chose to respond by attacking an antislavery pamphlet recently published by one of the court's most prominent jurists, Samuel Sewall. In *The Selling of Joseph*, Sewall had drawn an analogy between the biblical tale of the "manstealing" of Joseph by his jealous brothers and the African slave trade, concluding that "all men as they are the sons of Adam are Coheirs, and have equal Right unto Liberty." It was this conclusion that most rankled Saffin. The notion "that all men have equal right to Liberty" was false, he argued in his *Brief and Candid Answer,* for it denied "the Order that God hath set in the World, who hath Ordained different degrees and orders of men." Saffin then recited the traditional litany of social relationships. Some were born to be high and honorable, he wrote, "some to be Low and Despicable; some to be Monarchs, Kings, Princes and Governors, Masters and Commanders, others to be Subjects, and to be Commanded . . . yea, some to be born Slaves, and so to remain during their lives." Otherwise, the author concluded, there would be "mere parity among men."[1]

Saffin was no original thinker. Indeed, many of his fellow colonists would have agreed with his philosophical premises. The belief that a highly structured social order was natural—in fact, divinely inspired—had arrived in the New World with the earliest English-men and eventually became the basis of a paternalistic defense of bondage. It was the ideological offspring of a nobility for whom it was less an ideal than a simple description of reality. The paternalist ethic that influenced many colonial slaveholders was thus an English legacy, and it was elaborated most explicitly in such seventeenth- and eighteenth-century tracts as Richard Brathwait's *The English Gentleman,* Henry Peacham's *The Compleat Gentleman,* and Daniel Defoe's *The Compleat English Gentleman.* Although particulars changed with the passing generations, the essentials of paternalist dogma remained as Brathwait had outlined them in 1633.[2]

Brathwait began with the assumption that the social order was divinely ordained and therefore immutable. The gentleman's disposition could be nurtured only in those who were naturally endowed with special capacities. A benevolent Deity served as the supreme model for the "munificent" earthly father, and the patriarchal family in turn furnished the example for all social relations. "Wives are to submit themselves unto their Husbands; and again . . . Husbands should love their Wives." It was the duty of children to obey their parents, just as it was the father's responsibility to raise his children *"in instruction and information of the Lord."* So, too, did reciprocal obligations define the relation of master and servant. The gentleman never shirked his responsibilities as master of his household. Ideally, he ruled his estate with generosity, providing for the material needs of family and servants, never resorting to harsh treatment.[3]

The paternalist ethic implied an "organic" unity of interests within a social order, and indeed the biological metaphor was a common rhetorical device among paternalist advocates. Brathwait wrote that the gentleman's "vocation" in life was imposed by his social position. "For as in the mutuall offices of our *Body,* every member intends that peculiar function or office to which it is assigned or limited; so in the *Body* of the *State* (being all members depending and subsisting of that *State*) wee are all in our mutuall places or offices to discharge that Taske which is injoyned us." Hence it was "duty," rather than the prospect of fame or the lure of material reward, which called the gentleman to the exercise of political power.[4]

For Saffin, and many other colonial slaveholders as well, the principle of social equality was not only alien; it was the equivalent of disruption, chaos, and anarchy. "There is no truer Emblem of Confusion," George Alsop had warned, than an attempt by subject or servant "to be equal with him, from whom he receives his present subsistence." Perhaps for this reason, slaveholders sought to demonstrate the practical benefits of the traditional social order for those on the bottom as well as those on the top. In so doing, they laid the groundwork for one of the most persistent themes formulated in defense of slavery: that it was good for the slaves. To this contention was added the equally popular notion that the best slaves were those who had enjoyed the least autonomy in Africa, that blacks who "have been *Kings* and *great Men* there are generally lazy, haughty, and obstinate." Others believed that blacks born in America and reared under the "civilizing" institution of slavery were better adapted to the social hierarchy and so made "more industrious, honest, and better Slaves than any brought from Guinea."[5]

The fact that so few masters felt compelled to justify their behavior even as they actively participated in the construction of a slave society suggests the extent to which human inequality was simply taken for granted. To slaveholders, every assertion of the paternalist ideology was a tacit defense of slavery. Onto the traditional expressions of divinely ordained inequality they simply grafted references to the relationship of master and slave. Such expressions were everywhere to be found. Inequality was sanctioned from the pulpit by ministers, from the bench by judges, and in the legislative chambers by elected officials. Taken as a whole, the ideal of paternalistic hierarchy formed the nucleus of a complex and sophisticated social ethic that accommodated itself, albeit with some difficulty, to the emergence of chattel slavery.

When the Maryland slaveholders in the Episcopal parish of the Reverend Thomas Bacon went to church on a Sunday morning in 1742 and heard their pastor declare that God had "laid the foundation of justice and equity between man and man, by making each in his several station," they were being instructed on how to behave as well as how to save their souls. The honor and obedience owed to rulers, Bacon said, should be reciprocated by the protection of a subject's rights and liberties; the duty and respect owed by children should be repaid by the "support, education, and other advantages" provided by parents; neighbors should offer and expect mutual friendship and assistance. Finally, Bacon reasoned that in the providential order of things it was the duty of slaveholders to feed, clothe, and shelter their bondsmen and to educate them in Christianity, even as masters were entitled to expect "care, fidelity, and honest labour" from their slaves.

But Bacon was not merely waxing eloquent here on the wondrous "schemes of an all-wise Providence." He was, in fact, chastising his congregation for its failure to behave in accordance with the designs of God, for succumbing to the ruinous temptations of a "covetous world." Wealth and power, Bacon complained, had become distinctions used to "set persons above the ordinary precepts of social virtues." After all, the hierarchy of humanity was really a social fiction designed to meet the temporary needs of a dependent world. "For, when we die and are laid down in the common bosom of the earth," Bacon concluded, "all outward distinctions vanish, and the rank we held in the world, will be no farther concerned in the question, than whether we have behaved well or ill; whether we have done what was just and equal in it or not."[6]

Thus did Thomas Bacon unwittingly address himself to the central dilemma of the slaveholders' colonial experience. Implicit in the paternalistic ethos was the denigration of materialistic motives in all of life's pursuits. "For these earthly *Moles,* who are ever digging, till their graves be digged," Brathwait reserved his most bitter scorn. "Their *Dispositions* are of a baser temper: for they can taste nothing but *earthly things."* Yet from the earliest years of colonial settlement, the paternalistic ideology came into competition not only with a conflicting world view but with a historical experience that in fact contributed to the destruction of traditional values. With the advance of the market economy in the Old World and the New, paternalistic writers tried to reconcile the ideals of social inequality, stability, and organic unity with the conflicting principles of individual enterprise and material acquisition. Thus George Alsop, who so decried the notion of human equality, nevertheless discarded paternalism's traditional anti-materialism and spoke with enthusiasm of "Trafique, Commerce, and Trade" as "the very soul of a Kingdom."[7] As the South approached the revolutionary era, those who clung to the paternalist world view found themselves increasingly outnumbered by slaveholders who were more receptive to the seemingly inappropriate doctrines of individualism and equal opportunity.

This emerging majority of slaveholders had embraced the values implicit in the promotional literature written to entice European emigrants to America. The authors who wrote of the colonial South did not describe it as a "city upon a hill" wherein devout Puritans could escape the corruptions of the Anglican Church. Nor did they advertise anything akin to William Penn's godly community of Quakers. What these promoters stressed most of all was economic opportunity in an environment, both natural and political, that encouraged the materialistic aspirations of newly arrived settlers. As early as 1649, William Bullock had confidently declared that Virginia "is abundantly stored with what is by all men aimed at, viz. Health and Wealth."[8]

Through the eighteenth century such arguments remained the stock-in-trade of the South's boosters. In 1737, John Brickell pronounced North Carolina's "the best established Government in the World." Cheap land and widespread opportunity meant that in three or four years North Carolinians released from their indentures could, with good management and industry, save the capital necessary "to purchase a Plantation by which means many are become as wealthy and substantial Planters, as any in the Government." Such were the natural advantages of the climate of South Carolina and Georgia, another writer contended, "that Charles Town has now near six hundred good houses, and the whole population has above forty thousand negro slaves, worth at least a million pounds sterling."[9] Well before the end of the colonial period, the American dream of upward mobility became implicitly linked to land and slavery in the minds of many white Southerners.

Though few were aware of it, what promoters depicted was a world in fundamental conflict with paternalistic values. They advertised a fluid social order while tradition glorified social stasis. They spoke of equality of opportunity where paternalism assumed inequality and stratification. The pamphlets they distributed among anxious Europeans stressed the importance of individualism and hard work with the promise of material reward, but paternalist ideology stressed the mutual obligations of all members within a community. In short, the ideals implicit in the promotional literature were far different from those assumed by the slaveholding "gentlemen" who had fitted bondage so neatly into their conceptual order.

Few promoters consciously rejected the principle of human inequality. Yet in the more fluid circumstances of the colonial South, new rules for determining an individual's status needed to be understood if the concept of a social hierarchy was to have any practical force. In Elizabethan England, most people understood that those who owned land also held power. It was land that sustained the aristocratic pretensions and political power of the nobility and, generally speaking, those who held the most land were the most influential. By the time Englishmen began settling the southern colonies, landholding was the necessary qualification for the franchise. The practical effect of such requirements in Great Britain was to limit the electorate to a small fraction of the population. But in the southern colonies, despite concerted efforts by the wealthiest to take advantage of the free market by hoarding vast tracts of western lands, the property-based franchise was extended so broadly as to include the majority of white men.[10]

Hence the inevitable paradox of life in the colonial South: while a relatively small percentage of white immigrants survived their indentures and prospered, the slaveholding class emerged from the ranks of these lucky few. Their success derived from the fluidity of colonial society; their experience convinced them of the superiority of a social system that practiced what the South's earliest promoters had so earnestly preached, equality of opportunity. As these slaveholders took their places as leaders of southern politics, they pushed its ideological basis away from the paternalistic emphasis on stratification and stasis. Thus it was that even as slaveholding became the basis of social status and political power in the colonial South, the origins of the slaveholding class tended to dilute the influence of paternalist ideology.

Change came slowly, however. In accordance with the traditional rules of society, the wealthiest slaveholders held most of the major political offices in the southern colonies. The persistence of the idea that some were entitled by virtue of their wealth to the perquisites of power is clear in southern voting patterns. Nevertheless, there were sporadic political conflicts whose origins were at least partially to be found in the typical slaveholders' sense that power in the colonies was not properly apportioned. As early as 1700, so many settlers had purchased their own land, so many had become slaveholders, that the traditional link between wealth and political power precluded popular acquiescence to a circumscribed ruling elite.[11] It is hardly surprising that the democratization of southern politics was so forcefully advocated by the slaveholders themselves.

As EACH of the southern economies became dependent on an agricultural system based on slave labor, a contradictory pattern of wealth distribution emerged that was capable of sustaining both paternalistic and democratic ideals. Huge concentrations of land and slaves were amassed within a society that otherwise distributed its wealth quite broadly. Southern colonies eventually developed democratic political institutions based on widespread distribution of land, but at the same time they exhibited gross economic disparities. In Lancaster County, Virginia, in 1716, two-thirds of the taxpayers were slaveholders, eighty percent of whom owned from one to four bondsmen. Yet this was the birthplace of one of Virginia's wealthiest citizens, Robert Carter, whose holdings in Lancaster included 126 slaves. In the wealthy rice district of South Carolina, slaves were as inequitably distributed as anywhere. But in St. George's Parish in 1726, eighty percent of the households contained slaves. Sixty percent of the slaveholders owned between one and ten bondsmen, and forty percent owned five or fewer. Even so, twenty percent of the parish's slaves were owned by just three persons. As the poorest farmers picked up and moved farther south and west, the wealthiest families continued to enhance their landholdings with what was left behind. Yet the seemingly limitless supply of cheap land and the importation of tens of thousands of slaves allowed some colonists to build up huge plantations without thwarting the ambitions of the small slaveholders or yeomen farmers.[12]

In the eighteenth century, the wealthiest Virginia planters usually owned several estates, their home plantations averaging three thousand acres and eighty slaves. The median value of their taxable property was nearly 25,000 pounds. Similar concentrations of wealth could be found in Maryland, the Carolinas, and Georgia. The rich planters could thus afford a style of life that seemed appropriate to their disproportionately large role in colonial politics. It was in the middle decades of the century that South Carolina's rice planters began to build their Palladian townhouses around Charleston's battery, that ornate Virginia mansions at the Shirley plantation and Gunston Hall were created, and that the construction of Governor Tryon's spectacular palace at New Bern, North Carolina, was begun.[13]

The fortunes that sustained these enormous projects were rarely supplied by men who had worked their way up from indentured servitude. William Byrd of Westover was born in Virginia in 1674, the son of one of the most prominent planters in the colony. Educated in England, he returned to America in 1705, settled on his estate, and assumed his place as one of Virginia's most powerful citizens, a position he held until his death in 1744. Robert Carter's background was similarly auspicious. Born in Virginia in 1663, he was, like Byrd, a second-generation American who spent his life increasing the fortune bequeathed to him. After an influential career, he died in 1732, leaving to his children an estate estimated by *Gentleman's Magazine* to contain "about 300,000 acres of land, about 1000 negroes, and £10,000 in money." By the 1780's his descendants constituted by far the wealthiest family in the Old Dominion. The seven Carters who ranked among the forty richest Virginians had a combined worth that included 170,000 acres, 2,340 slaves, 450 horses, and 2,300 cattle. All told, their property was valued at nearly 500,000 pounds.[14]

Even those industrious planters who built up their own sizable estates rarely did so on their own. One of the most common features in the backgrounds of successful slaveholders was a generous patron who provided the contacts, the education, and often the capital to get the incipient planter going. Daniel Dulany arrived in Maryland penniless in 1704, but quickly secured a clerkship under the wealthy lawyer and planter George Plater. In 1709, at the age of twenty-four, Dulany was admitted to the practice of law and rapidly expanded his services over several counties and up to the highest level of the colony's courts. Substantial fees provided him the means to establish a plantation and to send his son to be educated in law not by a clerkship but by study at the Inns of Court in England. Devereux Jarratt lost out on his inheritance when both parents died without leaving a will. By hiring himself out as a teacher to a succession of wealthy planters, however, Jarratt established the contacts that secured him the private funding for a religious education in England. He returned to America as an Episcopal minister in Bath Parish, Virginia. From that office, he built up a comfortable estate that in 1782 included twenty-four slaves, eleven horses, and twenty-six cattle.[15] Hardly comparable to those of Virginia's "First Families," Jarratt's holdings were nevertheless far larger than the typical estate in Dinwiddie County at the time.

As the examples of Dulany and Jarratt demonstrate, a professional education in the law, the ministry, or medicine was one of the surest avenues into the slaveholding class. The high social standing of the professional could afford him more than just material wealth and access to power. In 1673, a tailor and a physician were each charged with horse racing in York County, Virginia; the doctor was acquitted, but the tailor was fined one hundred pounds because, the judge said, "it was contrary to law for a laborer to run races, it being a sport only for gentlemen." Such inequities diminished in the eighteenth century, but the importance of a good educational background did not. Professionals took refuge in their social standing whenever their excessive fees provoked popular indignation. Wealthy doctors in particular were frequently the target of the public's wrath. Lawyers also perfected the art of extracting profit from misery, by serving as debt collectors for wealthy landholders and merchants. Both Patrick Henry and Thomas Jefferson earned a considerable portion of their earliest fees as debt collectors. But most of the income that lawyer-planters derived from their law practices came from the legally regulated fees for criminal cases and the settlement of conflicting property claims. Their familiarity with property law made them especially active land speculators, and their services to the wealthier planters opened up avenues of political advancement as well.[16]

Of those who built up comfortable estates after migrating from Europe, few did not have some capital or a professional education.

William Dunbar emigrated from Scotland for reasons of health in 1771, arriving at Philadelphia with a noble birth and a good education to push his career along. Successful in the Indian trade, he sailed down the Ohio River in 1773, settled at Baton Rouge, Louisiana, on a huge tract of land, then went to Jamaica to buy more slaves. From these auspicious beginnings Dunbar made himself one of the most prosperous planters in that fast-growing region. In 1783 he moved to a plantation up the Mississippi River, nine miles south of Natchez, and by the end of the century he claimed to be producing 20,000 pounds of cotton a year.[17]

If the disavowal of materialistic aspirations was implicit in the ethos of the gentleman, few colonial planters fitted the paternalist mold. Neither Byrd, Carter, Dulany, nor Dunbar rested content with his inherited or acquired wealth. Like most prosperous slaveholders, they were "planter-businessmen" who continued to expand their enterprises, reinvesting their profits to amass more land and still more slaves. The most common venture of the large slaveholders was land speculation. They bought vast tracts in the West and waited for it to be settled—even encouraged its settlement—in an unblushing effort to beat the new immigrants out of the cheapest lands. Alexander Spotswood used his office as governor to facilitate the settlement of a colony of German immigrants on the thousands of acres in western Virginia that he claimed as his own. Then he rented it to the settlers as tenants, or worked it with their indentured service. William Byrd tried the same thing with less success. The wary Germans, educated by experience, simply pushed farther south and west to find land of their own. But the shrewd Daniel Dulany sold a large part of his western lands at a low price, deliberately incurring a substantial loss but knowing that once the Germans had settled, the rest of his land would become so valuable that he could still reap enormous profits from his investment.[18]

After land speculation, slave trading was one of the planters' most profitable and widely practiced enterprises. Byrd dabbled in it occasionally. Robert Carter was actively engaged in the slave trade and showed no signs of the reticence or moral distaste that would characterize later generations of Virginians. In a letter to George Eskridge, Carter spoke with no emotion, except perhaps annoyance, of the effect that lameness would have on one slave's retail value. With somewhat less detachment, William Dunbar reveled in the profits of the commerce. In 1776, when his plantation had fourteen working slaves, Dunbar also had "23 New Negroes for sale who are employed about the business of the Plantation." Only five small girls and two sickly men remained from the last cargo, he boasted later that year. "I flatter myself that the adventure upon the whole will turn to advantage."[19]

In the last half of the eighteenth century the boom subsided and gave way to stability. New immigrants pushed farther west and south in search of their own property, and the big landlords could no longer keep ahead of them. As America's participation in the Atlantic slave trade diminished, a major speculative enterprise was closed off to large slaveholders. They were settling down. Long before the cotton boom the wealthiest masters had established themselves on the South's most productive lands, forming a perimeter around most of the region. For good reasons they were attracted to water: it irrigated their crops, replenished their soil, and offered ready access to markets. The perimeter thus began at Chesapeake Bay, in the tobacco and grain producing counties of Maryland's eastern shore. In Virginia, where deep rivers extended inland for many miles up to the falls, they built their plantations at the edges of the Potomac and the Rappahannock —the northern neck—and along the James. They moved closer to the ocean as they expanded southward, but still took up land along the rivers that emptied into the sea at North Carolina's outer banks. They grew their rice on the great plantations of the South Carolina lowlands and spent much of their time and money in the coastal towns of Charleston and Savannah. They spread up the banks of the Savannah River and down the sea islands that dotted Georgia's coastline.

Blocked by the Spanish in Florida, they moved around the panhandle and began to settle in the two major Gulf Coast regions. As early as 1776, there were significant numbers of English-speaking slaveholders in the district of Mobile, where there were said to be 140 houses and plantations, 300 white men, 360 blacks, and 8,000 head of cattle. English slaveholders could be found in French Louisiana, where sugar plantations were already in operation. And in the 1780's, some had even gone up the Mississippi River and spotted Natchez

—destined to become the wealthiest area of the United States. "I verily believe, without exaggeration," one farsighted slaveholder at Baton Rouge concluded in 1783, "that one Negro at Natchez in the cultivation of the soil will do as much as five here."[20]

Before the close of the eighteenth century, then, the biggest slaveholders had settled or begun to settle in those areas that would in the long run prove the most consistently profitable. Their economic prosperity bred a kind of social stability that, as much as their sheer wealth, would separate them from the overwhelming majority of slaveholders. The great cotton plantations had yet to grow up along the Mississippi. The largest sugar plantations of Louisiana were not yet dominated by wealthy Americans. But the richest lands on the eastern seaboard were pretty much settled, and they would never feel the most intense effects of the spectacular inland cotton boom. The fortuitous combination of lengthy settlement, wealth, and unparalleled social stability isolated these areas from the young, speculative instability of the rest of the slaveholding South. Beyond the wealthy perimeter was a society of slaveholders whose characteristics began to take form in the great migrations of the eighteenth century.

IF THE THOUSANDS of men and women, free or indentured, who migrated from Europe to the southern colonies in the eighteenth century had carried with them no particular expectations about life in the New World, perhaps the material conditions in America would not have been so destructive of the paternalistic ideology. If the societies of the colonial South had been less varied, perhaps a monolithic slaveholders' world view would have survived the Revolution. But the emigrants whose descendants would be labeled a "planter aristocracy" came to America from myriad experiences and, once arrived, established a diversity that would never produce a unified slaveholding ideology.

Those who endured the hardship of separation and the frightful Atlantic crossing and who poured into the southern colonies in successive and overlapping waves brought with them perspectives scarred by their deprivation and often hostile to those entertained by the landlords they served in their American indenture. They came not only from England but from France, Germany, Scotland, and Ulster. They were Huguenot, Lutheran, Moravian, Baptist, and Presbyterian. Even the English immigrants were increasingly Methodist. The successful among them adapted themselves to slavery, sometimes haltingly, often after strong initial opposition. But they did so within the context of their own transformed cultures, and in most cases these proved more receptive to egalitarianism than to the principles of social hierarchy. When they adhered to the latter, they barely survived the Revolution.

The first permanent settlers in Virginia had among them a proportion of "gentlemen" six times as high as in England, an imbalance that had much to do with the way the colony's initial social structure evolved. But even in the earliest years, the majority of English settlers arrived in the New World unfree. If they anticipated paternalistic protection, they were quickly disabused of such notions. Death, re-emigration back to Europe or elsewhere, and insurmountable hardships ensured that barely one in five servants would survive their indenture and go on to anything like "prosperity" in America. By the end of the colonial era as many as ninety percent of the English emigrants described themselves as craftsmen, farmers, or laborers. These people left a society that was profoundly different from the one Elizabethan gentlemen had left in the early seventeenth century. For them, the traditional deference demanded by the upper classes had little practical force in everyday life. Theirs was the England not of Sir Walter Raleigh but of John Wilkes.[21] As they found their places in the slave economies of Maryland, the Carolinas, and Georgia, they helped chip away at the traditional emphasis on social hierarchy that was the first ideological foundation of colonial slavery.

Further erosion was effected by the significant emigration of Scotch-Irish throughout the eighteenth century. Immortalized by skeptics and romantics alike, from Wilbur Cash to Margaret Mitchell, the Scotch-Irish have become the very stuff of legend. They have fulfilled their role in popular mythology by assuming nearly every conceivable status, from "poor white trash" to sturdy yeoman, from parvenu slaveholder to gallant cavalier. No group before the Scotch-Irish had arrived in such complete destitution. Rack-renting, food shortages, high prices, and low wages pushed them out of Ulster at an accelerating pace throughout the 1700's. They almost invariably headed for the backcountry, commonly entering America through Philadelphia, making their way to western Pennsylvania, then turning southward and settling in a broad belt along the Blue Ridge and the Piedmont, from Maryland to Georgia. In later years, just before the Revolution, more and more Scotch-Irish came directly into Charleston, from which they likewise departed quickly for the back-country.[22]

Feisty and independent, the Scotch-Irish brought to the New World an almost religious devotion to the principles of free enterprise. Add to this their deep antipathy toward all things English and aristocratic, and they had no trouble choosing sides in the emerging conflict with Great Britain. As more of them joined the ranks of slaveholders, their sheer numbers helped change the character of the typical master from the haughty English gentleman of the seventeenth century to the democratic entrepreneur of the nineteenth.[23]

The German emigrants had a similar effect on southern society. They planted themselves in small settlements along the Piedmont plateau from western Maryland to Georgia. As the century went on, the isolated communities blended with one another as Germans who first went to Pennsylvania continued moving southward along the Blue Ridge until they almost reached the earliest settlements in Georgia. By the Revolution, the Germans and Scotch-Irish formed a demographic belt stretching hundreds of miles north and south at the foot of the Appalachian Mountains.

The Germans came in tightly knit groups of poor yeomen farmers who left their homeland to escape religious persecution and to find a better life for themselves. Their devotion to their community was nevertheless matched by an intense individualism and a deeply ingrained work ethic that originally made them hostile to slavery. But their culture could not be applied literally to the New World environment, and as the decades wore on, their resistance waned and they gradually made their way into the slaveholding class. Occasionally, a successful immigrant would amass a large plantation with a substantial slave labor force. Isaac Hite in Virginia, for example, owned thirty-eight slaves in 1782. But the dominant slaveholding pattern was the one that fit into the traditional German emphasis on the small family farm. A couple of slaves was most common, and even the wealthiest German settlers rarely held more than fifty bondsmen.[24]

What is significant is the way in which these immigrants found it increasingly difficult to sustain their initial hostility to slavery. The story of the German Salzburgers in Georgia is illustrative. Persecuted for their religious beliefs, these Lutheran emigrants were forced to flee the archbishopric of Salzburg in the 1730's and 1740's, before slavery was legal in Georgia. Industrious and thrifty, the devout Salzburgers tried their hands at the failing silk industry but eventually moved into milling, lumbering, and roadbuilding. Most, however, were small farmers. Because they were overwhelmingly poor, they were particularly fearful of the competitive threat of slave labor. The Reverend Johann Martin Bolzius, the wise and humane spiritual leader of the major settlement at Ebenezer, fifty miles up the Savannah River, saw the "great difference" between those colonists who came penniless and those who brought some wealth. "Our Salzburgers arrived very poor," Bolzius wrote, and they were friendless in a strange land where people spoke a strange language. They had "no good soil, nor horses and plow," and so after almost a generation in America, "most of them admittedly still belong among the poor."[25]

While the economy of their close neighbors in South Carolina was booming, Georgians found it increasingly difficult to attract new immigrants and sustain philanthropic contributions. Speculators and entrepreneurs angrily noted Georgia's troubles and pointed to the bans on slavery and land speculation as the cause. But Bolzius led the Salzburgers in their fight against the introduction of slavery. He experimented with the latest equipment developed by the British agricultural reformer, Jethro Tull, introducing his parishioners to a new plow that finally allowed them to cultivate the land in Georgia's pine barrens profitably and without slaves. But his efforts were to no avail. "Their strength is now used up," Bolzius reported in 1749; his "exhausted" people could no longer resist the pressure from without and the temptation from within. He allowed them to buy slaves. Ironically, Bolzius's successful agricultural experiments had only served to hasten the introduction of slavery to Georgia.[26]

Like the Germans in Virginia, the Salzburgers did not build huge plantations, and most of the slaves brought into Georgia worked on the coastal lands. But as the colony prospered, the Germans too made their way up from poverty to self-sufficiency to slaveholding. John Adam Treutlen was one of them. He was only a child when his parents left Germany for Georgia. His father died in a pirate prison and never reached America. But John Adam was educated by the Reverend Bolzius at Ebenezer, where he went on to become pastor of the local church from 1765 until his death in 1782. After his marriage, he became a merchant and a planter as well. Starting with a modest fifty-acre tract, Treutlen gradually added to his holdings until by 1769 he owned a thousand acres and twenty-three slaves. Increasingly active in politics, he sided with the patriots in the Revolution and assisted in the establishment of a state government. In 1777, Treutlen was elected the first governor of the state of Georgia.[27]

The German immigrants who found their place in southern society came to America with a set of ideas that differed significantly from those of their noble English predecessors. Although they recognized the class divisions about them, they hardly seemed willing to accept the status quo as divinely inspired, often resisting the efforts of wealthy South Carolina planters to have Georgia's ban on slavery lifted. They had come to America to escape persecution, and they seemed intent on preserving their traditional culture as much as possible in a radically altered setting. That they managed to adapt to slavery without abandoning their devotion to individual industry and liberty was of no small significance.

But there was one group, one major immigrant settlement pattern, that defied all these generalizations—a group whose remarkably swift adaptation to slaveholding put them quickly into the front ranks of wealthy and powerful slaveholders. Scottish settlement took two distinct forms: Highlanders rè-established their agricultural economy in the New World and built upon their experience as herdsmen to make their way into the slaveholding class. By contrast, the commercial activity of the Lowland Scots contributed incalculably to the expansion of slavery across the southern frontier before the Revolution.

The Highland Scots who trickled into the South in the eighteenth century left a society that is generally called "feudal." Land was held by large and hostile clans who dominated the lives of the Highlands' impoverished masses. Like so many other immigrants, Highlanders arrived in large groups but, unlike others, they came with their landlords. These "tacksmen" bought up huge tracts of land, especially around the Cape Fear Valley of North Carolina, between the tidewater and the Piedmont. Their anachronistic social system bred a fierce loyalty and a deeply rooted conservatism that made emigration harder for the Scots than for any comparable group of colonial settlers. They frequently considered their life in America a kind of temporary exile, and they came only after the most severe deprivation and the strongest urging by relatives and landlords. William McKay was typical. Thirty years old, a farmer with a wife and three children still living, McKay watched his crops fail year after year. Rents rose and the price of his cattle fell, until in 1775 he told a British customs official that "he could not have bread for his family at home, and was encouraged to emigrate by the Accounts received from his Countrymen who had gone to America before him."[28] It is no surprise that the Scots made a more than usual effort to re-create in America their homogeneous community life, with its stratified social structure and its unswerving loyalty to the British crown. *Quite new*

For the Highland Scots the major avenue of upward mobility into the slaveholding class was cattle-farming. The vast tracts of unsettled land in America had provided the earliest settlers of Virginia and South Carolina with the grazing area that made animal husbandry an easy and quick source of capital. Because Highlanders in the Cape Fear Valley came to America with long experience as cattle farmers, they found it the best way to build the reserves needed to buy their way into the slaveholding class. In Cumberland County, North Carolina, there was one bondsman for every four Highlanders, while the ratio of blacks to whites in the colony as a whole was less than one to three. Though the average Highlander slaveholdings were smaller than those in the coastal counties, they were larger than in the western region of the colony. And of course, there were several Highland Scots who had built up large plantations, men like Farquard Campbell with fifty slaves, or Alexander McAlister with forty.[29]

More impressive was the phenomenal rise of the Scottish merchants. Primarily Lowlanders, the great tobacco merchants were sent to America as salaried agents of the rising Glasgow trading houses. In several decades before the Revolution, the Scottish merchants developed two huge spheres of influence, which encircled most of the major southern settlements. The first stretched inland and northward from the Albemarle region of North Carolina beyond the fall line, surrounding tidewater Virginia and turning back toward Maryland's eastern shore to encompass the entire Chesapeake Bay. The second sphere, centered at Charleston, stretched southward in another half-circle from the Lowlander settlement at Wilmington, North Carolina, around the rice district of South Carolina and on into Georgia, returning to the Atlantic Ocean near the Highlander settlement at Darien.[30]

Setting up stores at strategic points between the great planters of the coastal lowlands and the small tobacco farmers of the upcountry, Scottish traders bypassed the usual consignment system of the London merchants. By perfecting a system of commerce more efficient than anything previous to it, the Scots ate away at the London trade. They purchased tobacco directly from the farmers who brought their goods to the conveniently located stores, which soon grew into huge, self-sufficient plantations with slaves of their own. By 1758, Glasgow had surpassed London as the chief tobacco port of Great Britain. The profits could be tremendous. In just sixteen years, Neil Jamieson of Norfolk built a string of warehouses in Virginia and amassed seven thousand pounds' worth of choice real estate. John Hamilton of North Carolina invested his profits in a number of local businesses, ships, and several plantations. As it expanded, the trade became intensely competitive, with merchants recklessly overextending credit in an effort to attract more of the business. When the Revolution broke out, so many influential slaveholders were in debt that when it came time to find a scapegoat for their sad economic condition, they quickly singled out their Scottish creditors.[31]

Political power, which gravitated naturally toward wealth and status, moved with special quickness to the Scottish slaveholders. Their trade kept them in such close association with Great Britain, they maintained such steadfast loyalty to the English monarchy, that royal governorships fell into Scottish laps with remarkable facility. Intensely devoted to their kinsmen, Scottish officials distributed polit-

ical plums with shameless favoritism. By the 1760's up to fourteen
of twenty-six members of Georgia's Assembly and six out of nine
members of its Royal Council were Scottish or of Scottish descent.
Wealthy Scotsmen like Henry McCulloh used their influence to
command special favors from imperial commissioners. After piling up
hundreds of thousands of acres of land in North Carolina, McCulloh,
a die-hard mercantilist and stout defender of British economic policy,
left America in 1747 and spent the next fifteen years protecting the
quit-rent exemptions he had wrested from his close friends on the
Board of Trade. In Georgia in the 1740's, wealthy Highlanders from
South Carolina pressured most persistently for the admission of
slaves. Thwarted by popular opposition and stubborn trustees (particularly the Earl of Egmont), they removed to Charleston, where they
published harshly critical pamphlets. Under the auspices of the notorious St. Andrews Club, several Highlanders sent Egmont "a very
sawcy letter . . . villifying Col. Oglethorpe, and divers of the Trustees
for not allowing them Negroes."[32]

By 1776, the Scots were in general not very well liked in America, and their popular image was hardly enhanced by their behavior
during the Revolution. Their close ties to the imperial economy,
intense loyalty to the King, and deeply conservative social ethos
pushed them naturally into the Tory camp. The Cape Fear Valley was
a hotbed of loyalism until February 1776, when the most vocal of
the Highland leaders were killed or taken prisoner at the Battle of
Moore's Creek Bridge. The following year there were reports that
up to two-thirds of the Scottish immigrants intended to leave America, and indeed they departed by the boatload. Most of the tobacco
agents went back to Glasgow. Their temporary exile was over.[33]

By the end of the Revolution, the Scottish trade was seriously
impaired, and the opprobrium heaped on the community as a whole
destroyed its political power as well. In 1782 the Georgia legislature,
angered by Scottish loyalism, passed a law providing that "no Person
a Native of Scotland shall be permitted or allowed to emigrate into
this State with intent to Settle within the same."[34] The immigrant
community, which adapted most readily to slaveholding and which
could have sustained the traditional elements of the paternalist ideology most effectively, could not survive the American Revolution.

Their very traditionalism had become an anachronism, placing the Scottish immigrants at odds with the prevailing sentiments of the age. Little more than the powerful legend of the Scottish clan survived the colonial ordeal.

Through the eighteenth century the working-class English, the Scotch-Irish, and the Germans had come to occupy a strategic geographic position at the western edge of the British colonies in North America. As Southerners poured through the Cumberland Gap into eastern Kentucky, across the North Carolina Blue Ridge into Tennessee, and down around the Georgia plateau into the nascent cotton belt, they were led not by the wealthy land barons of the Chesapeake or the would-be aristocrats of Charleston but by these new immigrants and their descendants. Egalitarian rhetoric and a social tradition that defied paternalistic assumptions emerged from a society in which freedom and bondage shared a common heritage. This advance guard of the slaveholding democracy felt perfectly at ease with its simultaneous devotion to slavery and freedom as it filled in the stable southern perimeter with a restless core of upwardly mobile slaveholders.

THE GREAT MIGRATIONS of the eighteenth century split the ranks of slaveholders along class, ethnic, and religious lines, which reflected in turn differences in economic patterns, geographic distribution, and social outlook. Yet there was much that was universal to the experience of slaveholding. In particular, no master could be isolated from the dehumanizing effects of the rigorous discipline of the slave regime or from the disruptive intrusions of the market economy upon which that regime thrived. These central features of slavery, punishment and profit, destroyed for most slaveholders whatever remained of the elemental principle of the paternalist ethos: that masters were obliged to look to the needs of the slaves in return for the diligence and fidelity of the bondsmen.

As an involuntary labor system, slavery was exploitative by its very nature, based ultimately on force, and so functioned in a way that made it all but impossible for either slaves or masters to fulfill their reciprocal obligations. In South Carolina, according to one observer, long hours of back-breaking work without pay, a general indifference to the slaves' religious concerns, and the slaveholders' disrespect for the bondsmen's marital and sexual needs created a "Foundation of Discontent" among slaves so that "they are generally thought to watch an Opportunity of revolting against their Masters." So widespread, in fact, was the fear of insurrection that in 1741 a Georgia inquiry commission reaffirmed the colony's ban on slaves, "for those are all secret enemies." William Byrd agreed. The "unhappy Effect of Many Negroes," he wrote, "is the necessity of being severe. Numbers make them insolent."[35]

So much of the slaveholders' energies were directed to thwarting real or supposed rebellions that the slaves commonly resorted to more indirect forms of resistance. From the very beginning, they seemed to go out of their way to frustrate the will of the masters. They stole food, broke tools, feigned illness, neglected their duties, and ran away, daily giving the lie to idyllic pronouncements of master-slave harmony. James Carter, a member of one of Georgia's wealthiest families, had so much trouble managing his slaves that he was at one point advised "to sell about half of his Negroes, those that are unfaithful, those women that pretend to be always sick and such rebellious fellows as Paris—it is dangerous to hold such property. . . . I have some that are objectionable and intend selling them." Inevitably, day-to-day discipline became as much a part of slavery as day-to-day resistance.[36]

In the eighteenth century, patterns of resistance reflected the diversity of both masters and slaves.[37] In Virginia, deep rivers extending inland dispersed the farms and plantations, and with them the slaves. Spread across the countryside in small, isolated groups, on plantations that depended on the slaves' skills as artisans, Virginia bondsmen resisted their oppression in patterns that suggested varying degrees of acculturation to American life. Whereas recently imported Africans would run away in small groups, a reflection of their communal heritage, highly acculturated slave artisans who had achieved some measure of independence tended to run away alone, in individual acts of resistance. But in South Carolina, the slaves were increasingly concentrated on large plantations in the lowcountry and so were able to retain more of their African customs and languages.

Acculturation therefore played a lesser role in emerging patterns of resistance, particularly after 1708, when blacks became a majority of South Carolinians. Indeed, it was the very concentration of this black majority in the expanding plantation economy of the lowcountry that helped provoke white fears and set off an escalating cycle of oppression and resistance.

Virginia planters often encouraged artisans' skills among slaves. But in South Carolina, after a period of crude frontier egalitarianism in which whites had relied heavily on peculiarly African skills, slave-holders were increasingly uneasy with persistent signs of black initiative. In both colonies, however, patterns of resistance were tied closely to the exploitation of the slaves' labor. The contradictions intrinsic to the lives of relatively independent slave artisans forced to operate within a severely circumscribed world help explain the Gabriel insurrection in Virginia. The intensified efforts to suppress black initiative by relegating most slaves to the routine drudgery of plantation labor played a role in provoking the Stono Rebellion in South Carolina. Whatever the differences from colony to colony, one pattern was clearly established in the eighteenth century: wherever there were slave laborers, masters had to deal with resistance.

From the daily demands of discipline and the periodic efforts to suppress insurrection, it was not a far step to the institutionalization of physical punishment. In 1775, the owner of twenty slaves at Jericho plantation in Virginia advertised for an overseer who "must be honest, sober, careful, and have Activity and Courage enough to correct an insolent or lazy slave." Some overseers abused their power and inflicted punishments that were little less than sadistic. Certainly there were limits on the slaveholders' behavior: William Pitman shocked even his family when he came home in a drunken rage one night and tied up a young slave by the neck and heels, beat the boy with a vine, and then "stomped him to death." Pitman's children testified against their father, and one newspaper editor declared that the convicted murderer had "justly incurred the penalties of law."[38]

Yet the open condemnation of extreme cruelty stands in contrast to the pervasive silence on the widespread use of harsh physical punishment. Even the best masters accepted whipping as essential to the maintenance of discipline. When William Dunbar found one of his slaves drunk, he had the bondsman "confined in the Bastile." The following day, Dunbar "ordered him 500 lashes . . . in order to draw a Confession from him." The slave acknowledged his misdeed and was promptly chained about the ankles. After several days, Dunbar had the irons "taken off, his leg being swelled, as I intend carrying him up to Point Coupee, where I shall sell him if I find an opportunity." Dunbar skillfully employed public punishment in an effort to terrorize all of his slaves. At one point he "ordered the Wench Bessy out of Irons, & to receive 25 lashes with a Cow Skin as a punishment & Example to the rest."[39]

It did not take much provocation for William Byrd to raise the lash. He whipped slaves for not reporting their illnesses, for "laziness," for wetting the bed, for "doing nothing." Byrd branded one slave with a hot iron and put a bit in her mouth. He forced another to take "a pint of piss to drink."[40] That Byrd does not appear to have been a particularly cruel master reinforces the conclusion that physical abuse was not an aberration, but rather a hallmark of slavery. As such, it contributed to the dehumanization of the slaves in the masters' eyes.

Such cruelty followed logically from the nearly universal goal of the slaveholders—material advancement. The poorest German or Scotch-Irish immigrant joined with the wealthiest English planters in viewing America as a land of unprecedented abundance. As slavery became the most popular means of acquiring wealth and status, the restraining force of reciprocal obligation gave way to the truly invisible hand of the marketplace. Hugh Jones reported that the "great Degree" of masters treated their slaves well so as to enhance their profits, although there were some who, "careless of their own Interest or Reputation, are too cruel and negligent." What Jones did not realize was that the pressures of the market could work just as effectively against the interests of the slaves. Negligence was not an uncommon trait among profit-conscious slaveholders. In North Carolina, for example, one observer reported that "many of the young Men and Women work stark naked in the Plantations in the hot Season except a piece of Cloath (out of decency) to cover their Nakedness, upon which account they are not very expensive to the Planters for their Cloathing." Some of the wealthier masters took pride in dressing their slaves "a little better than common," but even on the biggest plantations, fresh supplies of clothing might not be distributed until cold weather began to set in during the Fall. By that time James Habersham's slaves were "usually in rags." In 1764, he wrote to his agent in London asking him to speed up an order of slave clothing, "for I can almost say in regard to mine in particular that you will thereby be engaged in Cloathing the Naked." Even the kindest and wealthiest masters rarely provided more than a minimum of food, clothing, and shelter for their slaves. Philip Fithian was shocked by the slaves' meager weekly food allowance on Robert Carter's huge Virginia plantation. Doubly shocking was the fact that Carter was by all accounts "the most humane to his Slaves of any in these parts!"[41]

The distinguishing function of slaves in the South's market economy was to serve not only as a labor supply but also as capital assets. Consequently, the most distinctive feature of black slavery was the systematic effort to dehumanize the slaves by treating them as property. If slave women did not bear children after a year or two of cohabitation with their husbands, John Brickell reported, "Planters oblige them to take a second, third, fourth, fifth or more Husbands or Bedfellows; a fruitful woman amongst them being very much valued by the Planters, and numerous Issue esteemed the greatest Riches in the Country."[42] When the profitability of slaves as capital became that great, as it did very early on, the market economy came to intrude deeply into the most intimate of human relationships.

As capital, slaves became useful instruments of barter in the economy of the colonial South. One Virginia landowner advertised eight hundred acres of "good plantable Land" for which he would accept "ready Money, or young Negroes." John Geddy of Halifax, North Carolina, would "readily take either tobacco, hogs, negroes, or money," for his three tracts of land. Slaveholders paid off debts with bondsmen. Frances Christien wrote to Edmund Wilcox offering to "make any satisfaction" for his debt and to discharge the remainder of his bond "by selling two Negroes, a young Woman thirteen years of age, the fellow fifteen." William Bond willed that "my two old Negroes, Sip and Easter . . . be sold to pay my Loefell [lawful] Debts." Elizabeth Hudson's slave, Charles, was taken from her "to satisfy public taxes." In 1738, a Williamsburg matron entertained her guests by raffling off "a likely young Virginia Negro Woman, fit for House Business, and her child."[43]

In the profit-oriented market economy of the colonial South, the slaves' status as property stripped them of whatever protection the tradition of reciprocal obligations might otherwise have afforded. A few sensitive masters recognized as much. "It is a hard task to do our duty towards them," Peter Fontaine wrote of the slaves. "For we run the hazard of temporal ruin if they are not compelled to work on the one hand—and on the other, that of not being able to render a good account of our stewardship in the other and better world, if we oppress and tyrannize over them."[44] In the interests of economic survival, however, most slaveholders felt obliged to opt for temporal well-being.

Long before the American Revolution, the dehumanization of the slaves was institutionalized in law. "If the severest laws were not strictly put into execution against these People [slaves]," one writer warned, "they would soon overcome the *Christians* in this and most other Provinces in the Hands of the English." Virginia led the way in legalizing severity. Although various seventeenth-century statutes had restricted the rights of blacks and defined their status as slaves, it was not until 1705 that the first comprehensive legal code explicitly defined slaves as property. "All Negro, mulatto, and Indian slaves within this dominion," the statute read, "shall be held to be real estate and shall descend unto heirs and widows according to the custom of land inheritance." The principles of the 1705 slave code were similar to those incorporated into the statutes of most other colonies. A Massachusetts law of 1707 classified nonwhite slaves as personal estate. The South Carolina slave code of 1740 declared that unless they were born free or manumitted, "All Negroes, Mulattos, Indians and Mustees shall be deemed Slaves and Chattels personal in the Hands of their Owners."[45]

These were not simply labor laws governing the bondsmen as workers. They were also public declarations that blacks were, by virtue of their being black, slaves for life, and that their status was that of laborers held as property. Bondsmen and all of their descendants would enter the wills of their deceased masters and be passed from generation to generation along with houses, land, furniture, and livestock.[46] No white person—in any colony, at any time, anywhere in North America—ever suffered such a fate.

As HEIRS to the same political culture as Northerners, Southerners developed a similar sense of the distinctiveness of their new world. By the end of the Revolution, one slaveholder could write from London that a "people who has bin used to live in our Independent manner in Carolina can never like to live hear." Slaveholders resisted the same efforts at imperial expansion that angered other colonists; indeed, one minister suggested to the Charleston Planter's Society that Britain's actions were designed "to keep Us in abject Slavery" and to *"rule Us with a Rod of Iron."* Slaveholding Southerners had developed such strong devotion to the principles of liberty and freedom that they could join the Revolution without worrying about the significant sectional divisions that would become so troublesome in later years. "I have ever entertained a burning zeal for my Country & utter Detestation of the wicked Measures pursued . . . by the British Ministry," John Clopton wrote in 1775. "How can I be satisfied under these Circumstances," he asked his father in Hanover County, Virginia, when my own relatives have "fallen glorious victims of the noblest of all Causes, that of Liberty."[47] Slaveholders were no less enthusiastic in their support of the Revolution than other colonists.

Slaveholders were equally unified in their strong devotion to the protection of private property. Few things sealed this consensus more firmly than did Lord Dunmore's declaration that all slaves were "free, that are able and willing to bear arms, they joining His Majesty's Troops." Slaveholders were stunned by the proclamation, even those who never read it. Rumors of slave insolence and insurrection spread everywhere. In North Carolina, some slaveholders believed that Dunmore was ordering "the tories to murder the whigs, and promising every Negro that would murder his Master and family that he should have his Master's plantation." The *Virginia Gazette* reported that when a "gentlewoman" in Philadelphia reprimanded an insolent black for not stepping aside, he yelled back, "Stay you d——d white bitch, till lord Dunmore and his black regiment come, and then we will see who is to take the wall." Fomenting servile insurrection quickly became one of the slaveholders' chief complaints against Great Britain. Attached to the familiar lists of colonial grievances were complaints that "our negroes [are] taken from our plantations, many encouraged to leave their masters, and take up arms against us."[48] Slaveholders were doubly upset by Dunmore's proclamation because they saw Britain's economic policies as the cause of their dependence on slave labor. However naive their view of the origins of slavery, masters had enough resentment against England willingly to join the revolutionary cause.

And yet the consensus among revolutionary slaveholders was in many ways a fragile one. For while a majority supported the doctrine that "all men are created equal," there were those whose justification of the rebellion did not always involve the rejection of the paternalistic ethos of social hierarchy. Visiting from Boston in 1773, Josiah Quincy observed that although South Carolina had a popularly elected Assembly, "the representatives are almost wholly rich planters." Quincy added that "state and magnificence, the natural attendants on great riches, are conspicuous among this people." In Virginia he found that "an aristocratical spirit and principle are very prevalent in the laws and policy of this colony." A sermon delivered to the Charleston Planter's Society in 1769 demonstrates the tenacity of paternalistic ideals. "We observe amongst Men a *Variety* of GENIUS," the minister declared. "Some are framed with peculiar Talents for *forming* Plans, *making* Laws, *inventing* Arts, *taking the Lead.* . . . [Others] may be more prompt to *execute.*" According to the preacher, there are "Duties suited to our Station as Members of Society *in general*" as well as "to the Regard of the Planter's Society *in particular.*" Among these duties was a patriotic devotion to constitutional liberties. The recent actions of Parliament have violated "the very *first* Principles of the Constitution!" The minister asked the planters whether they were freeholders whose property was at their *"Own* or at the Command of *Others?"* As freemen, he wondered, would they be subject to their own laws or be "absolute Dependants on the Crown?"[49]

For such slaveholders, Great Britain had reneged on its reciprocal obligations. As the leading members of their community, they felt it was their duty to take the lead in resisting British assaults on liberty and the rights of private property. But liberty and property rights for these revolutionaries did not mean democracy and equality. Hence, many slaveholders continued through the Revolution to thwart the blacks' "genius for liberty" on the grounds that they were "not born to" it. Landon Carter, one of Virginia's wealthiest planters, initially opposed colonial moves for independence precisely because he feared that by breaking traditional ties to Great Britain, American politics would become too democratic. "Popularity" in politics, Carter wrote, "I long discovered to be an adultress of the first order." Although he had spoken out strongly against Britain's repeated assaults on the colonists' rights, he was appalled by the breakdown of the traditional "mixed government," which safely balanced the interests of monarchy, aristocracy, and democracy. "This republican form we all seem to be hurrying into" would be unable to contain the "internal Contentions" of society.[50]

Nevertheless, slavery itself had made it hard for most masters to sustain their devotion to the traditional rules of reciprocal obligation. They could accept the libertarian ideology of the Revolution because their colonial experience had provided them with the means to resolve the conflict between their simultaneous devotion to slavery and freedom. Many had arrived in America with the hostile prejudices and negative predispositions toward Africans they had inherited from their European ancestors. Europeans marked their differences from blacks by associating Africans with savagery, heathenism, and sexual promiscuity. Although they rarely denied the blacks' humanity outright, whites often professed to see relationships and similarities between apes and Africans that went beyond mere coincidence. The racist defense of slavery emerged from the interaction of such hostile predispositions with the dehumanizing effects of plantation discipline and slaveholding capitalism. It was precisely this interaction that came to define the institution of slavery to which the immigrants of the eighteenth century became devoted.

The American Revolution ratified this colonial experience. A political movement taken up in defense of property rights was no threat to slaveholders. The equality of all human beings could be widely proclaimed as long as it was understood that blacks were, somehow, less than human. It was no accident that the first systematically racist analysis of black slaves was written by the master who wrote the Declaration of Independence.[51]

To be sure, many revolutionary leaders did see a conflict between their libertarian ideals and their devotion to slavery. One Virginian suggested that his countrymen would have been "more strenuous in our opposition to ministerial Tyranny," and "manifested a more genuine Abhorrence of Slavery, had we not been too familiar with it, or had we not been conscious that we ourselves were absolute Tyrants, and held Numbers of poor Souls in the most abject and endless state of slavery." Chastellux reported that many Southerners in the 1780's "seem afflicted to have any slavery, and are constantly talking of abolishing it."[52]

Richard Randolph's will of 1796 reveals the inner turmoil of a revolutionary slaveholder unable to reconcile freedom and bondage. Randolph ordered that his slaves, "all of them," be freed as an act of "retribution." He chastised his countrymen for their exercise of "the most lawless and monstrous tyranny . . . in contradiction to their own declaration of rights." Randolph was motivated, he wrote, by his "abhorrence" of slavery as well as his desire "to exculpate myself . . . from the black crime which might otherwise be imputed to me, of voluntarily holding the above mentioned miserable beings in the same state of abject slavery in which I found them on receiving my patrimony."[53]

But most slaveholders who expressed misgivings about bondage used religious rather than revolutionary arguments, and a high percentage of the manumissions during the revolutionary era were made by ministers. "I am more & more convinced it is wrong," one Methodist clergyman in Georgia wrote of slavery, "though I feel a great Struggle in my minde about it." A Baptist minister admitted that "holding, tyrannyzing over, and driving slaves, I view as contrary to the laws of God and nature." In 1776, Henry Laurens told his son that "I abhor slavery." Born into a society in which "the Christian Religion and Slavery [were] growing under the same authority and cultivation," Laurens explained, "—I nevertheless disliked it."[54]

It may have been the recognition of this contradiction that inspired revolutionary slaveholders to liken their colonial status to bondage. In 1770 Richard Cogdell worried that his fellow North Carolinians would tolerate British depredations for fear of economic loss. "Liberty in Retail is but another Term for Slavery," he warned. "It would be highly dishonourable to sink into a slavish Inactivity." But if the analogy to enslavement struck masters with particular force, it was not usually because they were confounded by the inconsistency of their behavior. More often, they simply resented being treated as though they were black. "The British made war upon us because we and our women and children would not be their slaves & work for them the same as the negroes," the governor of Georgia declared in 1782.[55]

Two years later, over a thousand Virginians petitioned their legislature to cease considering a gradual emancipation bill by explicitly appealing to the rights of property that had only recently been secured by the Revolution. "We were put in the Possession of our Rights of Liberty and Property," the Free Inhabitants of Amelia County declared. "But notwithstanding this, we understand a very subtle and daring Attempt is made to dispossess us of a very important Part of our Property." If property rights sustained the slaveholders' devotion to the revolutionary cause, emancipation, however gradual, seemed an awesome threat. They insisted that slavery was sanctioned by Scripture and was essential to southern prosperity. Emancipation would unleash "the horrors of all Rapes, Murders, and Outrages, which a vast Multitude of unprincipled, unpropertied, revengeful, and remorseless Banditti are capable of perpetrating."[56]

Every proposal for gradual emancipation in southern law failed because of popular opposition, and most of the slaveholders who did come to oppose slavery felt compelled to leave the state or country in order to free their bondsmen. It was precisely this popular resistance to emancipation that concerned Henry Laurens as he contemplated freeing his own slaves. "Great powers oppose me," he wrote in 1776. "I shall appear to many as a promoter, not only of strange but of dangerous doctrines." In the end, Laurens resolved to "do as much as I can in my time and leave the rest to a better hand."[57]

A good deal of the opposition to slavery that surfaced at the time of the Revolution had less to do with the hatred of tyranny than with the abhorrence of blacks. When various Virginia counties resolved their opposition to the Atlantic slave trade, they argued that it was harmful to whites rather than Africans, that it was "most dangerous to virtue and the welfare of this country." The freeholders of Prince George County resolved that the African slave trade was "injurious to this Colony, obstructs the population of it by Freemen, prevents Manufacturers and other useful Emigrants from Europe from settling amongst us, and occasions an annual increase of the Balance of Trade against the Colony."[58]

If opposition to the slave trade was viewed by Northerners as a preliminary assault on slavery itself, it was rarely interpreted that way in the South. When the delegates to the Continental Congress from Georgia and South Carolina thought the Declaration of Independence did not make the distinction between slavery and the slave trade clear enough, they insisted upon and received an alteration. In adhering to this distinction, revolutionary Southerners inaugurated a powerful tradition. In 1807, John Mills, a Louisiana master, explained his position to a northern cousin: "I am a slave holder myself, and have increased the number within two months past, to 25 in the field, besides house & Body servants. yet you must not think that I approve of that Inhumane commerce, of tearing them from their native country and friends by force of arms, or by treachery or finesse. no I assure you that there is no man on earth, that can see it in a more horid light than myself." Two decades later, A. L. C. Magruder sounded the same theme in his defense of "those who are seized by the rapacious hands, of barbarous and inhumane men!" Appealing to his listeners' "consciences," Magruder asked for a law to restrain those "who call themselves civilized," even as they illegally import slaves "almost every day, by boat loads, from their native soil, from their Parents, and from their kindred." Yet Magruder was careful to explain that he did "not mean that those should be emancipated, who are now the inhabitants of the state," nor did he desire to interfere with the interstate traffic in slaves.[59] The distinction endured. Proposals to reopen the African slave trade were resoundingly rejected by the same secession conventions called to bring the southern states out of the Union so that slavery itself might be preserved.

THE PATTERNS of slaveholding that emerged in colonial America were not profoundly altered in the nineteenth century. Long before the

Revolution, the cash-crop economy had encompassed small slaveholding farms and large plantations alike. Cotton technology did not yet dominate southern agriculture, nor was there a workable marketing system that could service the cotton economy. But if the specific crops changed, if the South's physical boundaries expanded, most of the fundamental aspects of the slave system were in place by 1800, and they remained virtually intact through the antebellum years. Nearly a century before the United States officially withdrew from participation in the Atlantic slave trade, American blacks had begun to distinguish themselves among New World slave populations by achieving a birthrate that permitted southern bondsmen not only to reproduce but to expand their numbers at an unparalleled rate. Thus the debate over the closing of the slave trade followed rather than precipitated this major demographic development.[60]

By that time most slaveholders had rejected the paternalistic ideology and allied themselves with the revolutionaries who upheld the principle of human equality. But they could do so only after they had incorporated into their thinking the assumption that blacks were a "wretched Race" enslaved by virtue of their color. "White people were unequal to the Burthen in this Climate," James Habersham wrote from Georgia in 1768, "and therefore it was absolutely necessary to allow us the free use of slaves."[61] Having rejected paternalism, revolutionary slaveholders developed an entirely new defense of bondage, which was at base racial, and which took form in the great political controversies of the nineteenth century.

But if the structure of slavery was established, the ideology and culture of slaveholding were not yet fully developed when Americans declared their independence from Great Britain. The religious values of the master class were only beginning to emerge when the Revolution broke out; it would be a quarter of a century before evangelical Protestantism prevailed in the South. The spectacular westward expansion of the southern economy had yet to make its imprint on slaveholding culture. And the democratization of politics, a process which was to establish the tone of slaveholding ideology, had barely begun.

PART II

~

The
Market
Culture

~

Chapter 2

⟋⟍

Master-class Pluralism

I N WHAT HAS SINCE BECOME one of the most influential defenses of southern life ever published, Daniel R. Hundley attacked abolitionists for their failure to recognize the unique blend of aristocracy and democracy that characterized the pre-Civil War South. Republicans, Hundley charged, "pretend that Southern slaveholders are an exclusive class." They "fail to note," he added, "that it is not an *exclusive* aristocracy . . . but that every free white man in the whole Union has just as much right to become an Oligarch as the most ultra fire-eater. In truth, there are thousands of Southern slaveholders more democratic in their instincts than these very ultra Republicans."[1] Hundley had little trouble grasping the concept of a democratic oligarch. For even before he published his book in 1860, the tyranny of slavery had become separated from the question of whether southern white society was more aptly described as egalitarian or aristocratic. In large measure, this was because the contradictory patterns of wealth distribution that emerged during the colonial period persisted until the Civil War. There were huge concentrations of land and slaves in a society which nevertheless distributed its wealth quite broadly among whites. Depending on which evidence one chooses to emphasize, the Old South can be described as a society dominated by a slaveholding aristocracy or as an agrarian democracy.[2]

The statistics demonstrating a slaveholding aristocracy are of two kinds, the strongest showing the unequal distribution of wealth that gave the richest few the best lands and a disproportionate share of the slaves. In 1860 perhaps a third of all southern whites owned little more than the clothing they wore, while fewer than four percent of the adult white males owned the majority of black slaves. In Hancock County, Georgia, in 1860, the wealth of fifty-six planters averaged over $65,000, while nearly three hundred farm laborers and factory workers had virtually no wealth at all. The unequal distribution of wealth within the slaveholding class was less striking, but nonetheless evident. The majority of slaves were held by the one-fifth of slave-holders who owned twenty or more bondsmen. A sample of over five hundred masters from ten counties across the South in 1850 reveals that while fifteen percent of the slaveholders owned real estate valued at $5,000 or more, nearly one in five masters in this "landed" class owned little or no land.[3]

The evidence that slaveholding wealth became concentrated over time has also been used, with less success, to support the thesis that a slaveholding aristocracy prevailed. Evidence of increased concentration is important because it appears to indicate general trends in the slave economy and suggests what might have happened had the Civil War not interrupted southern development. The tax lists from Perry County, Georgia, indicate that in the thirty years following 1829 the planters—those with twenty slaves or more—increased their share of the slave population from twenty-five to seventy percent. In Harrison County, Texas, planters held nearly half the bondsmen in 1850. Ten years later they held nearly two-thirds.[4] But these statistics do not really prove that wealth became concentrated so much as they reveal the growing affluence of the communities under study. Nevertheless, if economic democracy is defined as the equal distribution of wealth, there was nothing like it in the antebellum South, not even among slaveholders themselves.

The statistics demonstrating the increasing concentration of wealth are of limited usefulness precisely because they depend upon local studies, and so miss geographical variation. There was probably no significant concentration of wealth within the slaveholding class across the South in the nineteenth century. What concentration there was varied enormously from place to place. In Montgomery, Alabama, more than half the white heads of families held slaves and there was no concentration of wealth from 1830 to 1860. In Onslow

County, North Carolina, the percentage of white families owning slaves increased from 14.9 in 1790 to 27.7 in 1860, with no significant concentration of wealth among planters.[5]

But the economic structure of antebellum southern society was considerably more complex than the statistics on concentration and maldistribution of wealth reveal. The proportion of slaveholders among southern whites was shrinking even as the absolute number of masters grew by seventy percent in a single generation, to nearly 400,000 in 1860. This expansion suggests widespread opportunity for upward mobility, and among slaveholders the evidence for social fluidity is convincing. There are strong correlations between youth and poverty, and between old age and large slaveholdings, suggesting that as individuals matured there was a good chance for economic advancement.[6]

Slavery created wealthy whites, not poor whites. Indeed, the unequal distribution of wealth in the South may have had little to do with slavery. Throughout America, equally large proportions of whites were impoverished—as many as two out of five. And, as in the North, southern poverty was as much a phenomenon of cities and immigrants as of rural destitution. What slaveholding did to the economic pyramid of white society was to expand its highest stratum. In 1860, the twelve wealthiest counties in the United States were below the Mason and Dixon line. Adams County, Mississippi, had the highest per capita wealth of any county in the nation.[7]

The median slaveholding rarely strayed far from four to six bondsmen per master. In 1850 half the slaveholders owned five bondsmen or fewer. Small holdings were not only the rule among the foreign-born but among the native-born white, Indian, and black slaveholders as well. In cities, on farms, in the old slave states of Virginia and North Carolina and in the frontier states of Missouri and Texas, the typical slaveholder did not own more than ten slaves. Three out of four masters owned fewer than ten in 1850. Even in the extraordinarily wealthy rice-producing counties of the South Carolina lowcountry, nearly half of the masters owned ten slaves or fewer.[8] Statistically, at least, the typical slaveholder was not even a planter, much less an aristocrat.

If the slaveholders were an aristocracy, they may well have been the most broadly based aristocracy in Western history. For the first half of the nineteenth century, about a third of all southern white families held slaves, and the fraction never went below a fourth before the Civil War. But even this statistic misrepresents the actual extent of slaveholding. In some of the most heavily populated slave states—South Carolina, Mississippi, Alabama, Georgia—between thirty-five and fifty percent of the white families held slaves in 1860. It would be difficult to argue that forty-eight percent of Mississippi's white families were aristocratic simply because they held slaves.[9] Yet these numbers still underestimate the extent to which southern whites had a direct material interest in the perpetuation of black slavery.

It is clear that the majority of slaveholders who owned no more than five bondsmen were not a stable economic class. At that level it was quite common for owners to hold slaves only erratically, depending upon their seasonal needs or their immediate economic circumstances. Indeed, movement into and out of the slaveholding class may have been the rule rather than the exception for the majority of masters. The statistics for the number of whites who held slaves at the moment the figures were compiled do not account for the thousands who held slaves intermittently. In addition, there were large numbers of farmers, professionals, tradesmen, and even government bureaucrats who hired slaves on a seasonal or yearly basis. It could be argued that whites who hired slaves were reinforcing planter domination by their dependence on large slaveholders.[10] But as often as not, it was the planters who depended on non-slaveholding employers to train their bondsmen in a skill or to relieve masters of the burden of caring for more slaves than they could employ usefully. Like those who temporarily held no slaves, those who hired bondsmen did not show up in the statistics for slaveholding.

There was also a smaller but nonetheless significant group of young white Southerners who, by virtue of their education or family background, had every reason to expect that within a few years they would own slaves. One reason poverty corresponded strongly with youth in the Old South was that young professionals who had moved out to the frontier to begin their careers showed up on the tax returns and census records as propertyless. But the goal of many southern doctors and lawyers was to own a plantation worked by slaves, and in the sickly and litigious atmosphere of the antebellum South that goal was not unreasonable. While it is impossible to arrive at any accurate figures, it is likely that for most of the antebellum era, a clear majority of white families in the Deep South had a direct material interest in the protection and perpetuation of slavery. The paradox is extraordinary. If the Old South was dominated by slaveholders, that domination was in large measure the democratic reflection of white social reality.

Thus, the evidence is conflicting. Antebellum slaveholders counted in their ranks a disproportionate share of the nation's wealthiest citizens, yet this very concentration of wealth set the planter aristocracy far apart from most slaveholders. The economic structure of the slaveholding class changed little in the decades before the Civil War, indicating social stability. Yet there was a dramatic increase in the number of slaveholders, significant upward mobility, and pervasive demographic restlessness among slaveholders as well. Concentration and diffusion, stagnation and fluidity were all characteristic of the slaveholding class. What is missing from such dichotomies is the vast array of individual variations which, by their complexity, force a re-examination of the nature of slaveholding in America. With the economic paradoxes of the antebellum South, we have only begun to sense the diversity of American slaveholders.

TRAVELING THROUGH the trans-Appalachian west in the first quarter of the nineteenth century, Timothy Flint was struck by the "strong features of nationality" that characterized the settlers. "The Germans, the French, the Anglo-Americans, Scotch, and Irish, all retain and preserve their national manners," Flint recalled. A man of his times, he proceeded to rank the various nationalities according to prevailing prejudices. The Germans were a sober and thrifty people, given to neither luxury nor frivolity: "Silent, unwearied labour, and the rearing of their children, are their only pursuits; and in a few years they are comparatively rich." Next in prosperity were the Anglo-Americans, "then the Scotch," and beneath them all were the French. "Generally a poor race of hunters, crowded in villages with mud hovels, fond of conversation and coffee," the Frenchman "never rises from a state of indigence."[11] The one feature common to all these ethnic groups, so common that Flint felt no need to mention it, was black slavery.

The patterns of slaveholding among colonial immigrants were as tenacious as their ethnicity. A young Pennsylvanian visiting western Virginia in 1827 wrote that the "settlers are very many of them Germans & Dutch." Their "large barns," their "frugal & neat system of cultivation," even their names, reminded the traveler of his home state. Although there were fewer blacks than he expected on the small farms of western Virginia, he nevertheless found that "most of the farmers have a few slaves," adding that even their small use of bound labor made these Germans less prosperous than those in Pennsylvania. The Germans who came to America to escape the political turmoil and economic dislocation of the 1840's and 1850's were encouraged by those who had arrived in the South before them. As their country-men had been in the colonial period, many Germans were at first hostile to slavery, and, as with those predecessors, hostility soon gave way to enthusiasm. "It is true, there are many slaves here," one immigrant wrote to Germany from New Orleans, "but they are all Negroes, who know no better than to be slaves. In Germany, how-ever . . . all of you are slaves, a few well-to-do people excepted." A large portion of the German immigrant community never aban-doned its opposition to the use of slave labor. But such opposition was rarely expressed politically, for there were always Germans who had adopted the values of American society and found the use of slaves a great convenience. An innkeeper at Natchez, the owner of four slaves, assured one of his guests that he was not the only German prospering in the South. "Anybody who is not too proud to work can get rich here," he declared.[12]

Like the Germans, the Scotch-Irish who became slaveholders were those who were most amenable to the culture of upward mobility. Frederick Law Olmsted, the most astute and thorough observer of life in the Old South, noted that the Scotch-Irish came to America overwhelmingly poor, but frugal and industrious. They "are certain in a few years to acquire money enough to buy a negro, which they are said to be invariably ambitious to possess." Similarly, nearly all the Irish came to America in poverty. Like the Germans, they frequently brought with them an antipathy for slavery, and, as with all immigrant groups who had come to the South before them, their opposition gradually waned as the more prosperous among them certified their assimilation by becoming slaveholders. The largest bloc of Irish immigrants in the antebellum South went to New Orleans, where successful Irish merchants, members of the Hibernian Society, and even the trustees of St. Patrick's Church all owned slaves, as did the most industrious Irish draymen. By 1856, the New Orleans *Catholic Standard* declared that "we have never yet met a Catholic who was not true to his southern rights."[13]

The ownership of slaves became for many immigrants the single most important symbol of their success in the New World, although few of them ever participated in the economy of the large plantation. The small slaveholding culture of the colonial frontier had been largely responsible for the initial expansion of the antebellum South, and that culture persisted. The comments of travelers are confirmed by the census returns and tax records: these people only infrequently became large planters. Furthermore, their ethnicity survived until the last decades of the antebellum era, when large numbers of new immigrants swelled their ranks. In 1860, there were still pockets of Germans, Irish, and Scotch-Irish throughout the South, all of them represented in the slaveholding class. The statistics vary from place to place, but there is no question that in the 1850's, with the increase in the number of European immigrants entering the South, there was a corresponding increase in the number of foreign-born slaveholders. In Claiborne County, Mississippi, the white foreign-born population rose from 12.8 percent in 1850 to 31 percent in 1860. In the same period the number of foreign-born citizens of Texas jumped by 145 percent, accounting for more than one-tenth of the free population. By 1860, thirty-five of Houston's 265 slaveholders were foreign-born.[14]

Most immigrant Southerners left Europe in response to political or economic oppression, but the French had come to Louisiana as part of an imperial effort to maintain control of the lower Mississippi valley for France. Finally convinced that only slave labor could sustain settlement in a colony notorious for its sickness, inaccessibility, and relative unprofitability, the French began importing black laborers in 1719. No one thought to question the morality of slavery, and so no one, not even the Catholic clergy, sought to defend it. With unconscious determination, slavery was fitted neatly into a typically hierarchical but uniquely Creole slaveholding culture.[15]

As late as 1853, the majority of the planters in the sugar-producing parishes of Louisiana were Creole—descendants of Spanish, Indian, but more commonly French inhabitants of the area. Their history, their language, their religion, and the crops they produced separated this local majority from the dominant culture of the antebellum South. Perhaps because their initial settlement had less to do with individual initiative than with official French policy, or because they were culturally distant from the Protestant world of most American slaveholders, French masters often impressed observers as decidedly unambitious if not downright lazy. "The majority of wealthy Creoles," one Louisianian told Olmsted, "do nothing to improve their estate; and are very apt to live beyond their income." Creole slaveholders were uncommonly stable; they participated only negligibly in the westward expansion of the slave economy. "They will not part with their land, and especially with their home, as long as they can help it." They were said to make few provisions for the economic security of their children. By dividing their holdings over several generations, Creoles were reported to have reduced themselves to indigence and poverty.[16]

What irked observers most of all about the slaveholders of French descent was the durability of their rich cultural heritage and their seeming refusal to adopt as their own the overt materialism of the age. In the circumstances, the Creoles could hardly compete, and by the last decades of the antebellum era, Southerners began to take note of the decline of French influence among Louisiana slaveholders. "The French had a fair start of us by more than a century," one observer remarked. "They obtained possession of the richest lands yet are now fairly distanced in the race." When they go into debt and are forced to sell their best lands, he went on, "they do not migrate to a new region farther west, but fall back somewhere into the low grounds near the swamp. There they retain all their antiquated usages, seeming to hate innovation. To this day they remain rooted in those parts of Louisiana where the mother country first planted her two colonies two centuries ago." *DeBow's Review* was no more charitable when it explained why nearly all the large planters in Terrebonne Parish were "American," even though a majority of the population was Creole. Despite "many noble exceptions," the magazine reported, the Creoles were "an indolent, uneducated race." The unblushing prejudice of such contemporary observations does not alter the evidence that despite the continuing presence of French culture, the largest slaveholders of Louisiana were increasingly "American."[17] French slaveholders certainly survived until the Civil War, but like the Scottish masters of colonial America, their influence was diminished as the aggressive, expansive, and upwardly mobile culture of American slaveholding overwhelmed the conservative, hierarchical, and paternalistic culture of the Louisiana Creole.

The history of slaveholding among Native Americans, like that of the Creoles, is distinct yet intertwined with the history of southern slaveholding in general. Although slavery existed in Native American society long before European penetration, it was never a commercial institution. Among the Cherokees, for example, slaves, *atsi nahsa'i,* were unimportant to the subsistence economy and suffered primarily by their exclusion from the kinship system. But Europeans saw only slavery, and assumed it was identical to their own. As they introduced the market economy to the Cherokees, the traffic in Native American slaves captured in war became important to the tribe. With the advance of African bondage in the New World, many Cherokees found the trade in black slaves profitable and fitted "the peculiar institution" into their distinctive social structure. Many adopted the white racial attitudes that defined blacks as inferior, their skin color the outward sign of their predestined lot as slaves.[18]

But Native Americans had good reason to resist the assimilation of white cultural norms, and their antebellum history is rife with internal dissension that reached its climax at the intersection of two seemingly unrelated phenomena: Indian removal and black slavery. The forced, westward migration of thousands of Native Americans put 74,000 out of 81,000 colonized Indians below the Missouri Compromise line. As Southerners, they found their progress judged by their white neighbors according to the strength of their devotion to black slavery. The prevailing test of successful colonization was the

number of Native Americans who became slaveholders. Whites
might well anticipate success, for even before removal there were
slaveholders in most major southern tribes. In 1824 there were 1,277
black slaves among the 15,560 Cherokees. By 1861, there were 5,000
slaves among the 25,000 Choctaws and Chickasaws. After removal,
the pressure on Native Americans to certify their assimilation and at
the same time demonstrate their devotion to the South made it all
but impossible for many to resist the temptation to become slaveholders. Among the Cherokees a split developed between "progressives"
—who, being the most amenable to white slaveholding society, tried
to convince their compatriots to remove themselves voluntarily from
their homelands—and "conservatives," who rejected both slavery and
white culture and attempted to preserve the Cherokee heritage by
resisting both slavery and removal to the West.[19]

For the most part, the ownership of slaves was a reliable indicator
that the master had accepted many of the values of white society.
Indeed it was frequently asserted that the biggest slaveholders among
the Native Americans were those with one white parent. "A slave
among wild Indians is almost as free as his owner," one traveler
wrote. "Proceeding from this condition more service is required from
the slave until among the half-breeds and the whites who have
married natives, they become slaves indeed in all manner of work."
For this reason, the cultural passage from Native American to Anglo-
American society was relatively easy for many Indian slaveholders.
The chief of Mississippi's Choctaws, Greenwood Leflore, had one
white parent. He stayed behind when his tribe was removed to the
West in 1830. Having begun to purchase blacks in the previous
decade, he was soon reputed to be one of the most avid slave buyers
in the area. By 1860 Leflore owned over four hundred slaves, and he
wielded considerable influence in the local white community.[20]

Slavery among Native Americans varied from tribe to tribe as
much as between individuals. Seminole slaveholders were conspicuously humane, allowing their bondsmen to live with their families
on small farms with liberties virtually indistinguishable from their
owners'. According to one observer, "many of these slaves have stocks
of horses, cows and hogs with which the Indian owner never assumes
the right to intermeddle." The persistence of cultural traditions even

among highly assimilated Indian slaveholders was revealed in the pre-removal Cherokee slave code. The fact that there were so few laws governing masters and slaves is itself evidence that the historical emphasis on personal rule within a kinship system was not entirely lost. The responsibility of the master was stressed in laws penalizing owners for purchasing goods from slaves, selling liquor to slaves, or for marrying their bondsmen. In contrast to the slave codes of white society, Cherokee laws stressed the personal responsibility of the masters by reserving for them the majority of the punishments and by omitting all laws dealing with slave insurrection and insubordination. For all of its communalism, however, this was not the code of a plantation society. In 1835, only three of the 207 Cherokee slaveholders owned fifty or more bondsmen; eighty-three percent owned fewer than ten slaves.[21]

So widespread was slaveholding among Native Americans that when the Civil War broke out, southern tribes almost universally supported the Confederacy. To be sure, they had no good reason to side with the government that had oppressed them for decades. But their reasoning went well beyond revenge: "Our geographical position, our social and domestic institutions, our feelings and sympathies, all attach us to our Southern friends," the Chickasaw Nation declared. "As a Southern people we consider their cause our own."[22]

Free black slaveholders had considerably less devotion to the southern cause. The right of blacks to hold slaves had been recognized as early as 1654, when a Virginia court denied John Casor's suit for freedom from his "old negro" master, Anthony Johnson. But until the early nineteenth century, when southern legislatures re-enacted restrictions on the slaveholders' right to free their slaves, most of the bondsmen purchased by blacks were quickly manumitted. Thereafter, blacks who purchased slaves were forced to retain their property intact or move to a free state. By 1830, there were some 3,775 free black slaveholders across the South, eighty percent of whom lived in four of the oldest slaveholding states, Louisiana, South Carolina, Virginia, and Maryland. Nearly half of all black slaveholders lived in cities, primarily New Orleans and Charleston.[23]

The evidence is overwhelming that the vast majority of black slaveholders were free men who purchased members of their families or who acted out of benevolence. There were literally hundreds of petitions by black masters asking to be exempted from state laws barring manumission. Often such petitions were presented by elderly blacks who feared that after their deaths their relatives would be enslaved to white masters. There were, of course, a few black slaveholders who sold off their relatives themselves, particularly spouses with whom they did not get along. But there were even more successful blacks who regularly bought slaves with the expressed intention of manumitting them. John Barry Meachum, a minister in St. Louis, purchased slaves and granted them freedom for a nominal sum or after they worked off their cost on liberal terms. After purchasing his wife and two daughters, William Castin bought two more young slaves, both of whom he later manumitted. That free black masters were usually the owners of their families explains why their average slaveholding was only slightly more than three bondsmen.[24]

The few large slaveholders among free blacks were usually at least half white. "Many of them are separated from the white race by a line of division so faint that it can be traced only by the keen eye of prejudice," a St. Louis observer wrote. David Barland, for example, was one of twelve mulatto children born to William Barland, a white planter in Adams County, Mississippi, and his slave, Elizabeth. All the children were freed by their father in 1815, and by 1849 David Barland owned eighteen slaves, none of whom were his relatives. The tax rolls occasionally listed him as white, but to the United States Bureau of the Census, David Barland was the head of a free Negro household. Although the law said they were black, their ancestry and skin color defined them otherwise, and their own behavior indicated that many "free Negro" slaveholders did not consider themselves black at all.[25]

In 1830, William Johnson was freed by petition of his owner in Natchez, Mississippi. His mother and his sister, also a mulatto, had already been freed, and the latter was sent to be educated in Philadelphia. Throughout his life, Johnson emulated the racist principles of white society, aspiring to social acceptance by the Natchez elite. He disdained the lowly habits of the city's free black community, eventually dissociating himself from it completely. He was trained as a barber at his brother's shop, which he bought in 1830. Johnson hired and trained free black and slave apprentices, but only two of his own slaves ever worked for him as barbers. He bought property and supplemented his business income through rentals, a small farm, and land speculation. When he first took over the barber shop, Johnson owned four or five slaves and by the late 1840's he owned eight or nine. His mother died in 1849, leaving Johnson with the largest holdings of his life: fifteen slaves, whose services he enjoyed for only two years, before his murder in 1851.[26]

The largest concentration of mulatto planters was in southern Louisiana, where a long history of miscegenation left a legacy of "black" slaveholders with French and Spanish names like Ciprien Ricard, Marie Metoyer, Charles Roques, and Martin Donato. It was from this culture that such men as Andrew Durnford emerged. An avid slave trader who made as much money buying and selling blacks as he did from the proceeds of his large sugar plantation, Durnford's letters from Virginia during an 1835 buying trip reveal the concerns of a typical slaveholder: the high price of blacks and the problem of transporting his huge purchase of twenty-five slaves back to Louisiana. From this community came some of the strongest expressions of non-white support for the South during the secession crisis. In a communication to a New Orleans newspaper, some of the "free colored population" of the state declared their willingness to shed blood for Louisiana, because they "own slaves, and they are dearly attached to their native land."[27]

The anomaly of black slaveholders was highlighted by the hostility they met from whites and slaves alike. If free blacks were feared for their associations with slaves, black masters were often viewed with particular alarm: their mere existence was an affront to the principle of white supremacy. As the Civil War approached, there were increasing efforts to restrict the right of blacks to hold bondsmen on the grounds that slaves should be kept "as far as possible under the control of white men only." Black slaves were no less hostile. "One nigger's no business to sarve another," a Texas slave complained. "It's bad enough to have to sarve a white man without being paid for it, without having to sarve a black man."[28]

Ethnic and racial origins were not the only source of master-class pluralism. One of every ten slaveholders lived in the South's largest cities, and it was in this urban setting that the slaveholding class was most cosmopolitan. The fluidity of urban society made for huge fluctuations in the percentage of slaveholders over time and place. In Baltimore, in 1860, only three percent of the adult white males owned or hired slaves. Ten years earlier, fifty-nine percent of Charleston's adult white males owned or hired slaves. The average slaveholding was no less varied in southern cities. In 1850, Savannah's masters averaged nearly eight bondsmen each, but in 1860 the number in Washington, D.C., was fewer than two. Such variations were paralleled by extensive diversity among individual urban slaveholders. Among those who owned or hired slaves in Savannah were attorneys, bookkeepers, bakers, carpenters, clerks, druggists, grocers, machinists, merchants, physicians, the sheriff, a tailor, a jeweler, and a blacksmith.[29]

Women comprised another ten percent of the slaveholding class, and in significant ways they differed from male masters. Overwhelmingly, female slaveholders inherited their bondsmen from their deceased husbands. Thus the average age of slaveholding women was fifty years, seven years more than the average for all masters. Nine times out of ten, female masters were listed by United States census officials as having no occupation. Indeed, over ninety percent of the slaveholders who listed no occupation were women. Illiteracy was four times as common among slaveholding women as among men of the same class. More than one of five female masters could not read or write.

In other ways, however, patterns of slaveholding among women were similar to those among men. Land and slave distributions did not vary significantly between the sexes. On larger farms, women relied heavily on overseers, suggesting that plantation routine was not noticeably altered by the presence of a female master. Indeed, the letters of the slaveholders' wives suggest that women had a good deal of experience managing slaves in their husbands' frequent absences. Widowhood did not always bring with it new or unexpected responsibilities.[30]

Immigrants, Native Americans, blacks, urbanites, and women all contributed to the diversity of the master class. In strictly numerical terms, their significance can hardly be discounted. If the planters included all those with twenty slaves or more, there were no more planters than there were women or urbanites among slaveholders. Black, mulatto, and Native-American slaveholders were nearly as numerous as "planter aristocrats" with fifty slaves or more. In one sense, then, the typical master did not really exist.

But numerical categories reveal patterns as well as variations. A statistical portrait of typicality can provide the basis for a fuller examination of the patterns of slaveholding in America. The average slaveholder was forty-four years old, most likely male, still more likely white. Whatever his ethnic heritage, by 1850 he was almost always native-born, and more than nine times out of ten he was born in the South. The average slaveholding was eight or nine, but the typical master owned fewer than that. The median value of the slaveholder's land was just under three thousand dollars. Eighty percent of the time his chief employment was in agriculture, either as a farmer, planter, or overseer.[31] The only surprise in all of this is that the middle-aged white farmer with perhaps a handful of slaves quickly disappeared from the history books, replaced by a plantation legend that bears little resemblance to historical reality.

THE SLAVEHOLDERS of legend were men bound by tradition. Attached to family and community, they lived lives of stability and comfort. If they were hedonistic, the needs of their black and white dependents were nevertheless chief among their concerns. Solidly agrarian, they resisted the hectic materialism of the more urban and industrial North. The society they established was unique, marked by its gentility, its reverence for the established ways, and an admirable blend of self-discipline and civility. But this legend has served the purposes of proslavery ideologues and post-Civil War romantics more than the cause of historical accuracy. It distorts the past by dismissing almost entirely the experience of the vast majority of slaveholders who were not planters and who rarely lived in bucolic relaxation. It further distorts by presenting an idealized image of the plantation divorced from the mundane and oppressive realities of everyday life. Most slaveholders, including the planters, would have recognized little in the legend that conformed to their own lives.

To own twenty slaves in 1860 was to be among the wealthiest men in America, easily within the top five percent of southern white families. Barely one in twenty slaveholders owned that many bondsmen, and not one in a hundred southern white families was headed by such a man. Yet southern white society is frequently analyzed from the perspective of this tiny elite. Similarly, the distinction between "slaveholders" and "planters" has often disappeared, despite numerous efforts to establish precise statistical definitions.[32]

Arbitrary numerical boundaries serve well the needs of individual scholars whose differing definitions impel the exclusion or addition of large numbers of slaveholders from the planter class.[33] In each case the specific definition may be justified, but in their very proliferation simple numerical boundaries reveal their own limitations. In reality, the slaveholding class was fluid. Most slaveholders spent their lives defying the statistical boundaries historians so emphatically establish. Masters commonly entered the slaveholding class from the yeomanry; they moved from the ranks of small slaveholders into the middle class, and if they were lucky, they crossed from one definition of planter to the next in predictable patterns.

This is not to say that there were no class divisions among slaveholders. Rather, it is to suggest that of all the ways of marking those divisions, numbers may be the least useful. Even in the Old South the term "planter" did not simply mean a large slaveholder. The distribution of slaves among those who defined themselves as "planters" in the 1850 census did not differ substantially from that of "farmers." In some counties nearly all slaveholders were called planters, while in others all were farmers. Nevertheless, there were patterns in the lives of small slaveholders, middle-class masters, and planters that separate each group from the other. And there is historical significance in their differing experiences.

Small slaveholders were particularly mobile. Among them shifting jobs was common, and movement into and out of the slaveholding class was widespread. Under the circumstances, the master-slave relationship varied enormously from one small slaveholder to the next. Walter Overton, for example, was born in Virginia in 1830, and after graduating from Mercer College moved to Georgia, where he married and settled down. He does not appear to have suffered any severe economic setbacks in his life before the war broke out, yet Overton was not really a stable member of his community if his employment record is any indication. He moved from job to job, working at various times as a brickmaker, plasterer, teacher, magistrate, and post office assistant. In 1860, he owned one slave, John, a skilled brickmason with whom he worked closely. The slave's value to Overton was consequently high. In one instance he withdrew from the job of helping to raise a neighbor's house rather than "run the risk of getting hurt or having John crippled [even] for a good sum of money."[34]

In contrast was Samuel Edward Burges. His home was a small farm in Cheraw, South Carolina, where his single slave, Tom, worked virtually alone. Before the war, Burges spent most of his time on the road collecting subscription fees for his employer, the Charleston *Mercury*. His travels allowed Burges to see his relatives and friends more often than his slave. A pleasant and helpful man by nature, Burges could always be counted on for a favor. On one occasion he drove an incorrigible slave to Bennetville and sold him "for Aunt Mary." Another time he helped a friend find a runaway slave hiding in an old house. "We tied her hands behind her back and locked her up in the smokehouse," Burges wrote, whereupon she "pretended to be very sick."[35]

For the thousands of small slaveholders whose jobs kept them away from their farms, indifference to the slaves was probably the rule rather than the exception. Certainly this was the case with James Buckner Barry's slaves. Born in Onslow County, North Carolina, in 1821, Barry left for Texas when he was twenty-three. He joined the army for two years before returning to his father's home in North Carolina. In 1847, after his marriage, Barry, his wife, her brother, and two slaves set out for Texas. They settled in recently organized Bosque County, where they raised livestock. But conditions on the Texas frontier, as well as Barry's apparent love of army life, kept him from his home a good deal of the time. He spent most of his days hunting or patrolling the frontier in search of Indians. Whatever else Barry's few slaves did while he was away, they did not grow crops sufficient to feed his family. Thirteen years after settling in Texas,

Barry revealed in his diary that he was still obsessed with fighting Indians, while at home bread was "scarce" and his crops "blighted by the drought."[36]

Conditions varied over time as well, making the master-slave relationship even less predictable among small slaveholders. W. J. Simpson worked his two slaves on a small cotton farm near Henderson, South Carolina, in the mid-1840's. After ten years of struggling and stagnation, Simpson hired out one of his two slaves and became his father's overseer on a farm with about seven bondsmen. As the manager of a larger group of slaves, he faced new problems. At the beginning of the cotton season in 1855, for example, several of the slaves took sick, others were away or busy elsewhere, and "Jack, Leah & Ned not being field hands just work when it suits them." In January 1856, Simpson estimated his worth at just over four thousand dollars. He still owned two slaves: a "boy," Joe, whom he rented out yearly for $175, and a female worth $700. His father's farm produced about ten bales of cotton each year, and although it prospered, it did not grow. In late 1860 Simpson's father died, and his slave holdings reached an all-time high of ten. In January 1861, one year before he volunteered his services to the Confederate Army, Simpson estimated his worth at over $15,000. Just when it no longer really mattered, Simpson had achieved the kind of economic security that eluded most small slaveholders.[37]

If there is a pattern in the treatment of bondsmen by small slaveholders, it cannot be derived from the imperatives of the master-slave relationship. As on the largest plantations, the interracial relations on the smallest farms depended on the personalities of individual owners, their immediate economic circumstances, the economic structure of slavery itself, and the willingness of the slaves to cooperate. Walter Overton and W. J. Simpson worked closely with their bondsmen, but where Overton and his slave labored together as skilled artisans and regularly attended the same church services, Simpson hired out his one male slave and worked with his father's bondsmen as a frustrated overseer. Samuel Burges and James B. Barry, by contrast, saw their slaves only occasionally, and if Burges's attitude toward bondsmen other than his own is any indication, he treated his slave with callous indifference at best.

Among small slaveholders such variation was the inevitable product of a way of life marked by constant struggle, spurts of progress
and occasional setbacks, and seemingly endless physical movement.
These were the forces that shaped several generations of the Lincecum
family. Hezekiah Lincecum was the only surviving son of a small
slaveholding family that had fled Georgia during the American Revolution. His father and two brothers died in the war, and all of the
Lincecums' slaves ran away. With little reason to remain at home, and
"being of a restless spirit," Hezekiah stayed only two seasons on his
mother's farm, just long enough to court and marry his fourteen-
year-old wife, before moving out to the Georgia frontier. Chased
back to Hancock County by Indians, the still restless Hezekiah was
impressed by the repeated urgings of his Tennessee relations. After
three prosperous years in Georgia, he "sold everything he could not
carry with him." He and his wife left for Tennessee with four
children, four slaves, and his eighty-eight-year-old mother, whose
sickness prevented them from completing the trip. They rented a farm
for a year, grew a good cotton crop, then packed up and headed for
Tennessee.

Once again the Lincecum family did not reach its destination.
Instead, Hezekiah decided to buy a farm in Abbeville District, South
Carolina, where he planted cotton for a year, after which he bought
another farm in Athens, Georgia. The following year, 1805, they left
again for Tennessee, this time with only one slave. But an accident
along the way caused the family to settle on a farm in Pendleton
District, South Carolina, until pressure from relatives brought them
back to Georgia. There Hezekiah sent his children to school for five
months before moving again to the booming frontier town of Eaton-
ton, Georgia. The Lincecum family stayed there during the War of
1812, while the eldest son, Gideon, left home, worked for some local
merchants, joined the armed forces, served as a local tax collector, got
married, and moved back home to help out on his father's farm for
a year before going to work on someone else's farm. Gideon was soon
pressured to move by his restless father and his well-born wife, whose
relatives "had been mean enough to cast little slurs at her and her
poverty." They moved out of Georgia onto Indian land.[38]

Gideon's interest in learning had been piqued by his few months of formal education. He taught himself to read and began to study medicine. At his newest frontier home Gideon became a school teacher, a profession at which he was so successful that he was offered a thousand dollars to remain another session. But Hezekiah was anxious to move again and Gideon could hardly resist. "I had been reared to a belief and faith in the pleasure of frequent change of country," he wrote in his autobiography, "and I looked upon the long journey, through the wilderness, with much pleasure." With his two slaves, his father's six, and his brother-in-law's two, Gideon and the rest of the Lincecum family moved five hundred miles to the "small log cabin village" of Tuscaloosa, Alabama. Short of money and building materials for his own house, Gideon joined a lucrative partnership as a clapboard maker. They stayed for a few months before moving seventy-five miles to what would later become Mississippi. There Gideon prospered by selling whiskey to Indians for pelts. His family stayed for four years, but they were always sickly. "Great as was this location for making money," Gideon recalled, "we were so unhealthy that we were forced to leave it."[39]

In 1825, Gideon Lincecum took his family to the hill country, where they stayed for eight years. During that time, his trading business collapsed because of intemperate partners and the refusal of his customers to pay their bills. Completely impoverished, Lincecum roamed the woods hunting for food for his wife and nine children. He tried to put together a traveling road show of Indian ball players, but it did not pay. He attempted to use his reading in medicine to set up a practice but "it required money . . . and that was an article I did not possess." After five years of poverty, a grateful old patient lent Gideon one hundred dollars to buy medicine and set up a shop. Within a short time, "Doctor" Lincecum was prospering again. "It was an unusually sickly season," he wrote, "and almost everyone became indebted to me."[40]

In 1835, Lincecum visited Texas for seven months, but returned to Mississippi during a period of great sickness, where his business continued to flourish. After a few years he transferred his thriving medical practice to Columbus, and in seven years he amassed a small fortune. In 1848, with a good deal of money, no debts, "ten negroes and ten fine horses," Gideon Lincecum packed up and moved his family to Texas. Their small settlement developed "into a thriving little village," and again the Lincecum family flourished. "When the Civil War came, we labored to perform our part in the struggle for liberty," Gideon wrote, but "we lost our *cause.*" His mortified wife soon died, and Lincecum himself became so disgusted with his "Yankee masters" that at the age of seventy-five he sold all of his possessions and "left for Tuxpan, Mexico."[41]

The Lincecum family is more prototypical than representative. Few slaveholding families moved that much; still fewer slaveholders had that many different jobs. Although economic insecurity was common among small slaveholders, few experienced such radical and recurrent shifts of fortune. Still, by comparison with the image of the stable planter, born and reared on his father's estate and never wandering far from his place of birth, the experiences of the Lincecum family are considerably closer to the historical record. Gideon Lincecum was nearly sixty years old when he finally settled on his Texas farm, and it is fair to say that his world view was shaped by forces quite unrelated to plantation life. So it was for the vast majority of small slaveholders, who neither grew up on plantations nor achieved planter status. More typically, their lives were shaped by restlessness, drift, and economic insecurity.

IF THERE IS A LESSON in Gideon Lincecum's biography, it may be that what separated small slaveholders from middle-class masters was something more than just the number of slaves but something less than the plantation experience. The behavior of middle-class slaveholders whose success could well have permitted them the leisurely life so widely associated with the plantation South indicates that such an existence was neither common nor commonly sought. It was the rare master who ceased his quest for more land and slaves, and it was precisely this grasping materialism which stands out in the collective biographies of middle-class slaveholders. They tended to be well educated; they frequently were trained in the professions or began their careers as businessmen. They usually started life with all the advantages that small slaveholders struggled to achieve. Even when not career-oriented, they could generally rely on a small patrimony

allowing them to skip altogether the roughest years when the price
of a single slave seemed an impossible expense.

Yet, their lives were hardly those of princely heirs. Their earliest
years were difficult; they usually left home in young adulthood and
were expected to make it on their own. Like most slaveholders, they
were migratory, especially in their twenties and thirties. They often
sought their success in frontier towns where the amenities of their
childhood years, however limited, were nowhere to be found. But
they were not frontiersmen by temperament. After several years of
search, struggle, and accumulation, they began to purchase land and
slaves in small parcels, slowly building on the profit of their careers.
Those who made agriculture their only source of income traveled the
same slow, arduous road to prosperity.

Traveling through the backcountry in the 1850's, Frederick
Olmsted noticed that the slaveholders were "chiefly professional men,
shop-keepers, and men in office, who are also land owners, and give
a divided attention to farming." In 1850, one out of five masters was
employed in an occupation unrelated to agriculture, making the
slaveholders the least "landed" of all classes in the antebellum South.
Ten years earlier the United States census had reported that seventy-
eight percent of the northern workers were employed in agriculture,
a breakdown almost identical to that of southern slaveholders in
1850.[42] But while the North was only beginning to feel the effects
of the immigration, industrialization, and urbanization that would
transform its work force dramatically in the twenty years before the
Civil War, there is no evidence that the occupational structure of the
slaveholding class underwent any similar change. Indeed it had always
been one of the defining characteristics of middle-class slaveholders
that they combined careers to enhance their prospects for upward
mobility.

Artisan's skills or professional educations protected the slaveholding middle-class from the most severe instabilities of the agricultural
economy. The flexibility of a dual career was thus invaluable to the
aspiring slaveholder. The profits of a trade or a profession were
invested in the slave economy while the effects of economic dislocation in one sphere were softened by the middle-class master's ability
to fall back on the other. In sum, the lives of middle-class slavehold-

ers, who constituted perhaps a fourth of all masters, were shaped by a few significant historical experiences: struggle in the early years, migration, and upward mobility, often founded on a dual career.

Olmsted estimated that "of the class properly termed 'the planters,'" middle-class slaveholders "constituted probably nine-tenths." Indeed, middle-class masters held the majority of all the slaves in the South. For while most slaveholders held five slaves or fewer, most slaves were owned by masters with more than five bondsmen. The significance of middle-class slaveholders derived not from their numerical preponderance but from their economic power, their broad control of the slave labor force, and their political activity. In Alabama, for example, nearly all the antebellum congressmen and most of the state legislators had dual careers or had begun their adult lives in non-agricultural jobs that served to propel their later success. If there was any single class of men that set the tone of life in the antebellum South, surely this was it.[43]

In 1850 over 20,000 slaveholders were employed as skilled artisans or tradesmen, among them mechanics, carpenters, blacksmiths, tailors. Samuel L. Moore was typical. Within a generation, Moore brought his family from North Carolina to Georgia to Tallahassee, Florida. On a further move down to Tampa, Moore's wife and one of his children died in a shipwreck while he was taking his twenty slaves overland. Having lost most of his possessions in the disaster, Moore "had to sell a slave or two to furnish the cabins and support the family until they could make a crop." In 1844 Moore went to Monticello County, remarried, and relocated again in 1850 in Lowndes County, Georgia. Because he was a brick manufacturer by trade, most of Samuel Moore's moves were prompted by the availability of work. In 1853, for example, he resettled his family again, this time to the village of Greenfield, Georgia, where bricks were needed to build the local Presbyterian church. When that job was done, Moore went on to Brooks County where he set up a "crossroads" store, and in 1859, he took his huge family to the county seat, Quitman. By that time, he owned fifteen slaves, most of whom worked in the Moore brickyard while his numerous children tended the farm.[44]

After several false starts, Martin Marshall made his fortune by falling back on his skills as a mechanic, blacksmith, and weaver.

Marshall operated a blacksmith shop in Columbia, South Carolina, until 1808, when he invested his wife's inheritance in a nearby plantation complete with seventeen slaves. By 1815, burdened with debts and on the verge of bankruptcy, Marshall sold whatever was left and moved with his family to Fort Claiborne on the Alabama River in Mississippi Territory. Relying on the skills his father had taught him, his trade gave him a good life in the booming frontier community. Within ten years he had purchased several town lots and a large acreage along the river. After a career which brought him from economic independence to near-destitution, Marshall began to thrive, and by the time of his death he and his son had become two of the wealthiest planters in Alabama.[45]

Businessmen, merchants, and civil servants in the slaveholding class numbered nearly 21,000 in 1850. And like most middle-class masters, they commonly shifted careers, often moving logically into the planter class. Sherman G. Forbes left Connecticut in 1836 and settled in Sparta, Alabama, in his early twenties. A laborer, a clerk, a businessman, Forbes worked variously for the Conecuh County land office, as a justice of the peace, tax assessor, clerk of the county court, and more. Building up his wealth through business interests, he filled his letters with details about money matters, loans, speculations, and the like. "I bought me a plantation," Forbes wrote in 1855. He hired an overseer, moved to his farm, and struggled to make it work. The house on his original purchase was "out of repair," and it took Forbes months "to get it fixed so that it would do to live in." All the fences were down, and the land he had expected to cultivate turned out to be poor. So he acquired several adjoining parcels, amassing just over a thousand acres. At first Forbes seemed overwhelmed by the responsibility "to feed nineteen in Number myself Wife & child & Overseer & fifteen negroes." But he approached his new plantation as he had approached his previous business ventures, speculating, borrowing, taking calculated risks, and soon Sherman Forbes was a prospering slaveholder.[46]

The experience of Josiah Hinds was more common, for he never became a wealthy planter. Born in Tennessee, Hinds moved to Alabama in his early adulthood and set up a mercantile business. "J. Hinds & Co." prospered in Selma for close to fifteen years, and he became a prominent member of the community and one of the largest land-owners in the town. But the economic panic of the late 1830's destroyed his business, and in 1839 he set out for Arkansas. Hinds got no farther than Mississippi, where he decided to take up the practice of medicine. Accustomed to town life and community leadership, his family now lived "almost in the woods—one cabbin onley to shelter us and our little ones." Hinds helped set up a church, became active in local politics, and returned to prosperity. By 1846 he had eight slaves and was ready to move them to another home in Chickasawas County. In 1850, he moved again to DeSoto County, where his practice of botanical medicine flourished. Having begun his career in DeSoto County with six slaves, Hinds's success could be measured in the acquisitions of the next decade. By 1860 he owned fifteen slaves who worked three thousand dollars' worth of highly productive land.[47]

Professionals also prospered as slaveholders in much the same way as merchants, civil servants, and craftsmen. In 1850 more than 27,000 doctors, lawyers, teachers, and other professionals were included in the ranks of the slaveholding class.[48]

Slaveholding professionals were probably the single most influential class in the antebellum South. Their education and wealth gave them control of much of the southern press. They were elected to political office in staggeringly unrepresentative numbers by present-ing themselves to southern voters as living testimony to the validity of the American dream of upward mobility. A common career pat-tern was for a young professional to move to a newly settled town somewhere on the western frontier. If the town was a few years old, he often set up practice with the established lawyer or doctor or else he started on his own. Given the prevalence of sickness and death, and the endless squabbling over land, the opportunities for success among young professionals on the frontier were virtually unlimited, in good times or bad. A young Alabama lawyer in the 1830's ex-plained why his situation was so profitable. "They all run in debt—invariably," he wrote of his neighbors, "never pay cash, and all always one year behind hand. They wait for a sale of their crops. The roads are bad, the prices low, they cannot pay. They all wait to be sued. A suit is brought—no defense is made—an execution is taken out and is paid with all the costs and they even think it a good bargain. The rate of interest allowed is but 8 pr. cent. So much is this below the real value that a man will let his debts go unpaid, pay interest and costs and buy negroes for making cotton or land and think it even then profitable and will be much obliged to his plaintiff if he will wait for the due course of law and not personally fall out with him." If the merchant asks payment from his debtor, "his answer is 'you must wait, I *can't* pay you, I *must* buy a *negro*, it is out of the question, I have the money but I *must* buy a *negro*.' And with this excuse he has the face to put off the debt and the creditor is obliged to take it or go to the law, whichever he does is to the debtor almost a matter of indifference."[49] In such circumstances, how could a young lawyer fail?

With success in their careers, professionals built up the capital necessary to buy their way into the slaveholding class. Some began buying land as soon as they were established, gradually accumulating property from Indian or government acreage, or from small farmers who had settled first, tried their luck, then moved on. After a number of years they bought a few slaves to clear their recently purchased lands outside of town, sustaining their initial losses with their increasingly lucrative professional careers.

Benjamin Fitzpatrick was admitted to the practice of law in Alabama in 1821. Within five years, having participated in some law suits regarding conflicting property claims among slaveholders, he had built up a clientele sufficiently broad to allow him to begin acquiring slaves. In 1826 Fitzpatrick purchased three slaves for a thousand dollars; in 1827 he bought a fifteen-year-old boy for four hundred dollars. The following year he spent over five hundred dollars on a seventeen-year-old girl and her six-month-old son, $975 on a sixteen-year-old girl along with a twelve-year-old mulatto and a nine-year-old boy. Later in 1828, he added a boy named Peter and a woman named Betsey to his rapidly growing slave force. Within the space of a few years, Fitzpatrick spent thousands of dollars acquiring slaves through the profits of his law practice. Moses Bledsoe did much the same thing with the money he made practicing law in Raleigh, North Carolina. Through the 1840's and 1850's Bledsoe bought small plots in the city and large parcels in surrounding Wake

County. He owned at least seven hundred acres of land by 1852, and throughout that decade he added a number of slaves to his property holdings.[50]

Others waited longer and purchased plantations whole upon the death or removal of a local slaveholder, or else they moved once more to set up a complete plantation farther west. Many simply shifted their major occupation from lawyer to planter, though few gave up their initial careers entirely. Most continued to invest in land and slaves with the profits from their practices. Thus a young Tennessee lawyer worked as a prosecutor collecting debts for local creditors, often taking small plots of land as payment. His law practice prospered, and by 1794 he owned ten slaves. By 1798, according to the Davidson County tax rolls, he owned fifteen. Despite a serious setback in the late 1790's, his prosperity continued until, in 1820, the census reported that he held forty-four slaves. By the time Andrew Jackson was elected President, there were ninety-five slaves on his plantation, the Hermitage. A few years later there were 150. When he died, the self-educated Tennessee lawyer owned almost two hundred.[51]

No less lucrative than the law was a career in medicine. As with lawyers, doctors did best when times were worst. Dr. Thomas Gale moved to Mississippi in 1816 and, like so many others, used his professional career to build up a plantation. "This country has been very unhealthy this season," Gale wrote in 1817. "My business has been very extensive and profitable in a short time. I hope to secure an interest that will be sufficient to settle me for life." As the yellow fever "swept off great numbers" of his neighbors in Natchez, Dr. Gale counted up his money and started buying land and slaves. By 1833 he had a plantation that was producing 150 bales of cotton each year. W. P. Graham did not become that wealthy, but he did well enough. He graduated from Cumberland College in 1812, moved around a bit, and in 1820 set up a lucrative medical practice in Salem, Georgia. He owned a few slaves and planted a small amount of cotton, but it was not until he moved to Covington, Georgia, in 1834 that Dr. Graham truly prospered. He began buying land almost immediately, and by 1838 his farm produced thirty-three bales of cotton; forty-two bales five years later.[52]

When the sons of planters did not go to college or did not train in a profession, they were often given a few slaves or capital to take with them to their prospective western destination. Establishing a plantation was fraught with obstacles, both natural and man-made. Everard Green Baker began with a few slaves in the late 1840's. He tried to expand his small farm near Natchez, battling floods that rotted his cotton, storms that blew it down, and rain that drowned his hogs. But after several years of debt, natural calamity, and prudent land trades, Baker moved to Panola County in north-central Mississippi in 1852 and ended up doing quite well. "I feel much better satisfied with my situation," he wrote in 1854, "and hope for better progress since I have bought Joe. He is very handy in many ways." By 1859, Joe and the rest of Baker's slaves were making fifty-five bales of cotton a year.[53]

Alex Allen of Bainbridge, Georgia, was equally typical. He borrowed a few slaves from his brother and worked hard to make his farm productive. "I expect to get two more in Oglethorpe so that we shall be able to make a right clean farm after your hands is withdrawn." But though Allen's law practice prospered, his farm did not. When winter came, he discovered the prices of land and slaves were rising too rapidly. "It is very doubtful whether I buy any men this winter," he wrote his brother. "Our farming operations will now be of a diminutive character but we think of enlarging as ever means may allow."[54]

Expansion and prosperity were characteristic of most middle-class masters, including well-to-do planters. James Torbert owned a sawmill and a plantation in Macon County, Alabama, in the 1850's, and though he visited his farm only once or twice a month outside harvesting and planting seasons, its prosperity can be measured in yearly increments. In 1856, his slaves produced twenty-nine bales of cotton; forty-nine in 1857; fifty-three in 1858. There were impressive, if less spectacular, rises in the production of corn, pork, and wheat. And although Torbert was clearly making money from his farming operation, he wrote in his journal in 1858 that his mill "pays well as Makeing Cotton." James Monette's Hope Plantation in Louisiana also expanded in the 1850's. He sold forty-six bales of cotton in 1852, fifty the following year, sixty-two by 1858, and seventy-two in 1860.

Growth and prosperity can be measured in other ways. James Harrington kept the records of his numerous land purchases in Mississippi and Alabama from 1832 to 1849. Barely a year went by that he did not buy plots ranging from forty to two hundred and forty acres.[55] Of such men was the planter class composed.

WHAT DISTINGUISHED the planter aristocracy from the slaveholding middle class was not any lack of accumulation but a lack of struggle. Only a small fraction of the slaveholders, less than two and a half percent, ever owned fifty slaves or more. Their relatively small number alone suggests the difficulty of achieving such heights of wealth. However, these richest of planters rarely had to rely on an alternative career to reach their positions. If the middle-class master began his adult life where most small slaveholders ended theirs, so too did the wealthiest planters start out with all the advantages middle-class slaveholders struggled to achieve. Yet comfortable beginnings did little to stem the acquisitiveness of the planter aristocracy.

Even small patrimonial gifts could be of considerably more substance than they might otherwise seem. In 1850, Dugal McCall was just setting up his plantation in Rodney, Mississippi, and he borrowed slaves from his father to clear his land, selling the lumber for profit. At first McCall grew only corn, potatoes, and a few other staples, to which he soon added peaches. His wife and child did not yet live on the plantation, residing instead in a nearby town. After a year, McCall began building slave quarters and smokehouses. In 1851 he fenced in his property and constructed his own home. By 1852, when he first planted cotton, he already owned sixteen slaves, and his first crop was huge for a beginner, fifty bales. The following year McCall doubled the number of plows he owned, and in 1854, with thirty slaves, his plantation made 165 bales of cotton—an astonishing increase.[56] If McCall's unusually swift entry into the planter class confirms the complaint that a lack of money at the outset of a career could be critical, it is his unrepresentativeness that is most significant. It was the rare slaveholder, even among the sons of planters, who could count on so much initial support that within five years his farm could produce over 75,000 pounds of cotton a year.

Rapid growth from lucrative beginnings was one of the out-standing traits of the planter aristocracy. The most significant indica-tion of a slaveholder's growing wealth was neither the increasing size of successive harvests nor the steady accumulation of land, but the increase in the number of slaves. In this the planter aristocracy was not alone. Where many middle-class masters remained in non-agricultural careers and so bought little land, the accumulation of slaves was a lifelong occupation for virtually all masters.[57]

But only the wealthiest planters had the means to accumulate slaves swiftly and in great numbers. Even so well-born a planter as George J. Kollock, who inherited large numbers of slaves and owned several plantations near Savannah, Georgia, never ceased adding to his holdings. In the dozen years following his acquisition of Rosedew Plantation, Kollock's force of fifteen and one-half full hands grew to fifty-six slaves in all. From 1849 to 1861, Kollock's slave force at Ossabaw Island grew from fifty-six to seventy-two. John Houston Bills never stopped buying slaves either. In 1845 he counted forty-five bondsmen on his Tennessee farm. With his remarriage the following year, Bills stepped up his interest in accumulating more lands, larger harvests, and a bigger slave force. The growing concern with his own economic advancement seemed to coincide with an increasing interest in his legacy to his heirs. Whatever the reason, he began to attend slave auctions regularly and watched more closely his annual profits. He complained that from his 1853 cotton crop he "got 78 bales only." By 1858, his slaves numbered eighty-four, and in 1860 the value of Bills's eighty-seven bondsmen was $79,950, a nearly five-fold increase in fifteen years.[58]

The habit of accumulation passed through the generations and did not stop with the achievement of planter status. John Arrington, who paid forty pounds for a slave boy in 1789, continued to purchase bondsmen in small parcels throughout his lifetime. By 1830 he was able to bequeath substantial holdings to his children, including twenty slaves to his son, Archibald. Archibald, however, was not content with his huge inheritance. He became a lawyer and used his experi-ence with conflicting property claims of other slaveholders to enhance his own wealth. With the combined profits of his plantation and law practice, Archibald Arrington continued to buy slaves throughout the

1840's and 1850's, long after he had established himself as one of the wealthiest planters in both North Carolina and Alabama.[59]

The zealous pursuit of wealth by Arrington and others like him was far too commonplace to be considered the holding action of a planter aristocracy digging in its heels to maintain its power. For most slaveholders acquisition was a way of life. If there was any tendency for the acquisitiveness of the slaveholding class to wane over the generations in the most successful families, it was slight at best. The sons of slaveholders, as much as any other group, were products of their upbringing.

BETWEEN 1830 AND 1860, in all the southern states, at least 170,000 people entered the slaveholding class. Between 1790 and 1860, there was no increase in the concentration of wealth within that class. As time went on, in other words, the percentage of the slave population controlled by the wealthiest masters did not significantly increase. If upward mobility was not the norm, if slaves were simply controlled by the richest planters who passed on their property from generation to generation, there would not have been such a substantial growth in the number of slaveholders. Neither would the statistics indicate as they do that the older southern men got, the more likely they were to become slaveholders, and the more slaves they were likely to own.[60]

Wealth, particularly slaveholding wealth, was never equally distributed in the South. But there was always substantial mobility into and out of the slaveholding class. If marriage patterns are any indication, it appears that white Southerners paid little attention to class distinctions in choosing mates.[61] Thus, despite huge disparities of wealth, it is futile to locate clearly delineated boundaries between slaveholders and non-slaveholders, just as it is difficult to draw simple numerical distinctions between small slaveholders and planters. How many slaves did a small farmer need to acquire before he ceased to behave like a yeoman? Or an artisan? At which point in his career did a lawyer begin to act like a planter? Did a merchant's life become "agrarian" when he bought a farm but kept his business? There is, in fact, no convincing body of evidence to demonstrate that the mere ownership of slaves, even in large numbers, automatically entailed the embrace of a distinctive world view.

This is not to say that no slaveholding culture emerged in the Old South. It did. But that culture developed from historical conditions that were only in part related to the ownership of slaves and only minimally associated with plantation agriculture. The dominant slaveholding culture grew out of the colonial experience in America and embraced the diversity of southern society. It took form in the rapidly expanding slave economy of the antebellum period and so produced a world view that equated upward mobility with westward migration. For unlike plantation life, physical movement, upward mobility, and social fluidity shaped the destinies of the vast majority of American slaveholders.

Chapter 3

~⟋

The Slaveholders' Pilgrimage

S AMUEL MOORE'S RECOLLECTIONS of his childhood were similar to those of many slaveholders. "My father was a baptized believer in the use of the rod, and when he told me not to do a thing, I knew what disobedience would cost me." Slaveholding parents, particularly those influenced by the middle-class precepts of antebellum America, took a keen interest in the moral and material development of their children, and in many cases their interest was doting and persistent. Nearly forty years after his father's death a Mississippi planter remembered his parent as a man "who never knew what it was to relax in the training of his children. He was *strict,* perhaps he erred, yet it was his belief it was for the best."[1]

Slaveholders pressured their sons to go to college, to be prudent in their investments, to live according to the dictates of Christianity, but above all else to succeed. Not surprisingly, most young slaveholders were deeply religious and at the same time obsessed with their own economic advancement. They were imbued with a materialistic ethos that ruled their lives, pushing them from their homes in search of prosperity, causing many to live in a style that belied their own wealth.

To be sure, there were slaveholders who defined success in terms other than material prosperity. William Byrd, a wealthy Alabama planter, impressed upon his son the same lessons to which he had been reared: "gallant chivalrous" conduct was of paramount importance. But the pressure to succeed was still apparent. "You do not know how much the hearts of your Mother and Father are set on your success," Byrd wrote to his son at the University of Virginia. "You are our only boy—the representative of the family name." While such aristocratic concern with the "family name" was rare among slaveholders, many parents were influenced by their close association with the military or the clergy and stressed the cultivation of such higher virtues as dignity, honor, and duty. When John Isaac Guion announced his plan to go to law school rather than West Point, his father, Isaac, promptly attempted to disabuse John of his misconceptions about military life. Writing from his plantation near Natchez, Mississippi, Isaac told his son that he would "in no wise endeavor to bias or govern your choice in the election of your future profession." Nevertheless, should America be invaded, his sons would be called upon to serve their country out of gratitude as well as "by imperious *duty* to defend her as his *mother* from whom he inhaled his first breath." As if patriotism were not enough to persuade John to go to West Point, Isaac went on to burden his son with the pressures of sibling rivalry. "Your brother Frederick," he wrote, was "crowned with success" following his general examinations at the academy. Frederick believed "that if Brother John should become a member there is no doubt but he will be well pleased with his situation." Not only is your brother flourishing at the military school, Guion wrote his son, "your cousin Thomas . . . seems strongly desirous to obtain his father's consent to go to West Point." Then, too, there was the "son of one of my good neighbors, and your old companion," whose father was preparing to take his son to the academy.[2]

John Guion was not the only young Southerner who felt the force of his father's concern. The Reverend Charles Pettigrew of North Carolina was prepared to influence his children from the grave. Seemingly haunted by visions of his imminent death, Pettigrew prepared a pamphlet containing advice to his children and then continued to suggest strikingly specific courses of action for his sons to follow. "Should it please God to prolong your lives," he wrote in 1797, "you may think it best to sell your possessions in this low country, and to move westwardly. If you should, be sure to procure a good and convenient spot, and well situated for health; that is *high* and not having any low or marshy ground to the southward of the house."[3]

The high point of parental pressure came when the sons of slaveholders left home to pursue careers of their own. Free from the constant gaze of their fathers' eyes, young Southerners were nonetheless rarely far from their parents' thoughts. In 1816 Isaac Guion wrote to his two sons in Tennessee. "Nothing affords me more *real pleasure* than to find that *the object* for which you are both separated from me is your steady and unworried pursuit: go on my *sons,* persevere in every laudable and worthy endeavour, & *success* will be the certain reward of your constant industry." Laurens Hinton was troubled by an intrusive father who signed his letters "your anxious parent." In 1836, the harried Laurens had left his father's home in Raleigh, North Carolina, settling in Mobile, Alabama. "I hope you will recollect that without prudence, industry and a close attention to business you cannot expect to be successful," his father wrote. He begged Laurens not to venture into the "extravagant speculating" then prevalent in Alabama. He asked for specific information about the prices Laurens charged for hiring out his slaves. After waiting a month without getting any response, the elder Hinton sent another fretful letter. He repeated his fears about the wildness of the Alabama frontier and asked Laurens about rumors that the Mobile bank had failed. He spoke of the sound and prudent business ventures of his other son, Henry, and then warned Laurens "never to contract a regular habit of drinking ardent spirits" as "the people of that country" generally do. "You are now far removed from me and have to act for yourself," Hinton wrote dejectedly to his son a month later. "I hope your course will be prudent." Several equally anxious letters followed, and though Hinton's desperate tone moderated somewhat, he never stopped worrying about his son's progress.[4]

James T. Harrison seemed destined for success from the start of his career, yet his father constantly worried about him. After his graduation from the University of South Carolina in 1829, Harrison studied under the prestigious Charleston lawyer, James L. Petigru. In 1834, he moved to Columbus, Mississippi, set up a practice and, following the pattern of so many others, began buying slaves. "I am

afraid your change of residence will not be advantageous," Thomas
Harrison wrote to his son. He counseled "steadiness, sobriety and
attention to business," but quickly relieved himself of responsibility
for his son's affairs. "Every thing depends on yourself," he wrote. "If
you fail it will be your own fault." But James's success was altogether
predictable, and within a year his father was congratulating him.
"You can't conceive how much your success has gratified me." Yet
the very instability on which frontier lawyers thrived continued to
worry James Harrison's father. He remained convinced, in the face
of all evidence to the contrary, "that money cannot be made at the
law in a new-settled country."[5]

Pressure from parents was reinforced by the influence of friends
and relatives and by social norms that placed a high premium on
individual achievement. As a result, materialism passed from one
generation of slaveholders to the next with all the certainty of a
genetic trait. Only a small fraction of masters ever stood aloof from
the avid pursuit of wealth. Indeed, far from witnessing a melioration
as time went on, most antebellum slaveholders became, if anything,
increasingly obsessed with economic prosperity. "The people think
more of money here than of Education," Henry Watson complained
from Alabama in 1831. "The truth is," a British traveler concluded
after touring the South, "this passion for the acquisition of money
is much stronger and more universal in this country than in any other
under the sun, at least that I have visited."[6]

The emphasis was less on the achievement of economic stability
than on material advancement. In 1853 a Tennessee planter attended
a sermon in which the preacher stressed "the passing away of time
& the value of it, the great propriety of improving every year upon
the past." An Alabama master, convinced that his slaves were not
working in his absence, reformulated the preacher's advice: "Time's
money, time's money!" he kept telling a traveler, " 'cause I left my
niggers all alone, not a dam white man within four miles on 'em."
Joseph Ingraham summarized the concerns of Mississippi slaveholders.
"To sell cotton in order to buy negroes—to make more cotton to
buy more negroes, 'ad infinitum,' is the aim and direct tendency of
all the operations of the thorough-going cotton planter: his whole
soul is wrapped up in the pursuit." A Maine-born farmer with no

slaves "sneered" at his Texas neighbors for sacrificing their own comfort to spend all their money on "more nigger help."[7]

Raised in a society where the pressure to succeed was brought to bear from every direction, slaveholders quite naturally were intrigued by the various devices available to them for making money. Young Oscar Hamilton found it difficult "to determine what labor I shall pursue." Although he wanted to attend medical school, Hamilton worried that it would require "some sacrifice of time and money in order to do so." Instead, he thought he might "commence farming" at his new home in Mississippi. "The only article of production in Kentucky that will bring the Cash is Tobacco," he observed, "and I am satisfied that hands can earn more in this country [Mississippi] by raising cotton." So Hamilton decided to forgo medical school and instead mapped out a career for himself as a cotton farmer. He reckoned that "by making a purchase here at this time (if it were small) the value would increase 100 per ct Annually for the next four years." Having only a "verry small capital," Hamilton wrote, "it behooves me to turn it to best Advantage. . . . I expect to buy one or two more negroes shortly if I can collect some money that is coming to me. I do not think at present that I shall ever visit Kentucky again until I shall have made a fortune," the young slaveholder concluded, "and that may never be the case."[8]

Land and slaves became the two great vehicles through which slaveholders realized their ambitions of fortune. After "Jackson and the Banks," an Alabama master wrote in 1834, what most concerned his neighbors was the distribution of public lands. "The people cannot be satisfied till they get them for nothing," he complained, or "next to nothing." The usefulness of land increased in proportion to the availability of black slaves. Consequently there was as much concern with slave trading as with land speculation. "For a young man, just commencing life," James Steer wrote from Louisiana in 1818, "the best stock, in which he can invest Capital, is, I think, negro Stock . . . ; negroes will yield a much larger income than any Bank dividend."[9]

All of the pressures to succeed that were so much a part of life in nineteenth-century America were epitomized in the private correspondence of migrants, a body of literature without parallel in its influence, except for the Bible. Letters from friends or relatives who had migrated west, encouraging old acquaintances to follow suit, represent one of the great cultural artifacts of American history. Only their widespread dissemination can explain the remarkable similarities of form and phrasing. Only the universality of their message explains why syntax and grammar are virtually identical in letters separated by half a century and a thousand miles. And the message was always the same: move and make your fortune, further west and further south.

In 1849, after Phillips Fitzpatrick graduated from school and was unsure of how to go about pursuing his career, he solicited the advice of his Uncle Alva. Come to Texas, his uncle told him. Get yourself a good piece of range land in a healthy location with plenty of timber and water. "Stick down upon it with some good woman as your wife for without a good wife it is hard to get along and raise every thing," Fitzpatrick continued. "Get as many young negro women as you can. Get as many cows as you can. . . . It is the greatest country for an increase that I have ever saw in my life. I have been hear six years and I have had fifteen negro children born and last year three more young negro women commenced breeding which added seven born last year and five of them is living and doing well." Come out for a visit, he advised his nephew, and if you like it "then stick down and attend to the foregoing instructions and in ten or fifteen or twenty years you will do as well as any other man in this or any other country."[10] Alva Fitzpatrick was more crass than most, but his message was typical.

Between 1800 and 1860 the "West" of the slaveholders' dreams included everything from Kentucky to California. Letters from the frontier follow a few simple patterns, dividing their praise of the new country between practical advice and outlandish exaggeration. If the letters are a reliable guide, prospective migrants were interested first in the availability of water and the health of the new region. Most were reassured. The land available in Tennessee was "convenient to the navigation of the Cumberland River," James Winchester assured his North Carolina friend in 1806. In Mississippi, C. C. Campbell wrote almost forty years later, "we have as good spring water as [there] is in this world." Indeed, it was so much better than South

Carolina water that merely to drink it was beneficial. "We have no tallow faced looking folk here," Campbell wrote to his old friends. The water in Arkansas is "as good as any I ever drank anywhere," Rufus Amis wrote his wife in 1857. In a fertile Bayou region of Louisiana one doctor found "perfect health enjoyed by the community." Frederick Bates in Missouri assured a friend that "we have more comparative health here than we have in Virginia."[11]

If the area was healthy and there was good water for navigation and survival, all that could keep a person from moving was the lack of cheap land, and in this, too, most prospective migrants were reassured. Land in the West was consistently declared to be fertile, cheap, and going fast. "The soil is light" in Missouri, Frederick Bates wrote, "and attention rather than labour is necessary in cultivating it." One Tennesseean claimed that "in the course of 5 years" land that recently sold for a few dollars "will be worth 50 dollars per acre." There were government lands still available in Louisiana in the 1830's, W. P. Graham was told, "which land will soon command from ten to seventy dollars—this advance often occurs in a few weeks." There were some bargains left in Arkansas in the late 1850's, one interested slaveholder wrote, "but of late there is a great rush for these lands and they will soon all be entered."[12]

The urgent tone of these letters reveals the depth of the slaveholders' concern with the idea of westward migration. Indeed, what stands out most is not the delineation of the practical benefits of moving but the gross exaggeration of those benefits. Letters told of the superiority of western "society," which in any case was constantly "improving." David Meade declared that life in Kentucky was "greater . . . than [in] any part of the habitable Globe." A Missourian preferred his new home "to all other parts of the U. States which I have visited." A transplanted New Englander believed that the chances for success were so great in Alabama "that every young man should emigrate if he is poor." James Barrett was ecstatic about his new home in Mississippi. "I tell you," he wrote, "it's enough to make one walk tiptoe to see his labours prospering so abundantly."[13]

The climax of these enticements was the inevitable and invidious comparison between West and East. Distinctions were commonly drawn in multiples, the new country being so many times better than the old. Of Tennessee's superiority over North Carolina: "I Can do better hear then I can thear & worke half of my Time Salley Can make more hear in Three mounths then She Can thear in Twlve." Of Mississippi over South Carolina: "You can repair your affairs in one year here as much as you can there in three." Of Louisiana over Georgia: "One Negro hear will make you more than four will in Georgia." Of Arkansas over North Carolina: "I am satisfied that a person can do better most anywhere here than they could in N. C. and on good land they can make three times as much." Of Texas over Alabama: "I can take one fourth dollar out of what it cost me in Alabama and mantain my [slave] family hear with it."[14] For as long as there was slavery, there were letters like this to and from slaveholders.

After the Mexican War, the emphasis was on Texas. "Take my word for it," Ariella Hawkins wrote in 1847, Texas "is the greatest country in the world." Whatever the "inconveniences" of the new country, they would be "doubly and triply paid for" in a short time. My husband "expects to get so rich," she wrote to her mother, "that he will be able to drive sixteen horses in hand when he pays a visit to North Carolina." As the Civil War approached, slaveholders extended their sights to the Pacific Coast. A Louisiana planter who had taken a slave with him to San Francisco found the West Coast "better than I could have thought. . . . If a man is able to work and will do it," he told his son, "he need not suffer heare."[15] It was in such letters as this that the distinction between social and parental pressure broke down. Before they reached their adulthood, most slaveholders had been conditioned to accept migration as the prerequisite to success. It is no surprise, therefore, that the antebellum master class was one of the most mobile in history.

WHAT UNITED SMALL SLAVEHOLDERS with the sons of planters was the goal of purchasing land and slaves and moving west in pursuit of that goal. By the nineteenth century, westward migration had become so much a part of upward mobility in the South that it took on a lure almost independent of the profitable potential of the actual move. Wives complained that their husbands and children seemed determined to move every time they got the chance. Success seemed as much an excuse for packing up and leaving as did failure. Entire communities in many eastern states were virtually emptied by the mass emigration of slaveholders and non-slaveholders alike.

James Rowe Coombs of Twiggs County, Georgia, recalled the days when "whole settlements moved off together, believing the best places were a long way off." He told of the occasional neighbor who would return from a trip to the "New Country" with tales of cheap and fertile land and the opportunities available to the energetic and industrious settler. Then "a panic or moving fever would soon break out," and the peaceful old community would be left emptied. Coombs's recollections were typical. J. H. Bills recorded in his diary the return of a former neighbor who had left for California some years earlier. Like several others before him, the neighbor returned to Tennessee in improved circumstances, advertising the glories of the golden state. "The *Alabama Fever* rages here with great violence and has carried off vast numbers of our citizens," one North Carolinian complained. "I am apprehensive if it continues to spread as it has done, it will almost depopulate the country." In northern Virginia a slaveholder told a visiting Englishman in 1835 that the local plantations rarely stayed in the hands of a single family for more than a few generations. Instead "a perpetual interchange was going on," he said.[16]

That seems to be what was happening in the cotton belt of the Deep South even through the last ten years of the antebellum period, when society might have been expected to stabilize. In some of Alabama's richest counties the majority of the wealthiest planters left the area in the ten years from 1850 to 1860. In Dallas County alone, fifty-four percent of the sons of planters were gone; over sixty percent of those whose fathers owned between ten and nineteen slaves had left by 1860. But of the sons of the largest group of slaveholders, those who owned between one and nine slaves, three out of four left Dallas County in their young adulthood. In this they merely followed the example set by their parents. For in Jasper County, Georgia, at the heart of that state's cotton belt and long past its frontier days, nearly sixty percent of the 1850 slaveholders were gone ten years later. Half the 1860 slaveholders had not been in Jasper

County ten years earlier.[17] If such rates of persistence and change were typical, it is likely that between eighty and ninety percent of the slaveholders did not stay in one place for more than two decades, even in the wealthiest areas of the cotton belt.

Perhaps these turnover rates are best read in comparative perspective. Interestingly, they reveal that slaveholders were no less mobile than antebellum northern urbanites. The persistence rate of Bostonians from 1850 to 1860 was thirty-nine percent, indicating a rapid turnover in the city's population. Yet this was very close to the persistence rate of forty-one percent for Jasper County slaveholders. In Newburyport, Massachusetts, during the same years, only thirty-two percent of the unskilled laborers stayed for the entire decade. But again, their persistence was not much different from that of small slaveholders in the antebellum South. These comparisons, it should be stressed, are between poor or broadly based populations in the North and the wealthiest—and presumably most stable—class in the South.[18]

Rapid changes in the local population were a part of life for most slaveholders, whether they participated in the movement or not. Letters to and from slaveholding families provided the details. In the years since she had left her home in Montgomery, Alabama, there were many changes in Mary Bailey's old community. "Mr. and Mrs. Rogers and family left last Tuesday for Florida. Martha hated to go very much. . . . Dr. Lucas has gone to Arkansas to look at the country. . . . I do hate to see [Margaret and John] go to Florida but I part with them with the hope that they may make a living." People were always moving in and out of Chestnut Grove, Alabama. "We live in a very public place," one mistress wrote, "a road passes right close by and a great many wagons pass. Some one is passing nearly all the time." Indeed there was so much movement at her new home that "we have got acquainted with no person at all."[19]

From as far as two hundred miles upcountry, great numbers of migrating slaveholders would converge on ports like Charleston and New Orleans on their way west. On his second visit to America Charles Lyell saw a group of "movers" on the dock at Mobile, Alabama, including one family "carrying away no less than forty negroes." Lyell called them "resolute pioneers of the wilderness." The

Southerner, he concluded, spends his lifetime moving and "though constantly growing richer, [is] never disposed to take his ease." Not all observers were distressed by such movement. The Arkansas *Gazette* was impressed by the "renewed vigor" of migration in 1845. The ferry at Little Rock "has been crowded, for several days, with movers, going South, some to Texas, but principally to settle in the fertile lands of the Red River district. Among those who have passed through town since Sunday morning we presume there were not less than 300 negroes."[20]

There was no period before the Civil War when this massive movement of slaveholders slowed down for long. Indeed, it reached its climax with the migration into Texas in the 1850's. The state's population tripled in just ten years, and half of the increase was in slaves. The number of slaveholders jumped from just over eight thousand to nearly twenty thousand, the overwhelming majority of whom owned fewer than ten bondsmen. In the antebellum South there never was a stable slaveholding society that was not, almost by definition, atypical.[21]

Movement disrupted the lives of individuals; it strained marriages; and it made transience a normal part of existence in the Old South. "The great objection to this country, to my mind, is that the population is so changeable," Henry Watson complained in 1836. He had moved from a small town in New England and was writing to his mother about life in Greensborough, Alabama. "Nobody seems to consider himself settled, they remain one, two, three or four years & must move to some other spot. Since I came here the entire population of this town, with a dozen or two exceptions, has changed. It is even notorious here, & if a man is away six months & returns he must expect to find himself among strangers. This of course has its effect upon the feelings of the community. No man knows when he gets acquainted whether he will ever know him long enough to make it worth his while to cultivate his friendship. The whole of these new states are in the same moveable state. Their restlessness brought them here and the same cause carries them on."[22]

Watson's reaction was typical of those who were born to stable families or raised in those parts of the country, particularly along the eastern seaboard, that were least affected by the turbulence of westward migration. James Davidson was twenty-six years old when he left Virginia to tour the South in 1836. Throughout his journey, he stayed with friends from his native state who had moved to Kentucky, Mississippi, and Alabama. Davidson, just out of college, had no trouble accepting the prevailing ideology of upward mobility. "A young man of energy and good character in the South can make a fortune," he wrote. Yet Davidson himself was not especially interested either in moving west or in making a fortune. Indeed he was offended by much of what he saw on his trip. "The people here are run mad with speculation," Davidson wrote from Vicksburg, Mississippi. "They did business in . . . a kind of phrenzy." The city itself was "full of strangers. In fact the South is crowded with strangers; gentlemen adventurers who have dreamed golden dreams of the South, and who think they have nothing more to do than to come South and be the Lord of a Cotton Plantation and a hundred slaves."[23]

If the complaints of men like Watson and Davidson were justified, their frustration was also predictable. Massive demographic dislocation was inevitable in a slaveholding culture that glorified movement, viewed westward migration as inextricably linked to upward mobility, and made material success the nearly universal pursuit. Yet the goal of economic advancement did not always manifest itself in purely material greed. Some slaveholders moved because they felt they had no choice. To one observer, the slaveholders of the Cape Fear Valley in North Carolina were "evidently losing ground from year to year." They talked of "abandoning the exhausted soil, and migrating with their slaves to the southwestern states." By 1854 H. C. Anderson of Haywood County, Tennessee, was "sick and tired" of cutting and rolling logs for a living. I "begin to wish I really was in Texas—I am completely broken down." Twelve months of backbreaking work "& at the end of the year we make nothing," Anderson wrote. "I must see Texas—I want prairie land."[24]

Some moved to be with relatives and friends who had already left. An old farmer planned to leave his Alabama community of twenty years hoping to feel more at home in Texas, "for all my old neighbors have gone there, and new people have taken their place here."[25] Others simply went along with the community rather than remain by themselves.

Charles Caleb Cotton moved to South Carolina from England in 1789 hoping to make enough money as a cotton planter to enable him to return to England and support his parents in their old age. More often it was the parents who moved in order to provide for their heirs. George Allen's "large supply of children" prompted him to move from Alabama to Texas in 1850 "to provide a few acres of land . . . for the benefit of the rising generation." Only the prospect of a rich harvest kept one Georgia planter from leaving for Texas, Charles Lyell reported. "He complained of a want of elbow-room, although I found that his nearest neighbor was six or seven miles distant." But the Georgia slaveholder had a large family, and he was anxious to sell his plantation so he could "purchase a wider extent of land in Texas, and so be better able to provide for them."[26]

If some slaveholders moved out of concern for their children's future, others moved at the insistence of their children already grown. James Lide, a well-to-do planter on the Pee Dee River near Mechanicsville, South Carolina, sturdily resisted the westward "fever" that infected his friends and relatives. He even extracted a promise from his son-in-law not to take his daughter west. But when he was sixty-five years old, Lide's son convinced him to move the plantation to Alabama, forty miles south of Montgomery. With six of his twelve children and six more grandchildren, James Lide and his wife left their South Carolina home with several other local families, virtually transplanting an entire village to Alabama. After James Harrison moved to Mississippi, his father wrote him several interested letters. "Are there any more Indian reserves to be had?" Thomas Harrison asked. "What chance is there of getting good land and on what terms?" He was anxious to quit his job at a Columbia, South Carolina, bank. "No consideration could induce me to remain in it *permanently*," he told his son. "I would rather grub for my living."[27]

THE WILLINGNESS to sacrifice, to forgo "conveniences," to "grub for a living" somewhere in the West was common among slaveholders, so common that for many voluntary deprivation was a way of life. They lived, Timothy Flint recalled, by the "influence of imagination," dreaming of the great West and subjecting themselves to real hardship. After "painful journies" and the difficulties of settlement, "a few weeks' familiar acquaintance with the scene dispels the charms and the illusions of the imagination." Simply moving a household several hundred miles over unpaved roads was itself an ordeal. Whole families stayed on the road sometimes for months, camping out every night. Wagons broke, boats sank, food supplies dwindled. "We found water very scarce in some portions of the country we passed through," Sarah Thompson wrote after reaching Texas. "We drank from Mineral to Hog Wallow. Some of it so stagnant we were forced to hold our breath until we quenched our thirst."[28]

The living conditions after slaveholders arrived at their new homes were rarely better than tolerable. "Every thing is so unhandy," one settler complained. He had to walk five miles to work some of his fields, and water was four hundred yards from the cabin. But what stuck in the minds of slaveholding settlers before all else were the miserable homes they lived in. "I am at this time living in an open Cabin that keeps But little wind out," a young Louisiana slaveholder wrote, "and it is very chilly and cold at this time." When the Lides arrived at their new home in Alabama, they lived in a double log cabin full of air holes but with no windows, "which makes it very dark." Nevertheless, "our house is considered quite a comfortable one for this country," Maria Lide wrote. Her sister, Sarah Jane, lived at the bottom of a cotton field "in two decaying leaky cabins . . . which are infested with snakes, lizards, mice & c., we feel very much confined." After nearly a year in Alabama, none of the Lides had finished constructing permanent homes. "If we can only enjoy health," Sarah wrote, "we are willing to suffer all these inconveniences."[29]

Even the largest slaveholders had to wait before the legendary amenities of plantation life were available. In Mississippi, "many of the wealthiest planters are lodged wretchedly," Joseph Ingraham reported, "a splendid sideboard not unfrequently concealing a white-washed beam—a gorgeous Brussels carpet laid over a rough-planked floor." Ingraham attributed this "ludicrous contrast" to the nature of frontier society. For slaveholders determined to make permanent homes at their new locations, the inconveniences of frontier life were temporary. As an area was settled, the local town developed and "society" improved. In time the log cabin was sealed and whitewashed. Rooms were added, or a more comfortable frame house would be built, "not unlike the better class of New England farmhouses."[30]

But it was not clear to most observers that wretched lodgings were a passing thing. On many plantations in the cotton belt the "Big House" was little more than a cramped, filthy hovel. "Very many of the houses, even of the wealthy and respectable planters, are built of rough and unhewn logs," Philip Gosse declared. Dark, windowless cabins were common, as were ill-fitting doors and roofs through which shone the only available light. This type of home was "not inhabited by poor persons," Gosse went on, "nor is it considered as at all remarkable for discomfort; it is, according to the average, a very decent house." Frederick Olmsted repeatedly confirmed Gosse's observations. In the Lower Mississippi Valley: "The plantations are all large, but . . . display few signs of wealthy proprietorship. The greater number have but small and mean residences upon them." In Alabama: "Much the larger proportion of the planters of the State live in log-houses, some of them very neat and comfortable, but frequently rude in construction, not *chinked,* with windows unglazed, and wanting in many of the commonest conveniences." In North Carolina most slaveholders lived in ramshackle dwellings. A few large planters were "gentlemen of good estate. . . . The number of these, however, is extremely small." In Texas a wealthy planter with a large income lived in a well-constructed, two-story home, yet "out of eighty panes that originally filled the lower windows, thirty only remained unbroken. Not a door in the house had been ever furnished with a latch or even a string. . . . The furniture was of the rudest description."[31]

In most parts of the South, Olmsted reported, such homes as these were considered the best. And by comparison with the dwellings of many small slaveholders, they were indeed comfortable. In southern Virginia, James Silk Buckingham found both the slaveholders and their homes "dirty, and comfortless in the extreme." In Alabama the "people in the country live altogether in log houses. In towns they have a few poor brick houses. They are made double for the white planters." On a trip from Baltimore to Savannah in 1824, Daniel Lord found the houses "miserably poor," yet surrounded by slave huts that were still worse. "Some slave holders also live thus meanly," Lord wrote "—in log houses, clay chimneys, with no cellar; many have their oven out doors." A prosperous Tennessee slaveholder lived in a run-down and disorderly home. "It was dirty," Olmsted recalled, "and the bed given me to sleep in was disgusting." The furniture of one small slaveholder in North Carolina "was more scanty and rude than I ever saw before in any house, with women living in it, in the United States. Yet these people were not so poor but that they had a negro woman cutting and bringing wood for their fire." Although most of the turpentine farmers in that region lived like "the poorer class," Olmsted wrote, "their property is, nevertheless, often of considerable money value, consisting mainly of negroes."[32]

Slaveholders' diets were appropriate to their homes. Although the southern food supply was varied, it consisted overwhelmingly of pork and corn. There was certainly no shortage of food, but its monotony struck visitors almost as often as did the poor housing. The "eternal fry, pone and coffee" was served throughout the South to disgruntled visitors perplexed by the anomaly of low standards of living among slaveholders of considerable wealth.[33] Even if the slaves lived in homes identical to many of their masters' and ate the same food, they cannot be said to have been well treated.

Scenes of seemingly inexcusable deprivation were so widely noticed in all parts of the South and were recorded so late in the antebellum period that they could not be explained away as temporary manifestations of frontier life. Certainly it took time to build a comfortable home and set up a productive farm on the frontier. And many recently settled slaveholders worked diligently to reduce their discomfort by rushing to build their homes and clear their fields. But it was the slaveholders' frequent lack of interest in improving their circumstances that struck so many observers; sooner or later they felt compelled to speculate as to why this was so.

A popular theory among English travelers was that owning slaves made whites lazy. Every time he saw a group of men "lounging idly" on a "veranda or piazza," James Buckingham concluded that they did nothing "because the negro slaves can do the work; and what they do, though done badly, contents them." Sir Charles Lyell, no stranger to upper-class snobbery, was offended by the living habits of Georgia "crackers." Although he referred to them as "poor whites," they were, he explained, "a class of small proprietors, who seem to acquire slovenly habits from dependence on slaves, of whom they can maintain but few." Neither Lyell nor Buckingham could reconcile such observations with their admiration for the refinements of planter aristocrats, who by their association with large numbers of slaves ought thereby to have lived lives of unrelieved squalor. The paradox remained as Francis Kron described it in his diary after he saw the "desolation" of a North Carolina plantation: "What renders the neglect in this case more remarkable is the ability of the proprietor to do better for he is an intelligent and industrious man, and his force of boys enough to show fairer sights. It seems indeed as if the abode was intended as a contrast with the character of its inmate."[34] The fact is that slaveholders were no lazier than any others, and their willingness to give up the simplest luxuries cannot be explained by their proximity to black laborers.

Other observers suggested more reasonable explanations. According to one traveler, slaveholders took a certain "pride of the privation, which they, without any necessity, continue to endure with their families." They cared little for fine homes, fancy clothing, and refined diets. Instead, "it is their pride to have planted an additional acre of cane-break, to have won a few feet from the river, or cleared a thousand trees from the forest; to have added a couple of slaves to their family, or a horse of high blood to their stable." When Lucy Clanton moved from her North Carolina home to Madison County, Mississippi, she found that her new neighbors "don't care much about show, a great many wealthy people live in log houses, some few have them well furnished, some don't seem to care." If ostentatious display was an essential element in the maintenance of the planters' authority, many appear to have been unaware of it. Rather than move out of their original "log huts," Joseph Ingraham explained, the slaveholders' "whole time and attention were engaged in the culture of cotton; and embellishment, either of their cabins or grounds, was wholly disregarded."[35]

There were less charitable explanations of the slaveholders' habits. When Olmsted visited a Red River plantation in Texas, he found the owners living in a filthy one-room cabin. The mistress described the atrocious food she served as the "Bes we've got." Her little daughter, though severely ill, was unattended by a physician, and a drawer full of medicine bottles was unusable because, the mother explained, "I can't read writin." Yet the family owned more than ten field hands, who raised sixty to seventy bales of cotton a year. After figuring the expenses of the farm, Olmsted concluded that in two years the family's profits should have been six thousand dollars. "What do people living in this style do with so much money?" he asked. "They buy *more negroes* and enlarge their plantations." Henry Watson saw the same thing in Alabama. "The Farmers in the country live in a miserable manner," he wrote. "They think only of making money and their houses are hardly fit to live in."[36]

Many slaveholders would not live in a place long enough to care whether it was comfortable or not. The favorite topic of conversation among western settlers in Kentucky, Timothy Flint recalled, was the lands still further west. "They talk of them. They are attached to the associations connected with such conversations. They have a fatal effect upon their exertions." Consequently, Flint explained, "they only make such improvements as they can leave without reluctance and without loss." Slaveholders who had no intention of remaining on their farms permanently were still less inclined to improve them. "Every planter considers himself only a temporary occupant of the plantation on which he is settled," Buckingham observed. "He thus goes on from year to year, racking it out, and making it yield as much cotton or corn in each year, without considering the future, holding himself ready to sell at a day's notice to any one who will give him what he considers to be the increased value of the estate."[37]

It was their obsession with the acquisition of land and slaves, not their laziness, that caused wealthy men to live so poorly. And it was their incessant desire to move in search of greater opportunities to use their slaves that made masters live like paupers. John and Polly Colvin, for example, left their home in South Carolina to settle in Mississippi with their slaves and children. For nearly two years they lived in a "very old and dilapidated double log house" until a modest, one-and-a-half-story wood-frame home was completed. But no sooner were they settled in when "the call of the west" pulled them further. They sold their Mississippi farm and moved to Texas. Thus, a good deal of the poverty attributed to the Old South is based on descriptions of some of its wealthiest citizens. "Many of those who live in this way, possess considerable numbers of slaves, and are every year buying more," one shocked traveler declared. "Their early frontier life seems to have destroyed all capacity to enjoy many of the usual luxuries of civilized life."[38]

DEMOGRAPHIC MOBILITY was so much a part of life in the slaveholding South that those who yearned for stability were often frustrated. Complaints were most common among the wives of slaveholders who missed the society they left. "I feel almost friendless," a Tennessee mistress wrote to her Virginia friend. "The intimacy of dear and loved relatives have been broken by the bitter pill of separation leaving a faint hope of meeting on earth. I feel exceedingly desolate and lonely." On the road to Alabama Sara Jane Lide wrote that "when I think of my dear friends behind, I feel gloomy and depressed." She was no more satisfied when she reached Pleasant Hill, her new home. "Oh! how I would rejoice if I were only back to good old Darlington again." In 1839 Mary Drake explained to her relatives in North Carolina why she was so "discontented" in Alabama: "To negroes who have been always accustomed to little smoky cabins & the coarsest fare, to the lover alone of money, to hardy industrious men . . . Creek and Choctaw Nations present perhaps as many charms as my dear native soil. but to a female who has once been blest with every comfort, & even luxury, blest with the society of a large & respectable circle of relations and friends . . . to such people Mis. and Ala. are but a dreary waste."[39]

It was women who most consistently protested the wandering ways of their slaveholding husbands. They wrote of their loneliness on the frontier, complained of being left alone for long stretches while their spouses searched for lands out west, and objected when the decision to move was announced. Having made the difficult adjustment to life in Alabama after a major move from South Carolina, Maria Lide was distressed to hear talk of yet another move. "I expect to spend the remainder of my days in moving about from place to place. . . . Pa is quite in the notion of moving somewhere; he is urging brother Samuel to sell his land. . . . His having such a good crop seems to make him more anxious to move. I don't know why it is but none of them are satisfied here. . . . You have no idea how tired I am of hearing about moving; it is the subject of conversation every time pa and brother meet and that is very often." She tried to convince her brother to go all the way to California "because I think he would be obliged to stop then for he could go no farther, and I think he would be far enough away from society to be satisfied to settle himself permanently." Alex Allen's wife prevented him from moving west with his brother in 1850. "I fear Maria will not be willing to leave Ma in case I get matters so arranged that I could go to Texas," Allen wrote. "I am not satisfied to remain here but it will be difficult to get away."[40]

Demographic instability eventually provoked an agricultural reform movement in the South, particularly on the East Coast, the states from which slaveholders most frequently emigrated. The editors, if not the readers, of the agricultural periodicals saw the restoration of exhausted soils and the advancement of internal improvements as the means by which "to stop this current which is annually sweeping away so many thousands" to the West. "These things would soon put a smiling face upon our country," the *Farmers' Register* declared, "and take away the inducements to emigrate."[41]

Reformers analyzed the motives of those who left. They cited the "restless disposition of the people of a new country—the greedy avarice of the acquisition of land—and the strong propensity (to some extent commendable) to accumulate wealth." What was particularly troublesome to reformers was that the West was not simply attracting the poor and indigent. One writer complained that the "majority of emigrants" were young men "at that period of life when their labor is most valuable to society." In addition, those who left were usually "the most efficient and enterprising." They included the best educated Southerners, and they took with them "a considerable amount of the accumulated capital of the state." The *Southern Cultivator* agreed that this was a movement of slaveholders as much as non-slaveholders. "I speak not of those who were driven from their homes by the union of pride and poverty, or those who sought professional employment; but of planters."[42]

The *American Farmer* blamed poor childrearing practices for the removal of so many young men. "The most intelligent and enterprising of our sons are lost to the Old States," one writer explained, because our "home education is deficient." Rather than teach the young boy to accept the prospect of "moderate wealth" in his home environment, "he is taught by marvellous tales of fortune made in a day, to turn his longing eyes 'to the ends of the earth.' " Reformers deflated the exaggerated accounts of the wonderful fertility and incomparable climate of the West. Such inducements were "too strong to be resisted by a people who find it laborious to earn a mere subsistence in the land of their fathers," one editorialist complained. He called the "mighty west" a "fairy land of imagined manna, and of milk and honey."[43]

Opponents of emigration not only questioned the claims of western settlers, they suggested that the disadvantages of migration outweighed the benefits. "Do fathers of family reflect, when they remove to the West," the *Southern Agriculturist* asked, "that they condemn their posterity for two or three generations, to the ills and hardships to which frontier countries are necessarily exposed, to a state short of barbarism, destitute of that amenity which has been the delight of their lives?" Reformers appealed in vain to the slaveholders' sense of family and community. "Led captive by an excited imagination," the *Southern Cultivator* declared, migrant slaveholders "abandoned friends and relatives, their old homestead, tolerable lands and reasonable prospects, here, for an *ignis fatuus* of wealth in distant parts."[44]

Motivated largely by the desire to keep their best young men from abandoning the old slaveholding states, editorialists tied the reform movement to the enhanced profitability of eastern soils. "A farmer had better emigrate, than continue to cultivate exhausted lands," the *Southern Agriculturist* admitted, "but would it not be preferable to remain at home without exhaustion?" The *American Farmer* agreed: "Our system of agriculture is responsible in some measure, for the evil [of emigration], and agriculture will be the greatest sufferer, if it is not checked." If there was diligence, and a willingness to implement the techniques of scientific farming, the "enterprising agriculturists on old farms in eastern Virginia, will do better for themselves, their families, and the community in general, by remaining at home and improving their lands, than they could possibly do by emigrating to the south-west."[45]

If conservatives are those who revere tradition and stability in the face of "rapid social change," these reformers may be so classified. Yet their arguments reveal that they accepted the prevailing commercial assumptions and so suggested sweeping changes designed to enhance slavery's profitability. After all, the essence of their attack on westward migration was that it simply did not pay. "Count their slaves, count their acres, count their children," the *Farmers' Register* summoned its readers; ask those who have moved "how much clear money they have on hand each year, *after all is paid,* and then inquire how much property they can purchase with it." A Mississippi editor agreed. "Let any man 'cypher' up the cost of moving," he wrote to his brother. "I venture on it, no sane man will move."[46]

In their zeal to tout the profitable potential of the old slave states, reformers revealed what poor conservatives they were. For in resisting economic decline, they were not arguing for social stasis. Instead they railed against popular resistance to modern management techniques that would make farming more lucrative. They proposed the building of railroads and canals to facilitate the growth of a flourishing market economy, and in many cases they suggested alternatives to agriculture itself. "Turn your attention to every new branch of business that is honorable and remunerative," a correspondent for the *Southern Cultivator* advised his young readers. "Build up manufactories of every kind. Introduce the culture of everything that yields a large return from a small extent of land."[47]

In the end, reformers did not so much try to suppress the boundless energy of migratory slaveholders as to redirect it toward the transformation of slaveholding culture itself. If they failed, it was because the patterns they sought to reverse were too much a part of the slaveholders' ethos to succumb to the force of mere logic. By the late antebellum period, movement meant more to slaveholders than the rational pursuit of economic goals. Migration was a part of their ideology, a product of their rearing, a response to social pressures and psychological impulses that reduced the complaints of wives and the strictures of reformers to feeble gestures. "We have been doing so all our lives," one slaveholder explained, "—just moving—from place to place—never resting—as soon as ever we git comfortably settled, then, it is time to be off to something new."[48]

As if to counteract the anomie of antebellum life, Southerners fabricated a kind of stability by drawing closely to themselves the basic institutions of their society. In terms of population density, local governments were closer to southern people than to Northerners in most agricultural areas. Every county had a county seat, and if there was a navigable river within its borders there was probably a shipping port as well. The state maps of the antebellum South were thus dotted with hundreds of small towns from which emanated the only sense of community most slaveholders could ever know. "Each town is the centre of a circle which extends many miles around it into the country," Joseph Ingraham observed, "and daily attracts all within its influence."[49]

Around the South's perimeter, fertile lands and lucrative crops sustained unusually large plantations, which in turn sustained much of the South's urban economy. Cities like Richmond, Charleston, Savannah, Mobile, New Orleans, and Natchez served as entrepôts for the South's staple-producing economy as well as social centers for its wealthiest citizens. Where there were large plantations there were cities, and where there were cities there were few small towns.

But if there was a focal point for the social life of most slaveholders it was neither the big city nor the large plantation. The growth of the nearby town was a significant development in a frontier community. When John Fraser tried to convince his old friends in South Carolina to come to Mississippi, he told of the "public place known as Gray's Post Office Port," where "Grocerys and Domestics and all of the Store Combustibles can be bought." At places like Warrenton and Staunton, Virginia, farmers dealt with merchants, smiths, lawyers, barbers. It was here that they went to church, heard politicians speak, and sold their produce. As he traveled through Mississippi, Ingraham visited towns like Raymond, Clinton, Washington, and Port Gibson. They had a post office, a courthouse, a jail, a doctor's office. Some were pretty, with town squares and attractive public buildings; others were dilapidated, little more than a short row of buildings along a roadside or at the crossroads. The population of a rural village could range from one or two hundred to several thousand people. New towns were filled with young unmarried men, professionals looking for a place to start a career or open an office.[50]

Slaveholders looked to the town as a social anchor in a world that seemed always to be adrift. Even though they complained about their severed relations, the lack of amenities, and the absence of an established church in their new Alabama home, the Lide family was not completely isolated. Frances Jane Lide spoke anxiously of nearby Nubbin Ridge as "almost a town" that was "very thickly settled."[51] Most of the slaveholders' social, legal, political, and religious activity took place in the small town. But with its merchants, shippers, and country stores, the town served primarily as the nucleus of a vast and decentralized marketing system that tied the products of slave labor into the international economy.

Not all slaveholders marketed their goods through small towns. The wealthiest masters who owned the best lands along the major waterways were able to ship their goods directly to a "factor," or purchasing agent, downriver at a major port city like New Orleans or Mobile. Small slaveholders who lived near a river or a major port also bypassed the middlemen and brought their goods directly to the market. Often slaveholders simply hauled their merchandise overland to a small inland city like Vicksburg, where they either sold it or sent it downriver themselves. Sometimes such trips were necessary because there was no town convenient to the slaveholder; sometimes it was more economical to bring the goods directly to the market. For others the trip was an annual event. Whatever the reason, slaveholders who carried their own cotton, hemp, or tobacco overland rarely had an easy time of it. The roads were bad in the best of weather, and the journey usually took several days or longer. Wagons broke, mules went lame, oxen had to be fed and watered, and when the weather was poor roads were frequently impassable. "No finished public roads, no regular taverns at convenient distances," Francis Kron remarked; "all is done with the greatest labour, the worst hardships and money and time consuming motions." Occasionally the expense of the journey outweighed the benefits. In North Carolina, Olmsted saw three thousand barrels of pitch worth $4,500 dollars in New York "thrown away, a mere heap of useless offal, because it would be more to transport it than it would be worth."[52]

In wealthy areas with large plantations, small slaveholders who did not go directly to a merchant or factor sometimes sold their produce to the planters, who in effect acted as middlemen by setting a fee to gin cotton for neighbors. William Moseley in Florida charged by the pound or accepted a share of the cotton he ginned. For Moseley and other planters like him, this service was just another part of the business. In December 1850, for example, his slaves ginned cotton for several neighbors, and Moseley recorded the transactions in his diary: "Higgs paid me the money due by Jason and William Wages for ginning three bales of cotton at $30.50. . . . Rec'd from J. Higgs my share of the three bales of Jason Wages cotton."[53]

Once the cotton was ginned, many small growers sold their crops to the itinerant merchants who traveled through the undeveloped areas of the antebellum South, where no small town economy was yet established. But as with planters who offered ginning services for a fee and slaveholders who hauled their goods overland, itinerant merchants were exceptions to the usual pattern of cotton marketing. With the rise of the small town economy in the nineteenth century, itinerants gave way to small merchants, gin house operators, and store owners. Cotton speculators working through the store continued to buy cotton from small growers, but speculators, merchants, and store owners all sold their cotton directly to factors by shipping or bringing the crops to the major port cities, the same way wealthy planters did. As the antebellum years passed, most slaveholders came to rely on the town store as their closest link in the chain that connected them to the cotton economy. "Wherever the middling classes are a considerable proportion of the population," J. W. Dorr wrote in 1860, "there the country stores are numerous."[54] More than the courthouse, the post office, or the church, the southern country store attracted slaveholders and non-slaveholders alike into the small towns, reinforcing their place at the center of the slaveholders' social universe.

The town store was the most readily available agency of credit, supplying farmers with groceries, tools, and other goods for twelve months, accepting crops in payment at the end of the year. Those farmers and slaveholders who did not own their own cotton gin usually went not to a nearby planter but to the local gin house or country store, where ginning was frequently provided as another service. Finally, store owners marketed the crops of small slaveholders, accumulating large concentrations of cotton and selling it to their own factors. It could be a very lucrative business, and store owners were often among the most influential men in the community. They frequently possessed large numbers of slaves. "Sometimes three or five years business would be so profitable to a sober and prudent merchant as to enable him to retire," H. S. Fulkerson observed. The store owner would then "sell out to his clerks or go to planting, or to New Orleans to engage in larger operations." Fulkerson recalled one store in which three sets of partners made their fortunes in less than fifteen years. Thus the one institution that might have brought some stability to the slaveholders' world was caught up in the same restlessness that kept the slaveholders forever on the move and on the make.[55]

Town life was as unstable as rural life in the Old South. Businesses changed hands over and over, particularly among innkeepers. The same credit system that kept the stores going and created so many small fortunes was particularly vulnerable to the boom-and-bust cycle for which the credit system was largely responsible.[56] The mobile society which the small town was uniquely capable of serving could also be the town's nemesis: one sweep of "Alabama fever" might empty a village, leaving a hull where once there had been a thriving community.

LIKE A SACRED PILGRIMAGE, westward migration justified itself. In many ways, the perpetual exodus of American slaveholders was a futile effort by a highly structured society to fulfill its own egalitarian ideal. For movement generally necessitated the abandonment of the settled community, the destruction of established relationships, and the reduction of the physical environment to a universal level of subsistence. In part, the slaveholders' restlessness reveals the ambivalence that arose as slavery drew more and more Southerners out of the subsistence economy and into a market culture.

Raised in a society that promoted slavery as a bulwark of equal opportunity, slaveholders acted out their ideals in corresponding contradictions, abandoning their homes to re-create the experience of their parents, accumulating wealth but living like paupers, constantly moving because the implications of settlement were too unpalatable, always searching for something they would never find. Almost sixty years old, on his way to Texas in 1854, Eli Lide wrote to his aged parents in Alabama: "I often think how can I do without my Father and Mother. I cannot I cannot do without them yet something within me whispers onward onward and urges me on like a prisoner who has been 58 years and idled in his Lords vineyard and lived on his bounty and made no returns for the favors received." Like the slave-holder who feared that at thirty years of age nothing had come of his life, Eli Lide wondered at sixty "what the Lord intends to do with me." One month later, he died of cholera, shortly after reaching Texas.[57]

The conflicting impulses Eli Lide felt within himself were im-plicit in the market culture of the slaveholding class and were rein-forced by southern parents who impressed upon their children the importance of personal achievement and material success. For the more intense the pressure to succeed, the more likely were parents to suffer from the migration of their children. In their inevitable search for relief from these contradictions, slaveholders turned for solace to the ambiguous message of evangelical Protestantism.

Chapter 4

∽

The Convenient Sin

E VANGELICAL PROTESTANTISM attracted most of the religiously inclined slaveholders. Episcopal orthodoxy remained strong in eastern Virginia and lowcountry South Carolina. A significant Catholic tradition persisted among the slaveholding descendants of the Maryland colonists and the French and Spanish settlers of Louisiana and Florida. And there were ethnic and regional variations as well. But the slaveholders who expressed religious convictions were overwhelmingly Protestant and practiced their faith in the diverse evangelical styles of Baptists, Methodists, Presbyterians, and some Episcopalians.[1]

This was not always true, and the timing of the slaveholders' conversion to evangelicalism is not without significance. The Great Awakening of the 1740's, which did so much to disrupt established religious practices in colonial New England, was not nearly as effective in converting Southerners. Appealing to a small community of Scotch-Irish immigrants, Samuel Davies led a brief Presbyterian revival in Virginia in the 1740's. But his influence did not extend much beyond Hanover County, and the revival collapsed with his departure in 1759. If the tradition-bound settlements along the southern Atlantic Coast resisted the lure of revivalism before the American Revolution, the inland regions of the same colonies were as yet too sparsely populated to produce the numbers of converts upon which revivalism thrived. In 1752 the Reverend Devereux Jarratt visited Albemarle County, Virginia, and found "no minister of any persuasion, or any public worship within miles."[2]

But in the decades immediately preceding and continuing through the Revolution, the population of these backwoods regions swelled with the arrival of large numbers of immigrants whose religious traditions were different from those of the Anglican Church. Scottish Presbyterians, English Methodists and Baptists, and German Lutherans all made it difficult for an established orthodoxy to prevail. If the huge crowds George Whitefield attracted to his northern revivals were nowhere to be found during his several visits to the South, his influence was nevertheless significant. Two northern preachers, Shubal Stearns and Daniel Marshall, who had been converted at Whitefield's Connecticut revival in 1745, settled in western North Carolina ten years later and began a series of "New Light" or "Separate" Baptist revivals. Although eastern North Carolina remained aloof, the backcountry proved receptive to New Light revivalism throughout the 1760's, converting as many as forty-two churches and 125 ministers. But, like the earlier revival in Virginia, North Carolina revivalism collapsed with the loss of its charismatic leadership. Daniel Marshall had gone to South Carolina in 1760; Shubal Stearns died in 1771. Within two years his Sandy Creek Church declined from its peak of six hundred members to only fourteen.[3]

Nevertheless, the tradition of southern revivalism had been established, and in 1776 Virginia witnessed its first major Methodist camp meeting. Thereafter evangelicalism flourished. The "Great Revival" —in reality a series of revivals throughout the last quarter of the eighteenth century, culminating in several spectacular camp meetings at the turn of the century—transformed the culture of slaveholding more dramatically than anything thereafter, until the Civil War destroyed slavery altogether.[4]

The majority of masters, small slaveholders and large planters alike, were evangelicals, and their presence at revivals attracted attention. In antebellum Mississippi the Methodist denomination appealed to "all ranks of society, embracing many of the affluent and a majority of the merely independent planters, throughout the state." Those who attended a revival in Tallahassee, Florida, in 1843 were among "the first and most influential classes in society. . . . There we saw Physicians, Lawyers, Merchants, Planters & Legislators," the minister boasted. In fact, evangelicalism had wide appeal among all classes in the Old South. In Georgia and South Carolina, one traveler wrote, "men talk in public places, in the churches, and in bar-rooms, in the stage-coach and at the fireside, of their personal and peculiar relationship with the Deity."[5]

Revivals were frequent and major occurrences throughout the antebellum South. A Texas pioneer recalled that in the 1830's "there were no churches but plenty of camp meetings." In 1841 a Lowndes County, Mississippi, slaveholder left his forty bondsmen to attend a camp meeting for four straight days. John W. Jones, a Kentucky slaveholder who regularly attended church services, prayer meetings, and revivals, was ecstatic in late 1859 when a camp meeting produced "more additions to the church." Revivals were common even at many universities in the southern states, reinforcing the conclusion that the slaveholding middle class was strongly attracted to evangelical Protestantism.[6]

Slaveholders often remembered the conversion experience as a central event in their lives, one which informed all subsequent thought and action. In 1839, Josiah Hinds returned to the campground at Ebenezer, Alabama. "This is where I first went up to be prayed for and joined the church, and near this campground I first found the Lord precious to my soul. While riding along the road by myself, the Lord spoke peace to my soul, and I bless God that I ever was permitted to join the church as a seeker of religion." Like Hinds, most slaveholders assumed that their conversion would manifest itself in "Christian" behavior. Observers were struck by the changes wrought by spiritual conversion. "Your Uncle Lewis . . . has lately become a member of the Methodist church," Sarah Guion wrote her son in 1818, "and is now as remarkable for his piety as he has ever been for the benevolence of his heart."[7]

The first evidence of Christian behavior—what most occupied the minds of slaveholding parents—was the moral and religious training of the children. The mistress of an Alabama plantation was "determined if the Lord spares me to live, to try and raise my children in the fear and admonition of the Lord. The greatest desire of my heart," she told her daughter, "is that you may be faithful Christians, that you may be useful, and happy, while you live, that you may die happy, and live with God forever." A slaveholding father warned his children that "The moment you become *irreligious* and insensible to your obligations to God, you will begin to grow remiss in your duty towards men, and cease to be happy." After their own and their family's conversions, what most interested evangelical slaveholders and their wives was the conversion of their relatives and friends. "I have not told you what my object in life is," Octavia Otey informed her mother. "It is to see my dear relatives, Uncle John, especially, get religion, and I feel certain they will do it." In 1852, a Georgia slaveholder told his brother of "a most precious Revival of Religion in Bainsbridge. The meeting continued two weeks. 32 were added to the Church. . . . I did not forget you, My Dear Brother in this precious season of grace. My poor prayers are for you daily and God grant that you and my much loved Sister may think of this all-important subject."[8]

For young Southerners, the pressure to accept Christianity was often as intense as the pressure to succeed. "My moral training has been equally good as my mental," Thomas Hobbs observed at nineteen years of age. "I have pious parents, strict Methodists, who have ever endeavored to lead me in virtue's path, both by precept and example; and I hope I have not been unmindful of their teachings." Eliza Burruss warned her son in 1825 that he was now "old enough to be accountable to God" for all his actions. "You must diligently seek a change of heart, for, according to the scriptures, you cannot enter the Kingdom of Heaven unless you are converted." In 1859 an Alabama slaveholder wrote anxiously to his son at the University of Virginia: "I am pleased to hear that you have a revival at Charlottesville and that some of the students have joined the church—it would be very happy news for me to hear that you had done so yourself —The experience of your father assures you that there is no blessing in this life to be compared with an early and thorough devotion to our *creator.*" When Mary Bethell's son Willy professed religion she was overjoyed. "I felt quite happy next day," Bethell wrote, "the thought of God's converting one of my children made me feel *so* thankful."[9]

WHAT WERE THE UNIFYING PRINCIPLES of evangelicalism, which cut across traditional denominational boundaries and effectively won the loyalty of most Southerners? At the risk of oversimplification, but for the sake of clarity, it is useful to begin with the principle of Divine Providence. God was believed to control all events on earth, and man was helpless before His powers. Yet as they looked around them, evangelicals saw a world seemingly overrun with evil and indifferent to religion. "Oh man when will thou meekly submit to God without a murmur," one slaveholder wrote in his diary. "His will be done should be our constant prayer." Thus, despite God's omnipotence, the state of human affairs was miserable, and for that evangelicals blamed mankind's sinfulness. Though defined in many ways, sin was generally equated with irreligiosity and was usually ascribed to covetousness, "worldliness," an inordinate, distracting, and ultimately immoral concern with material things. Sin was so prevalent in the world that only universal human degradation could explain it. Drawing on a centuries-old tradition within Christianity, evangelicals asserted that all human beings stood before an avenging God, equal in their helplessness and degradation, but not without hope. The conscious acceptance of Christ, symbolized most forcefully in the jolting ritual of conversion, offered the sinner release from the things of this world and an entirely new life, a spiritual rebirth, and with it the promise of eternal salvation.[10]

Southern evangelicalism grew from the same roots as northern and British evangelicalism; all were similar in many particulars. But the significance of any religion derives from its context as well as its content, and in the antebellum South evangelicalism took on a meaning that served the specific needs of a slave society. Evangelical churches and camp meetings provided slaveholders with a genuine sense of community in a frontier setting where tangible institutions were often ephemeral at best. Sometimes the social function of the churches was obvious, not to say banal. On a voyage up the Mississippi River in 1806, one traveler noticed several small, modest church buildings in a sparsely settled area. "The inhabitants find a great convenience in these Churches—Sunday the Church serving as an exchange." Camp meetings were suited to the needs of migratory slaveholders among whom it was often impossible to maintain a regular body of worshipers. One Presbyterian clergyman complained that the "instability of connexions" made it difficult to establish a local ministry, "which required such a length of time to acquire its proper strength."[11]

Changes in evangelical Protestantism from the Revolution to the Civil War did not alter the structure and function of revivals. Camp meetings would last for days, even weeks, and the participants would temporarily settle in what amounted to an artificial town. An astonished Norwegian settler described what he saw at a Texas revival. Five preachers sermonized "day and night for a whole week. The people in the vicinity congregate around the camp, where they remain: some in their wagons and tents and others in small log-houses, which they have constructed there for their own comfort,—all of them bringing along sufficient food products and household utensils for the length of time they intend to stay there."[12] Such events undoubtedly counteracted the loneliness of the slaveholders' rural lives, just as the wild and cathartic experience of conversion relieved, if only temporarily, the dull routine of their isolated existence. But in much more complex and subtle ways, southern evangelicalism offered the slaveholders a religious style uniquely suited to their psychological needs.

While a religion that emphasizes man's total depravity can hardly be called uplifting, there is no denying the profound sense of relief and even pride implicit in the testimonials of the converted. This tendency to recover a sense of superiority from a theology that seems at times frightfully degrading goes a long way toward explaining evangelicalism's attractiveness to the antebellum South. From a glorious tradition of political leadership in the world's most successful libertarian revolution, the South passed through the early national period determined to separate the question of slavery from the issue of democratic freedom and so entered the era of sectional conflict with a sullied reputation, its moral influence shattered by a tenacious resistance to the implications of its own egalitarian ideals. On the high seas Great Britain was making a kind of public penance for its earlier involvement in the Atlantic slave trade, while at home a few proslavery ideologues suggested that the South resume its participation in the shabby commerce. In the North, abolitionists passed grave moral judgment upon a once-great South, pronouncing the slaveholders guilty of cruel injustice and shameful sin. Ridiculed by a foreign power that thrived on the fruits of the South's slave laborers and by a North that treated its own blacks as beneath contempt, it is not surprising that slaveholders clung in vast numbers to the security of evangelical Protestantism. For this was a tradition which permitted them to deny the world around them, to proclaim their independence and individuality, to acknowledge their private guilt, and to transform that acknowledgment into visible evidence of their high moral virtue through public declarations of spiritual rebirth.

This tendency was most evident on religious holidays, which seemed to ease the masters' consciences, destroying temporarily their ability to ignore the humanity of blacks. "I love the sabbath," Jeremiah Clemens wrote from Lexington, Kentucky, in 1834. "It is a time when slavery itself is free—when it unlooses its shackles, forgets its horrors and tells its tales of love." No holiday was more widely celebrated among slaves than Christmas, few plantation routines more honored by slaveholders than the suspension of work on Sundays, and it was at such times that references to the happiness of slaves were most frequently made. "We have had a 'right merry' Christmas; and I do not know when I have seen such an expression of content and happiness as my negroes exhibited during the festival," John N. Evans wrote in 1836. "I am much more reconciled to my condition as a slaveowner when I see how cheerful and happy my fellow creatures can be in a state of servitude, how much I have it in my power to minister to their happiness."[13]

But the soothing message of evangelicalism came at great cost to the slaveholders' psychological security. As humans, masters were by definition complex beings, capable of holding to contradictory values, motivated by principles at odds with their behavior, torn by irreconcilable impulses intrinsic to their way of life. The slaveholders' religion addressed but never fully resolved these conflicts, for in its implicit egalitarianism and explicit rejection of materialism, evangeli-

calism questioned two of the fundamental tendencies of the slave
system: the dehumanization of the bondsmen, and the grasping materialism of their owners. Among its many rewards, slavery offered
masters the luxury of ambivalence.

Evangelicalism first addressed the ethical contradictions of slaveholding by countering the brutal implications of the gospel of prosperity. In its rejection of a sinful, covetous world, evangelicalism
carried a strongly antimaterialistic message that struck slaveholders
with peculiar force. Their society was founded upon the pursuit of
material wealth, and that was precisely what evangelical ministers
attacked so vehemently. "From the growing love of wealth, which
seems to be the all-devouring passion of our country," a Virginia
Methodist warned, "and from the corruptions and sins which this is
sure to bring in its train, I must believe that unless this be repented
of and abandoned, God will bring this nation also to the dust."
Another evangelical preacher complained of his constituents that "the
world is in their thoughts day and night. . . . The price of merchandise
and negroes are inexhaustable themes of conversation. But for them
the name of Jesus has no charms."[14]

Thomas Gale, a Mississippi slaveholder, understood that this was
a lesson masters had to learn if they were to be saved. "The things
of time, what are they? They vanish as the bubbles on the surface of
the water and why should we immortal beings feel so much interest
in them." Therefore, Gale declared, "let us pray to God to give us
reason and enable us to combat this world." E. G. Baker made a
similar prayer in his plantation diary. "Oh God may I turn from
worldly ways, to the love of those Heavenly. . . . May I renounce
ever more that which is sinful and only cling to that which is holy."
John Houston Bills, a Tennessee slaveholder, expressed "disappoint-
ment . . . in *man* pretending to be governed by Correct christian
principles when their actions prove the controlling principle to be
Money."[15]

Thus the moral lesson slaveholding parents stressed most strongly
within their families was in sharp contrast to the secular emphasis on
individual achievement and material success. A wealthy Alabama
slaveholder sternly warned his son against the dangers of covetousness. "Don't let this world, or the honors of the world, yea I would

add the Riches too, cheat you out of the love, and of course the favour of your blessed Saviour. Recollect what *he* says. Son give me thy heart and if any man (no matter who) love the world the love of the father is not in him. . . . I know it is not sinful to be rich, or honourable, but Mr. Wesley says it is extremely dangerous, therefore we should watch and pray *much* in order to keep humble and devotional—this you must do or your Pappa says you will backslide."[16]

Evangelical Protestantism sparked in slaveholders an intense fear that they were unworthy of the prosperity born of slavery and that their children would be unable to resist the materialism that was so much a part of the market culture. "Oh my God," one successful master prayed in his diary, "may I deserve this prosperity." When wealthy masters rejected worldly luxury by living in ramshackle homes, wearing tattered clothing, and dining with dreary monotony, they were, in a sense, acting out these religious principles with singular literal-mindedness. "I have made some money and a good crop," a Mississippi slaveholder wrote in 1847, "but what is all this life when compared to eternal things." In 1858, C. P. Pettit wrote to a friend from his new home in Texas. "I am now worth between 5 and 6 thousand dollars and is making Money fast yet and Josh what affords me more pleasure than all i feel that i am a Christian and that is worth more to me than all the welth of Texas." To reject worldly luxury in this way was to repudiate implicitly a fundamental element of slave society. Thus one slaveholder in the Old Southwest freed his slaves out of "a sense of right, choosing poverty with a good conscience, in preference to all the treasures of the world."[17]

Attacks on materialism were part and parcel of Christian tradition; but within the context of a slave society they served as a psychological medium through which masters expressed their misgivings about bondage. They complained repeatedly about the "difficulty of serving both God and mamon." Slaveholding ministers felt most strongly that Christianity could not be reconciled with the treatment of slaves. "It is exceedingly difficult to use them as money," one preacher admitted, "to treat them as property, and at the same time render to them that which is just and equal as immortal and account-able beings, and as heirs of the grace of life, equally with ourselves."[18]

THE IMPORTANT PLACE of religion in the proslavery defense is an indication of how deeply slaveholders felt the need to bring their ethical convictions into line with their daily practices. The only philosophical justification of slavery that ever gained any real popularity among slaveholders was the religious one, and a high percentage of proslavery tracts were in fact written by clergymen.[19] Theirs was not an easy task.

From the earliest decades of the colonial period, slaveholders associated Christianity with freedom. The practice of distinguishing "slaves" from "Christians" in colonial slave codes met no protest until the implications of black baptism made it untenable. Masters were so fearful that Christianized slaves could no longer be held in bondage that, beginning in the 1660's, southern legislatures were compelled to resolve the issue. "Whereas some doubts have arisen whether children that are slaves by birth, and by the charity and pity of their owners made partakers of the blessed sacrament of baptism, should by virtue of their baptism be made free," the Virginia legislature declared in 1667, "it is enacted that *baptism does not alter the condition of the person as to his bondage or freedom; masters freed from this doubt may more carefully propagate Christianity by permitting their slaves to be admitted to the sacrament.*" Several other colonial legislatures passed similar laws, hoping to relieve the masters' "doubts." But the doubts persisted, and many colonial slaveholders continued to resist the baptism of their bondsmen, because they feared their slaves would become "saucy." Apparently convinced that Christianity had a dangerously liberating effect, many slaveholders believed that "a Slave is ten times worse when a Xn, than in his State of Paganism."[20]

The American Revolution did not significantly alter this situation, for not until and unless a master's religious principles convinced him of the slaves' humanity did the revolutionary ideal of human equality have any genuinely liberating force. In 1775, at the climax of the ideological war that formed the backdrop to America's conflict with

Great Britain, a Maryland slaveholder, Freeborn Garretson, rejected secular principles in explaining his decision to free his slaves. "It was God, not man, that taught me the impropriety of holding slaves," Garretson insisted shortly after his own conversion. He related the religious circumstances of his decision: On a Sunday morning spent in worshipful solitude, reading the Bible, Garretson, "under a sense of duty, called the family together for prayer. As I stood with a book in my hand, in the act of giving out a hymn, this thought powerfully struck my mind, 'It is not right for you to keep your fellow-creatures in bondage; you must let the oppressed go free.' I knew it to be the same blessed voice which had spoken to me before—till then I had never suspected that the practice of slave-keeping was wrong." Garretson's action promptly eased his conscience. "I was as clear of them in my mind as if I had never owned one.... I was now at liberty to proceed in worship. After singing, I kneeled to pray."[21] Certainly the political climate in the wake of the American Revolution was more favorable to slaveholders who freed their bondsmen than it became in later decades. But as the cotton economy expanded and ultimately prevailed, private manumissions declined, and the psychological conflicts instilled by religious principles intensified.

Yet the revolutionary ideology had its effect, if only because it was often bound up closely with the evangelical impulse. An Anglican minister complained in 1767 that in the Carolina backcountry "Itinerant Presbyterian, Baptist and Independent Preachers . . . traverse this Country Poiso[n]ing the Minds of the People—Instilling Democratical and Common Wealth Principles in their Minds—Embittering them against the very Name of Bishops, and all Episcopal Government and laying deep their fatal Republican Notions—Especially—That they owe no Subjection to Great Britain—That they are a free People." This "democratical" tendency was reinforced by the structure of the camp meeting. Following an Arkansas revival, for example, a Baptist minister reported that "the master and servant, the child and parent, the self-righteous moralist and the profane sceptic bowed at the same altar." In contrast to the secular principles of liberalism, evangelical egalitarianism resisted the convenient distortions of racism by actively embracing black worshippers as fundamentally equal in the sight of God.[22]

Consequently, the antislavery sentiment implicit in evangelical Protestantism was strongest in the late eighteenth century, when the revolutionary doctrine that "all men are created equal" made it logically necessary to define blacks as an inherently inferior race and therefore undeserving of basic human rights. In the wake of the Revolution, the Methodists openly banned slavery while other denominations prohibited at least their ministers from owning slaves. Yet these were precisely the denominations into which large numbers of slaveholders were moving at the time.

Well into the last decades of the antebellum era, many masters remained fearful of the implications of slave conversion. By that time, however, evangelical churches had become actively engaged in missionary activity among the bondsmen. For Charles Colcock Jones, such activity seems to have mitigated his youthful misgivings about slavery. As a student at Princeton, Jones had joined an antislavery society and wrote letters explicitly questioning the morality of bondage. Later, as a wealthy and devout planter, he was among the most vocal advocates of religious education for slaves. In *The Religious Instruction of the Negroes in the United States,* Jones repeatedly assured slaveholders that, far from inspiring resistance, Christianity could be used to inculcate docility among slaves. That so many antebellum masters invoked biblical authority to preach obedience to their bondsmen suggests the spreading influence of men like Jones. And yet, his own arguments revealed a continuing inability personally to reconcile slavery and Christianity. Indeed, Jones came as close as any slaveholder to a philosophical recognition that the dehumanization of slavery was incompatible with his religious convictions. In preaching to the slaves, "we separate entirely their *religious* and their *civil* condition," Jones wrote in 1842, "and contend that one may be attended to without interfering with the other." In effect, the only way slaveholders could justify preaching Christian doctrine to their bondsmen was by ignoring their status as slaves. Yet this implicitly contradicted the widespread assertions by missionaries that Christianity could effectively subdue the slaves' resentment. The slaves knew better, and, if nothing else, it was their persistent refusal to succumb to the masters' use of Christianity as a weapon of indoctrination that sustained the slaveholders' awareness of the contradiction.[23]

As evangelical Protestantism became the dominant religion of the slaveholding class, the churches felt strong pressure to back down from their overt opposition to bondage. Later, when slaveholders were stung by an abolitionist movement that was itself religiously inspired, and whose major premise was that slaveholding was a sin, they naturally looked for a religious defense. The principle they found most useful to their needs was Divine Providence. "For the institution of domestic slavery we hold ourselves responsible only to God," one slaveholding politician declared, thus denying the abolitionists' right to condemn a divinely ordained social order. "No human institution, in my opinion, is more consistent with the will of God, than domestic slavery, and no one of his ordinances is written in more legible characters than that which consigns the African race to this condition."[24]

But this reasoning only enhanced the masters' fears that they would ultimately be judged by God for their behavior as slaveholders. For the invocation of Divine Providence in the proslavery argument had the residual effect of imposing great responsibilities on the masters. "No doubt the Lord has placed them under our charge for a wise purpose," one minister noted, "and how fearful the consequences if we withhold the means of salvation from them." In the first quarter of the nineteenth century, before the vigilant defense of slavery preoccupied southern intellectuals, local churches throughout the South regularly policed the conduct of slaveholders. The Hepzibah Baptist Church of Louisiana rejected William West's application for membership in 1819 "for whiping a black Brother of the church." A few years later the same congregation charged one of its members, Daniel Edds, with abusing one of his slaves "which was proven against him and he was Excommunicated for the Same." The contradiction between the implications of evangelical Protestantism and the religious proslavery argument tortured the souls of more than a few masters. *"Duty* plainly calls you to the station of a 'Planter' & a planter here is the *Master of slaves,"* Mary Burruss wrote her brother in 1836. "God knows I would gladly make them *freemen,* if I could. But in his Providence we are called to their care now & of course, their government."[25]

Thus for evangelical slaveholders the religious defense of bondage was never fully satisfying. Indeed, their deepest religious convictions exposed the slaveholders' most profound moral dilemma. For the structure of slavery tended toward the dehumanization of the bondsmen. Slaves were defined in law as real or personal estate, treated as property in the commercial market, bought and sold like so much merchandise. Slaveholders most often defended their ownership of slaves by invoking the rights of property, bolstering their defense with a racial ideology that declared blacks inferior. Slavery conceded the bondsmen's humanity only grudgingly; it denied their equality absolutely. But Christianity questioned slavery's implicit dehumanization, and evangelical Protestantism went on to assert a fundamental racial equality before God, if only in the afterlife.

Masters who had little trouble rationalizing the compatibility of slavery with their patriotic ideals found it hard to be a Christian and a slaveholder at the same time. A North Carolina master warned his children that "To manage *negroes* without the exercise of too much passion, is next to an impossibility, after our strongest endeavors to the contrary; I have found it so. I would therefore put you on your guard, lest their provocations should on some occasions transport you beyond the limits of decency and Christian morality." A Virginia master echoed these sentiments. "This, sir, is a Christian community," he wrote in 1832. "Southerners read in their Bibles, 'Do unto all men as you would have them do unto you'; and this golden rule and slavery are hard to reconcile."[26]

Throughout the antebellum period, slaveholders continued to show signs that, despite the best efforts of the proslavery apologists, evangelical Protestantism still carried an implicit antislavery message. A South Carolina slaveholder complained that his father "had too much religion to keep his negroes straight." Deeply religious slaveholders frequently complained about the cruelty that was built into slavery. A pious Alabama master found punishment "an unpleasant duty, but one nevertheless which in the present state of things, must be attended to." A North Carolina slaveholding minister believed it was a pity that "Slavery & Tyranny must go together—and [that] there is no such thing as having an obedient and useful Slave, without the painful exercise of undue and tyrannical authority."[27]

The suspicion that slavery violated fundamental moral dictates unleashed an undercurrent of fear and apprehension throughout the slaveholding South. Masters may not believe slavery to be wrong in principle, William Allen Smith observed in 1856, but they are "nevertheless subjects of painful misgivings. They *fear* it may be true." Philip Gosse found that slaveholders "tremble when they look into the future. It is like a huge deadly serpent, which is kept down by the strain of every nerve and muscle; while the dreadful feeling is ever present, that, someday or other it will burst the weight that binds it and take a fearful retribution." The Reverend John Witherspoon, a South Carolina slaveholder, impressed his apprehensions upon his daughter in 1836. "A gloomy cloud is hanging over our entire native South and indeed over our whole land," he wrote. "A miracle of mercy alone will prevent the disunion of our country. . . . To you my children I can safely say 'I would that I & mine— with all my relations & friends, were safely out of this inauspicious section of our country.' "[28] This pervasive sense of millennial retribution crystallized logically in the slaveholders' attitudes toward death, for it has always been one of religion's major functions to explain the enigma of mortality in a frightening world.

To FEAR DEATH in the antebellum South was to live in constant terror of the immediacy of one's fate. It was not a healthy place to live. Long, hot summers and vast areas of swampland were ideal for the proliferation of disease-bearing insects. Inadequate housing, poor diet, and simple ignorance left much of the South's population vulnerable. Periodic epidemics of cholera and yellow fever took thousands of lives, particularly in urban centers. In 1853 yellow fever afflicted nearly a third of New Orleans's 100,000 residents, killing over a thousand people each week in the month of August, until there were more corpses than there were graves to put them in. The Old South suffered as well from abnormally high infant mortality. In addition, a variety of ailments resulted from the slaves' poor diet, inadequate clothing and shelter, and miserable working conditions. Pellagra, a disease endemic to societies where pork, corn, and molasses form the bulk of the diet, appears to have been widespread among slaves. Blacks seem also to have been more susceptible to a variety of respiratory diseases. Thus, despite some resistance to two of the South's deadliest maladies—malaria and yellow fever—slaves had a lower life expectancy than whites.[29]

Epidemics were so common in the Old South that the stability of family and community were further disrupted beyond the already unsettled norm. The unexpected death of a neighboring doctor impressed a Mississippi slaveholder as a "striking *memento* of the instability of human existence." In the twenty-nine months covered by the first volume of Philip Pitts's diary, the slaveholder recorded the deaths of fifteen friends, relatives, and slaves in and around his home at Union Town, Alabama. They included Pitts's father, brother, cousin, doctor, the doctor's wife, "Suckie my nurse," and several of the neighboring children. He recorded the deaths of an additional fifteen of his father's friends and acquaintances who died in 1851 alone.[30] In this, Pitts was typical, for slaveholders' letters and diaries are often literally filled with horrifying descriptions of disease and death, along with equally atrocious home remedies.

There were those who believed the slaveholders' obsession with death was unwarranted. "I find the reports of sickness at a distance always exceed the truth," William Shepard wrote in 1817. "On the road Washington was represented, as a perfect Hospital, but I found it not so bad as the representation." Henry Watson went so far as to suggest that his Alabama neighbors actually encouraged the spread of cholera by their panic and hysteria. "You must know enough of the human constitution and of the history of such diseases to know the influence of the mind over the body. . . . How great then must be the effect of such extreme fright as must prevail among the ignorant."[31] It would not be surprising if slaveholders exaggerated reports of sickness. But it is less significant whether they did or did not have good reason to fear death than that they were consumed by their fear, and that in their obsession they exposed patterns of behavior and systems of belief which indicated deeply troubled consciences. The religious meaning that slaveholders gave to death is the key to understanding their discomfort with the institution of slavery. The same religious dogma that implicitly condemned slavery as sinful provided masters with a vivid picture of the eternal consequences of sin.

Death put the fear of the Lord into slaveholders. With his little son "quite unwell" and his wife sick also, E. G. Baker wrote privately that he was "now altogether sorry for all wrongs I may have committed in life—both from the fear & love of God." When Samuel Buchanan died in 1836, his brother Andrew was reminded of his own fate. "He is no more, and you and I and all of us must follow him. There is no chance to avoid it. O may I be as well prepared to meet the King of terrors as he was." In 1826 one of Lucy Horton's Alabama neighbors took sick on a Sunday evening and died before the night was over. "Good lord how awful it is to think of death and that so sudden," she wrote to her husband. "It convinces us that we all ought to be prepared to meet it at any time. Oh that it may be yours and my happy lot to be fully prepared to meet death whenever it comes and after death judgment."[32]

Thus, many slaveholders viewed death as evidence of divine retribution. "In portions of the Territory where disease was scarcely known, sickness and death appeared in their most formidable guise," the slaveholding governor told Florida's territorial legislature in 1840. "It is our duty to bow with fear, resignation and thankfulness before that great Being, whose wrath and whose blessings have been poured in a mingled stream upon our people." During the terrible yellow fever epidemic of 1853, Bishop Leonidas Polk of New Orleans asked God to "turn us from the ravage of the pestilence, wherewith for our iniquities, thou art now visiting us." Two years later the slaveholders of Fayette, Mississippi, heard "a sermon on the yellow fever being sent as a judgment to humble us." Even the deaths of innocent children were seen by slaveholding parents as a punishment from God. When Mary Carmichael's son died he "left his aged father and mother to mourn over the delight of their eyes—*But God took* him for he saw he was our idol."[33]

More than anything else, it was the egalitarianism of death that so frightened slaveholders. For if all men were truly equal in the sight of God, death was the moment when all earthly distinctions vanished, when the iniquities that slaveholders perpetrated throughout life were scrutinized and judged. "Death, the leveler," a devout Tennessee slaveholder explained, "has no respects for persons or positions." Consider the role of religion in your life, John Callaway, a Virginia master, warned his son, "for we must all die, come to judgment and give an account of the deeds done in the body: whether they be good or evil."[34]

For slaveholders, sickness and death mitigated racial distinctions and brought blacks and whites together as equals. "Influenzer or grippe prevalent still," one South Carolina slaveholder wrote. "All in house, plantation & yard have it, except Old Binah and myself." An Alabama master told his brother he had "two or three negroes sick, I think mostly cold, and I have a very bad one myself." In descriptions of death, slaveholders made few distinctions between black slaves and free whites. "It is with much sadness that I now seat myself to write of the death of our dear papa," Margaret Lide lamented in 1854. "He died last thursday morning. . . . Old Grannie Sarah died yesterday morning. She held out as long as Pa lived but as soon as he died she gave up. . . . Old Tom died the Saturday before Pa died. Tell Momma Dinah Kate died last Friday and Henrietta's baby Saturday."[35]

Nothing so effectively broke down the psychological barrier by which whites maintained their separation from blacks as did death. When "poor Jim languished night after night and day after day," Hugh Lawson wrote his sister upon the death of his favorite slave, "with sleepless vigilance I could not but compare his situation with your own, in December." Lawson had nursed his sister through pleurisy and pneumonia. While Jim *"was* a servant and you may be vexed and ashamed, that I should in my way compare him with yourself," Lawson remained struck by the similarity.[36]

What impressed masters most about the deaths of their bondsmen —significantly, in view of the slaveholders' racist assumptions—was the equality of whites and blacks at death. Slave births, when noted at all, were usually entered into the slaveholders' diaries like so many assets in a bookkeeper's ledger. "Some bad Luck," an Alabama master complained in 1857, "had one negro born dead." But the death of a slave could elicit a spontaneous outpouring of eulogy and emotion, often tied to a religious conviction that the deceased was in a better, fairer place. When one of his favorite slaves died in 1854, E. G. Baker wrote an obituary in his diary. "I shall ever cherish his memory," the master exclaimed. "He deserves a better reward than he can be given in this world." Rodah Horton was "sorry to hear of the death of poor old franky," he told his wife in 1836, "but poor old negro she is gone to a better world I hope." On a move from North Carolina to Georgia, James Rowe Coombs remembered, a slave child died of measles and was solemnly buried. "He had found a home," Coombs wrote. "The remaining portion of our suite were in search of one. . . . Perhaps this sable son of Africa may have been washed by divine Blood, and is now enjoying equal rights and privileges in the Celestial Kingdom." In 1853, Clement C. Clay, Jr., wrote his wife that "Poor little Cornelius died on the 3rd inst. We have lost 5 negros this year! Yet trusting that they are better off, I do not feel that we are worse off."[37]

The pervasive inner turmoil among the slaveholders is revealed in their startlingly frequent declarations that when they died they would go to hell. Slaveholders questioned the sincerity of their beliefs and bemoaned their lack of faith. Distraught for months by the death of his wife, a Louisiana planter wrote that "evry Where I turn I miss her. dreary is my lot, the world is cold and selfish, if I could only Believe we were to meet hereafter [it] would give me great relive." Robert R. Reid, a Florida slaveholder, was upset that his "prospects in this world—and *no prospects* in another—are all gloomy and fill me with dismay. Would I were a *Christian,* but I cannot be a hypocrite." James Barrow, a Georgia planter, was pained throughout his life by morbid fears of death. "I am now watching for the messenger which is to remove me to the other world," Barrow wrote in his diary, "but every day proves to me that I have a wretched wicked heart."[38]

In explaining why he could no longer attend revivals, a master in northern Mississippi echoed a widespread conviction among slave-holders about their eternal fate. "I used to go to the meetings with as much sincerity and soberness as anybody could. . . . I did think I was a converted man, but of course, I aint, and I 'spose 'twarnt the right sort, and I don't reckon I shall have another chance." Plantation mistresses felt no differently. "How many of those I know and loved have passed from the stage of life in the last brief year," Clarissa Town wrote. "Still I am spared; and for what? that is the question." Convinced of God's love for her, Mary Bethell of North Carolina was no less certain that she was "not worthy of his love. . . . If the Lord had treated me as I deserved he would have sent me to hell long ago."[39]

For evangelical slaveholders the fear of mortality was directly related to slavery, for their conduct as masters was subject to God's judgment at death. "Give your servants that which is just and equal," a Baptist minister declared in 1854, "knowing that you also have a Master in heaven." When they "remember their accountability and that they are to meet their servants at the bar of God," a Mississippi minister wrote in 1831, slaveholders "acknowledge their obligation to provide for the *spiritual* as well as temporal wants of those whom God has entrusted to their care." "Never forget to be kind to your inferiors," an Alabama mistress wrote her daughter in 1843. "Learn to govern yourself, get a habit of self-control while young, and you have no idea what an advantage it will be to you in after life." Minerva Cain was warned by her mother "to learn to treat your father's domestics (who are daily employed in adding to your *comfort* and *gratification*) with much feeling and give them as little trouble as possible, for place yourself in their situation, and how do [you] think you would bear it? Always bear in mind that you will have to answer at the bar of God, for your conduct towards them."[40]

Many masters never forgot the antislavery message of early evangelical sermons which suggested that, as one southern preacher flatly declared, "no slaveholder could be saved in heaven." The disappearance of such lessons was an indication of the intensification, not resolution, of the dilemma of slaveholding. "Always I felt the moral guilt of it," a Louisiana mistress admitted, "felt how impossible it must be for an owner of slaves to win his way to heaven." Ann Meade Page of Virginia prayed for deliverance from the moral burden of slaveholding. "Oh my Father, from the distressing task of regulating the conduct of my fellow-creatures in bondage, I turn and rest my weary shoulder on thy parental bosom. . . . My soul hath felt the awful weight of sin, so as to despair in agony—so as to desire that I had never had being. Oh God! then—then I felt the importance of a mediator, not only to *intercede* but to *suffer* under the burden of my guilt."[41]

Even if northern evangelicals exhibited the same morbid fears

about the afterlife, it would not alter the crucial fact that the circumstances in which such fears are expressed define their significance. In
fact, while Northerners and Southerners were equally obsessed with
death, they interpreted it in profoundly different ways. Unlike slaveholders, northern evangelicals were distinctly sanguine about their
own mortality. They accepted it calmly and without fear. Many
Northerners went even further. Popular novels published in the
antebellum North romanticized death, portraying it so favorably as
to make it seem an inviting prospect. Such visions could not have
differed more sharply with those of the slaveholders.[42]

Thus, in their conviction that they were destined for hell, the
slaveholders were not expressing a common evangelical belief about
humanity's fate in general. Masters were, after all, quite confident that
slaves went to heaven when they died, and evangelical Protestantism
was as much a pathway to salvation as it was a threat of damnation.
Nevertheless, identical sermons left masters and slaves with strikingly
different impressions of each other's fate as Christians. While masters
were convinced that death freed the slaves and made them equal,
many slaves believed that masters would suffer their just punishment
in the afterlife. "Slaves know enough of the rudiments of theology
to believe that those go to hell who die slaveholders," wrote Frederick Douglass, himself a former slave. Many years after he had been
freed, Louis Hughes wrote that "the master and most of his victims
have gone where professions of righteousness will not avail to cover
the barbarities practiced here." Martha Harrison remembered her
master as a man so frightened by his imminent death that he offered
thousands of dollars to secure his salvation. "But he couldnt'a got out
of hell," the former slave declared, "the way he beat my mammy."[43]

Conversely, many bondsmen had no doubts about their own fate.
Moses Grandy, for many years a slave in Camden County, North
Carolina, recalled that during violent thunderstorms, "when the
whites have gotten between feather-beds to be safe from the light-
ning, I have often seen negroes, the aged as well as others, go out,
and, lifting up their hands, thank God that judgment was coming at
last." Solomon Northup called the grave "the only resting place of
the poor slave." When one of his fellow bondsmen died, Northup
believed that "the Angel of the Lord . . . had silently entered the cabin

of the dying woman, and taken her from thence. She was *free* at last!"[44] Thus while it was not intrinsic to evangelicalism to instill universal fears of damnation in all of its adherents, there was something in it that caused bondsmen and their owners to agree that while death liberated the slave it doomed the master.

THE CONTRADICTION between evangelicalism's entrenched anti-materialism and the slaveholders' secular ethos was no more resolvable than the conflict between the racist dehumanization of the slaves and evangelicalism's recognition of the fundamental equality of blacks and whites. Slaveholding parents who taught their children by word and deed to accumulate land and slaves with voracious zeal also imparted to their children a religious dogma that promised damnation in return for the sin of greed. Slaveholders were raised to justify slavery by dismissing blacks as inferior, and they behaved on the assumption that slaves were chattels as much as humans. But masters were also taught that in the sight of God blacks and whites were equal and would be judged on that basis.

So fundamental were the psychological conflicts bequeathed to the children of slaveholders, so great was the rift between their religious convictions and their behavior, that for most the prospect of resolution seemed dim. In 1850 the average master was in his mid-forties, having reached adulthood well before the crises of the 1830's provoked the dissemination of the idea that slavery was a "positive good." Another generation might have seen the successful internalization of a proslavery ideology, but even that would have been unlikely. If secular proslavery ideologues never had a large following among slaveholders, the religious defense of bondage only served to highlight the moral contradictions intrinsic to slaveholding culture. And it was precisely the ancestral bridge across which these contradictions were carried to succeeding generations of slaveholders.

Under the circumstances, it is hardly surprising that so many masters expressed the fear that the rising generation would repeat the sins of its elders. A Florida slaveholder lamented as he considered the fate of his young nephew: "Shall the time come when his kind heart will become corrupt and his innocence give way to guilt? God forbid!" Like many slaveholders, Charles Pettigrew of North Carolina feared that his own behavior did not measure up to high Christian standards. He told his children that he was "mortified on a retrospect to think that my life has been so imperfect, and I wish you to improve on my imperfect example."[45]

More specifically, masters feared for the fate of their children in a slave society. "You know, my dear Son, I abhor Slavery," Henry Laurens protested. "I am not the man who enslaved them . . . nevertheless I am devising means for manumitting many of them and for cutting off the entail of Slavery. . . . [But] what will my Children say if I deprive them of so much Estate?" he wondered. "In this state of slavery I *almost feel* that every *apparent blessing* is attended with *a curse,*" a South Carolina slaveholder wrote, "and although their *wives* have no dread of the future—there are but few *husbands* and *fathers* of *daughters* who do not feel at times *dreadful apprehensions.*" Similarly, a Virginia master thought the South was "a bad country in which to bring up boys. I wish mine could be raised in the indigence and simplicity that you and I were," he wrote a northern friend. "You may feel very happy that you are not in a slave state with your fine Boys, for it is a wretched country to destroy the morals of youth." David Ross, a prosperous iron manufacturer and slaveholder, hoped that if he lived to see his son's education "perfected, he would never have any inclination to hold his fellow men in slavery." Another slaveholder freed his bondsmen not only because slavery was morally wrong but "because he was not willing to allow his children to be educated as slave masters."[46]

The most convinced slaveholders often remembered that they had grown up doubting the morality of bondage. No less a proslavery zealot than Edmund Ruffin conceded that "in the early part of my life, [I] was opposed to slavery and a speculative abolitionist." Remembering the lessons of his childhood, a Missouri slaveholder felt compelled to explain himself to his mother. "I recollect when I was very young you advised your children never to have a slave, because, for the most part nothing but discipline could make them profitable," Frederick Bates wrote from his new home in St. Louis. "I have been induced to purchase—and have been so fortunate as to get a family, which will not I hope ever require harsh treatment."[47]

It is no wonder that so many masters spoke apologetically of the abandonment of their youthful ideals. Born and raised "in the midst of slavery," Jeremiah Jeter never considered the question of whether human bondage "was right or wrong." Nevertheless, he was always moved by the "great severity" of slavery, and so "grew up with a determination never to own a slave." But when Jeter married a woman who owned bondsmen, he found himself in a dilemma. The laws of Virginia prohibited manumission unless the slaves were shipped out of the state, and the slaves made it clear they did not want that. He decided to sell or give them away, but the slaves did not want that either, for it would have involved the separation of families and friends. After a great deal of contemplation and reading, Jeter finally concluded that while slavery was neither "right . . . [nor] the most desirable condition of society," it was at least "allowable" under the laws of God. David Benedict underwent a similar transformation. He arrived in Charleston in 1776 with "every prejudice I could have against slavery," only to find his principles impractical. "Providence has cast my lot where slavery is introduced and practiced, under the sanction of the laws of the country," he wrote some years later. "Servants I want; it is lawful for me to have them; but hired ones I cannot obtain, and therefore I have purchased some: I use them as servants; I feed them, clothe them, instruct them, &c;—as I cannot do as I would, I do as I can."[48]

Inevitably there were slaveholders who felt they had inherited the very sins their fathers had tried not to bequeath. A Missouri master told Henry Clay Bruce that "he believed slavery to be wrong, but it was handed down to him from his father, and although he held and owned slaves, he had never bought or sold one, and had always treated them well." Likewise did John Witherspoon protest his innocence. "I never *willingly & heartily, bought* or *sold* a human being. I have done so, for the accommodation of the slave & my own domestick peace & comfort, but *never* for *gain*—'from the love of filthy lucre.' "[49] Such repeated assertions and disavowals on the part of some masters suggest how fundamentally the entrenched materialism of slavery conflicted with their religious convictions.

The paucity of open expressions of remorse among slaveholders, either before or after the Civil War, cannot be taken as evidence for the absence of guilt. For while remorse normally follows an avoidable misdeed, guilt is the product of a deeply rooted psychological ambivalence that impels the individual to behave in ways that violate fundamental norms even as they fulfill basic desires. This was precisely the predicament in which most slaveholders found themselves. All of their training, indeed their entire secular culture, pressured the slaveholders to behave in ways their religious convictions told them were wrong and sinful. Thus while few slaveholders expressed remorse, many spoke of themselves as trapped into slavery by the circumstances of their birth, and, not surprisingly, ministers felt these contradictions most acutely.

In the late eighteenth and early nineteenth centuries, slaveholders occasionally revealed their discomfort by explicitly refusing to talk about slavery. In 1807, a Louisiana master was "fearful that unless a stop is soon put to the encreasing number" of blacks imported to America, a bloodbath would ensue. "Much more might be said on the subject," he wrote, "but I must drop the curtain for the present." With respect to slavery, George Washington admitted, "I shall frankly declare to you that I do not like even to think, much less talk, of it."[50]

In later years, the psychological dilemma of masters was reflected in the frequently expressed wish to be rid of the slaves entirely. Completely ignoring the servants who stood right behind her, a Gulf Coast mistress declared that "it would be better if there wasn't any niggers in the world." "Lord send that there was no negro in all America," a Mississippi master prayed. "I sincerely wish there was not a slave in the world," Charles Pettigrew told his children. "I am more and more perplexed about my negroes," another master wrote. "I cannot just take them up and sell them though that would be clearly the best I could do for myself. I cannot free them. I cannot keep them with comfort. . . . What would I not give to be freed from responsibility for these poor creatures."[51]

The slaveholders confirmed the essential tragedy of their lives by declaring their inability and unwillingness to change. "We were born under the institution and cannot now change or abolish it," a Mississippi slaveholder declared. He would rather "be exterminated" than be forced to live in the same society "with the slaves, if freed." Although "we do not call ourselves abolitionists we look upon the Bondage of fellow beings as a great evil," a Florida plantation mistress wrote to her northern brother in 1855, "& would gladly advocate the abolishment of the system if we thought it could be done with safety to the Country."[52]

Slaveholders never did find a way to abolish slavery "with safety," and so the lure of prosperity continued to attract white Southerners to black slavery, despite the moral injunctions implicit in their religious values. Mary Burruss McGehee, the daughter of a prosperous slaveholder, understood well the fate of such convictions. "Fond benevolent feelings, tender regard for the good of souls, evils of slavery, &c. &c., are all less than dust of the balance when weighed against the charms of some wealthy heiress, possessor of slaves," she wrote her brother in 1836, and "the hope of winning her & enjoying the ease of the paternal mansion banishes all thought of Abolition or benevolence." One Southerner put the matter more bluntly. "A gentleman has the right to make the most of this life," he told Frederick Olmsted, "when he can't calculate on anything better than roasting in the next." Perhaps it was inevitable that a master who was conspicuously unmoved by the sentiments of evangelical piety, someone like Henry Watson, Jr., of Alabama, would reduce the moral dilemma of the slaveholders to the pathetic proportions of an epigram. "I abominate slavery," he had written in 1835, shortly after moving to the South. But within fifteen years, Watson had repudiated his youthful ideals. "If we do commit a *sin* owning slaves," he wrote his wife, "it is certainly one which is attended with *great conveniences.*"[53]

Not all masters, then, were conspicuously troubled by their religious convictions. Paternalistic slaveholders may have suffered less, precisely because their conception of slavery differed so radically from that of most others. Because they never believed in human equality to begin with, paternalistic masters were usually attracted to orthodox religious principles with no strong egalitarian tradition. Concentrated in the oldest, wealthiest, and most stable regions of the South, paternalists were less imbued with the feverish materialism that characterized the slaveholding class as a whole. Instead, it was the paternalists' peculiar fate to agonize over the failure of the vast majority within the slaveholding class to live according to the precepts of their anachronistic ideal.

If different masters manifested varying degrees of guilt, few escaped it entirely, for the elements of psychological conflict were intrinsic to slaveholding culture. But that culture also produced a secular ideology that explicitly repudiated the suggestion that slaveholding was immoral. Grounded in the historical and material experiences of the master class, this ideology contained a major ambiguity of its own: the more slaveholders glorified success, the more they feared failure. Thus did their secular ideology reinforce the slaveholders' moral dilemma: To succeed was to risk one's soul; to fail was a disgrace.

Chapter 5

~

Freedom and Bondage: Politics, Ideology, and the Implicit Defense of Slavery

SLAVEHOLDING WAS THE SYMBOL of success in the market culture of the Old South. It was an ambition, an achievement, a reward for diligence, hard work, and tenacity. As one Louisiana master wrote, "A man's merit in this country is estimated according to the number of Negroes he works in the field."[1] And as widespread as slaveholding was, it was no mean goal. From the recognition of their accomplishment, the sense of having prevailed over innumerable obstacles, slaveholders fashioned a world view that informed their public discussion of slavery, and made freedom and bondage inseparable in their minds.

BECAUSE THE STUDY of slaveholders is a success story by definition, it is difficult to understand the fear of failure that was part of the culture of slaveholding. "What shall I say at the commencement of the new year?" Henry Marston, a Louisiana slaveholder, asked in his diary at the beginning of 1827. "Am I better than I was a year since? I answer without hesitation that I am not." Marston then asked for God's help so that he might prosper "and at the close of the year find myself better in every respect." Like Marston, A. R. Boteler owned no more than ten slaves. A backwoods farmer in Shepardstown, Virginia, Boteler grew a variety of fruits and vegetables but seemed to get most of his money from cutting and hauling lumber. Nor was he a man at ease with himself. "My birth day—30 years of age!" he wrote in his diary. "30 yrs. & what have I done in all this time? — Nothing— absolutely nothing."[2]

There was enough failure among slaveholders to justify the concerns of men like Boteler and Marston. In 1842 William Mitchell Davidson's business in Waynesville, North Carolina, collapsed. All of his property—land, stock, and slaves—was sold at the sheriff's auction the following year. With his wife and three sons, Davidson moved off his homestead on Jonathan's Creek. For a year they farmed on rented land near Asheville, but Davidson was not satisfied. In late 1844, he sold everything he could not fit into a four-horse wagon and headed west. In Texas he leased more land and seemed to be doing well. But the region was sickly, his entire family was ill, and in 1846 Davidson died, never having recovered his losses of four years earlier. His sons remained long enough to gather the crops before returning to North Carolina.[3]

Slaveholding families were no more immune to failure than individuals. In Burke County, North Carolina, in 1820, the Greenlee brothers owned 184 slaves. A generation later none of the Greenlee heirs in Burke County owned more than five slaves. In the same county John Butler owned fifty bondsmen in 1830, making him one of the largest slaveholders in the area. But business reverses before his death left his widow without a single slave in 1860. Those who owned fewer than ten bondsmen in Dallas County, Alabama, in 1850, and who stayed there for the decade, were as likely to lose all their slaves as they were to end up owning more than ten.[4]

Slaveholders recognized the tenuousness of their economic security. Advertisements for the sale of slaves seized for back taxes appeared regularly in the southern press. Frederick Olmsted heard two men in the lower Mississippi Valley talking about an unlucky neighbor whose father had recently died. He had discharged his overseer and tried unsuccessfully to run the farm himself. "Finally the sheriff took about half his niggers. He tried to work the plantation with the rest, but they was old, used-up hands." Frustrated by the poor productivity of his remaining slaves, he "sold 'em all" by the end of the year. John C. Jenkins purchased a debt-ridden plantation and struggled to revive it after the panic of 1837 and the ensuing depression. But Jenkins himself signed two bad notes and after more than a decade he complained in his diary that he was "not yet out of debt by a long shot."[5]

Slaveholders often attributed their failures to the speculative credit system, which encouraged people to go into debt to build up their holdings. The "universal indebtedness" of Alabama farmers made Henry Watson's neighbors particularly susceptible to economic disruptions like the panic of 1837. In the depression of the early 1840's Josiah Hinds lost thousands of dollars when his mercantile operation in Mississippi went bankrupt. "I am getting tired of this credit system, and I think I shall change my plan of doing business," he complained, "neither credit nor be credited." Small farmers eager to become slaveholders frequently overextended themselves by taking up more land than they could pay for. "Many fail altogether, and quit their farms in about ten years," one land agent said.[6]

Those who analyzed their own failure, even those who were to prosper later on, usually blamed their immediate circumstances on the lack of capital. Alex Dortch left Virginia in 1845 and arrived in Arkansas "without one cent." For three years the country was virtually uninhabited, and Dortch wrote that he "could not more than support myself and my family." As immigration stepped up, he began to speculate in land but found it difficult to collect his profits. After five and a half years he still could not pay off the debts he had left in Virginia. "Could I have reached here with a few hundred dollars, I could have soon made enough (long since) to have paid off my indebtedness," he told his creditor in late 1850, "—but sir, you have no idea how hard it is to start on *nothing,* and I do hope *most sincerely* that you may never have it to try." Slaveholders were thus fully aware that success in their calling depended very much on the availability of capital. "Had I money enough I would turn cotton planter," a young lawyer wrote from Alabama in 1831, "but as I have not I must go to work some other way."[7]

The same message was stressed over and over again in letters from the West. Those coming to Texas "would do much better to bring some money with them," R. C. Clark wrote to his family in 1849. "It is true that they can and a great many immigrants do get along without it but the want of money is felt more here than any place I have ever seen." In a published letter of advice to his son, a slaveholding father declared that "one of the greatest errors committed in farming, arises from an erroneous impression that this business may be undertaken with less capital than most others. . . . Like every other producer, he is obliged to spend money before he can get it back, and it is the height of folly to commence the business without sufficient floating capital, to meet contingent expenses." Even established farmers were distressed by the expenses of slaveholding. "Negro women at a thousand dollars is extremely high," James Torbert wrote in his journal in 1856. Though interested in buying, he hated "to give a thousand dollars." Six years earlier a struggling slaveholder in Georgia looked over his books and declared it "very doubtful whether I buy any men this winter" because the price of slaves was so high. "I had thought of buying several."[8]

The difficulty of maintaining an economic foothold in a fluid and speculative society left slaveholders deeply conscious of the struggle that it took to achieve prosperity. "We have had some very hard years till last year," an Alabama master wrote to his cousin. "I think it was the best crop year that I ever saw we made." Joseph Thompson, a Louisiana planter, felt much the same way. "I have used every exertion in my power to do the best I could and for the three past years have made short crops," Thompson wrote to his aunt. "This year I have success in making everything in abundance in the way of crops. . . . I have I think worked hard enough to have some comforts around me." Thompson had no intention of ceasing his quest for ever more land and slaves. As with so many others, the struggle seemed as important as its outcome. "There is nothing valuable or worthy in the mere possession of property," one Southerner explained, "but everything in the effect of a prudent, rational, and just pursuit of it."[9]

Thus, hardship did not lead slaveholders to reject the ethos of individual achievement, but to justify and enshrine it. By a curious twist of thought, slaveholders emphasized the role of personal struggle in order to dismiss the same economic barriers that held them back for so long and continued to limit popular access into the slaveholding class. The crucial need for capital, which frustrated so many, found its way into optimistic statements about widespread opportunities. David Meade wrote from his new plantation in Kentucky that "newcomers can be at no loss (if they have Cash) to secure an Estate to their taste in any part of this state." Even Alex Dortch, whose long years of struggle in Arkansas left a cynical tone in his prose, remained convinced that "Enterprising men here with Capital, would soon make fortunes."[10]

THE SLAVEHOLDERS' GIFT for turning disadvantage into virtue culminated in a progressive ideology that looked to a future of unbounded expansion, unprecedented abundance, and white supremacy. Physical movement and personal struggle, upward mobility and westward expansion, molded the minds of slaveholders and shaped this southern gospel of prosperity. Its rhetoric was religious and patriotic, its components were democracy and equality of opportunity for whites, and its foundation was unlimited westward migration and a vast supply of slaves. It was intensely individualistic, and it incorporated most of the features of what is called the "Protestant work ethic." It was the southern version of the American creed. However much he may have disapproved of it, Governor John L. Manning recognized the power of the slaveholders' ideology when he spoke to the South Carolina legislature in 1854. "A strong inclination to progress is a characteristic of the race which you in part represent and is, perhaps, the secret of Anglo-American ascendancy," Manning declared. "Its spirit prevails over the continent, and is continually hurrying us into new positions of theory and of government. It pervades to a greater or lesser extent, every State in the American Union, and is incorporated into its laws, religion, industry and politics."[11] Thus, a social class dominated by upwardly mobile masters successfully translated its own prosperity and patriotism into a distinctive slaveholding ethic with human bondage at its base.

Pundits across the South subscribed to the gospel of prosperity. Southern agricultural periodicals were cluttered with articles like "Gold Mines in Virginia," "How to make Farming Pay," "Manure is Wealth." Others were contemptuous of the widespread passion for equal opportunity. "The white man who has to labor for his support, does it with an unwilling spirit," the *Farmers' Register* complained. "He sees the exemption enjoyed by others, and, if he does not fancy himself equally entitled to it, is too apt to repine at his lot, or migrate to some new state, where he will be upon a footing of greater equality with his neighbors. . . . All despise poverty and seem to worship wealth." But the same white egalitarianism that bothered the editor was an article of faith for most slaveholders. Antebellum rhetoric was infused with vigilance against creeping elitism. Only "the pride of honorable success" was justifiable, one writer insisted. "This is an important principle everywhere. In a republican government, where no aristocracy is supposed to exist, but an aristocracy of merit—it is *imperative.*"[12]

When slaveholders pondered their success they turned first to God and gave thanks. The wealth and population of Mississippi had "steadily increased," A. G. McNutt noted in 1842. "For these manifold blessings we are indebted to the superintending care of an all wise providence." The contentious behavior of his fellow Georgians could hardly explain "the flourishing condition of the country," Governor G. M. Troup warned in 1827. "That the Republic is yet safe, and that the country is still prosperous, we are indebted more to Divine Providence, than to our own merits." Whatever policies Southerners devised to ensure their "present enjoyment and future prosperity," George Crawford advised, their eyes "cannot be too often and intently turned to Heaven for guidance and guardianship."[13]

As convinced as slaveholders were that the prime mover of their success was an all-powerful creator, they were no less certain that hard work and individual effort were the keys to advancement. Perhaps for this reason, personal expressions of the gospel of prosperity were frequently rendered in quasi-religious rhetoric. "If we take care of what heaven blesses us with," a Mississippi mistress warned her son, "we shall always have something to bestow on the needy—but negligence and extravagance always keeps one poor and dependent." She reminded her child that "Frugality and Industry are the hands of fortune." Edward Harden opened his diary on February 9, 1839 with a personal logo. In a box drawn at the center of the page Harden carefully inscribed the words "Industry, perseverance, prudence, economy, temperance." To one degree or another, most slaveholders accepted the stern dictates of Harden's motto, although few ventured as far as his final stricture. This was, after all, an ideal. E. G. Baker, for example, "resolved" in 1850 "to pursue my business with a strict regard to honesty in my dealings with others—with humanity to my negroes, & a determination to live within my income, that I may have no temptation to do wrong. —And be enabled to have everything comfortable and prosperous around me."[14]

For many slaveholders, however, success was merely a spur to still more enterprise. As R. D. Spaight of North Carolina put it, "the increased value of the fruits of agriculture afford such ample remuneration to labor, as to give unexampled prosperity to the country, and to stimulate the enterprise of our citizens." At the age of sixty-five, James Lide was "the most busy man you ever saw." A successful planter in South Carolina, Lide moved his entire family to Alabama in 1835 where he worked with youthful diligence, excited by the great "prospects before him." For Lide, success was not enough; the pursuit itself counted for something as well. Thus prosperity seemed to feed on itself. Excited by the immigration and growth he saw about him, the governor of Texas gloated in 1853 that "a spirit of enterprise and improvement is now abroad among our people." The most debilitating calamity could not contain the slaveholders' boundless enthusiasm. Poor crops and disease stimulated "vigilance and exertion," William Rabun noted, even as they reawakened the sense of "dependence on the Almighty Disposer of events, of which man, uninterruptedly prosperous, is too prone to be forgetful."[15]

For as long as there were land and slaves enough to keep their society "uninterruptedly prosperous," exuberance would overwhelm the slaveholders' fear of failure. It was no wonder that every piece of new land was looked upon as the site of future wealth and greatness. Slaveholders were forever declaring the discovery of the new El Dorado, a dream world to which they were unswervingly attracted but which they never actually found. And with bondsmen to work the new land the prospects were all the more exciting. "If we had slaves enough to cultivate all of the cotton lands in the state," Governor Elias Conway declared in 1858, "Arkansas, alone, could supply annually, the market of the world with as much cotton as has ever been raised any year in all of the cotton growing states of the United States."[16]

Slavery gave southern whites enough prosperity to justify such hyperbole; it offered enough opportunity for advancement to allow them to feel comfortable with their gospel of prosperity. In this peculiar way, human bondage reinforced the slaveholders' devotion to the American way of life. Two years before the election of Abraham Lincoln to the presidency, Joseph E. Brown reassured the Georgia electorate that "there has been no lack of provisions in the land. The laborer of every class has been able to supply his necessities by the fruits of his labor. The barns of the husbandmen teem with plenty for both man and beast. . . ." A Tennessee politician went even further. "The artisan and the laborer find ready employment with increased and remunerating wages, and everywhere within our borders the comforts of life are being equally and generally diffused. . . . Our civil and religious institutions and privileges are extended to all classes of our people and contribute greatly to their happiness and welfare."[17]

For slaveholders, none of this could have happened without bondage. Responding to the free-labor ideology of antislavery Republicans, the Richmond *Enquirer* declared in 1860 that "at the South, free labor is the main support and stay of the institution [of slavery], because where the two races approximate equality in numbers, slavery is the only protection of the laboring classes against the evils of amalgamation and moral degradation."[18]

THE GOSPEL of prosperity and the defense of bondage were inseparable in the minds of most slaveholders. But when they made explicit reference to slavery, masters drew also from an intellectual tradition that reaffirmed their faith in the destiny of the white man as the harbinger of global wealth. In the antebellum South, racism and the gospel of prosperity were joined in symbiotic relation.

Slaveholders, like other white Americans, indulged in most of the popular prejudices of their day. It did not matter in the least that most of the groups slaveholders disdained were represented in their own class. They did not like Catholics. "O what horrid beings they are,"

Sarah Fountain declared, "and how much to be dreaded." A Mississippi slaveholder wrote in his diary that "for the three last centuries, the influence of the Catholic church has been to retard the march of intellect and human liberty." Such religious stereotypes were not only applied to Catholics. Esther Boyd recalled that as a child on her father's plantation her "idea of Jews was that they were usually peddlers who sneaked around negro quarters to sell goods to negroes."[19]

In the Southwest, slaveholders disapproved of Mexicans. They "are as bigoted and ignorant as the devil's grandchildren," one Texas master insisted. "They haven't even the capacities of my black boy. Why, they're most as black as niggers any way, and ten times as treacherous." The wife of a Gulf Coast sugar planter believed that Mexicans were getting "so impertinent" that the Americans were going to have to "get together and drive them all out of the country." Native Americans were no more tolerated by slaveholders. "Their *characters* have *not* been misrepresented," an Alabama slaveholder wrote to a friend in Connecticut. "They are a degraded set with little of pride, honor or generosity about them." Timothy Flint reflected the thinking of many slaveholders when he wrote that Indians "have not the same acute and tender sensibilities with the other races of men." Flint believed that the Indians were most like "the negroes. They have no quick perceptions, no acute feelings. They do not so easily or readily sympathize with external nature. They seem callous to every passion but rage."[20]

Slaveholders were thus accustomed to thinking in crude racial terms, and it was upon these assumptions that they rested their defense of black slavery. Most slaveholders probably never examined their racist beliefs critically enough to draw fine distinctions between cultural and genetic inferiority. Their casual remarks indicate that slaveholders had no trouble holding at once to environmental, religious, biological, and cultural explanations of black degradation. Few slaveholders ever bothered to offer a coherent racial defense of bondage in their letters or diaries. So ingrained were their racist assumptions that slaveholders were most likely to reveal themselves by recoiling in shock from the mere hint of racial egalitarianism or antislavery sentiment. Black equality was simply inconceivable, a subject not even open to discussion.[21]

As early as the 1780's, Thomas Jefferson had suggested that the divisions between whites and blacks could "never end but in the extermination of one or the other race." Thereafter, slaveholders echoed his conviction in their repeated assertion that racial harmony was simply not possible in America. "Unless there is order and subordination kept up, amongst negroes," a Louisianan wrote in 1807, "they would soon be masters instead of Slaves, for tho they are black, they have as great a propensity to command and be tyrants as white people generally has." There could therefore be no racial equality, John Mills concluded, "for if the negroes were free, the whites would soon be slaves, or their throats would be cut." The same fear haunted antebellum slaveholders, and that fear was evident in their politics. "No man that reflected about the matter . . . could believe that the two races could ever live together in the same community as equals," a Virginia congressman insisted in 1848, "they never did anywhere, and never could."[22]

Slaveholders frequently expressed their racism in words and deeds that had no direct bearing on the defense of slavery. They spoke of blacks in crude racial epithets. They burst into fits of denunciation, proclaiming their desire somehow to be unburdened of the need to live in any proximity with blacks. A Tennessee farmer and sometime slaveholder explained to Olmsted that highlanders were friendly and sociable because "there warn't no niggers here; where there was niggers, people couldn't help getting a cross habit of speaking." He went on to say that "he'd always wished there hadn't been any niggers here . . . but he wouldn't like to have them free. As they had got them here, he didn't think there was any better way of getting along with them than that they had." A slaveholder near Mobile, Alabama, told a British traveler that it was a "great blessing that we had no negroes in England, as he believed they were enough to destroy any country." Most commonly, whites spoke of blacks as animals, or at best somewhere between humans and beasts. Following the Nat Turner uprising in 1831, a southern editor called the black rebels "monsters. They remind one of a parcel of blood thirsty wolves rushing down from the Alps." In a proslavery tract written twenty years later, John Campbell declared that "there is as much difference

between the lowest tribe of negroes and the white Frenchman, Englishman, or American, as there is between the monkey and the
negro."[23]

Alexander Stephens came as close as any slaveholding politician
to articulating a racist defense of slavery. "As a race, the African is
inferior to the white man," he told the Virginia secession convention
in 1861. "Subordination to the white man, is his normal condition.
He is not his equal by nature, and cannot be made so by human laws
or human institutions. Our system, therefore, so far as regards this
inferior race, rests upon this great immutable law of nature." If few
slaveholders publicly carried the logic of racism as far as Stephens,
still fewer publicly disagreed with his conclusions.[24]

A purely racist defense of slavery was largely unarticulated by
most slaveholders, and not because they questioned its validity or
because their views were so universal as to require no explication.
Black inferiority alone was simply not an adequate justification for
enslavement. As many abolitionists noted, if blacks were as degraded
as the slaveholders claimed, that only made bondage more objectionable in its exploitation of the weak. Instead, masters used their racism
to construct other justifications of slavery.

Samuel Bass, a carpenter hired to build a new home for a Louisiana slaveholder, Edwin Epps, provoked his employer into defending
what Epps probably never thought to defend. "What *right* have you
to your niggers when you come down to the point?" Bass asked.
"What right!" the slaveholder shot back, "why I bought 'em, and
paid for 'em." For the free-thinking carpenter that answer would not
do. "Of *course* you did," Bass conceded, "the law says you have the
right to hold a nigger, but . . . suppose they'd pass a law taking away
your liberty and making you a slave?" Epps scoffed at the idea. "Hope
you don't compare me to a nigger, Bass." The carpenter remained
unconvinced. "In the sight of God," he asked, "what is the difference,
between a white man and a black one?" All the difference in the
world, the slaveholder answered. "You might as well ask the difference between a white man and a baboon." At this point the argument
had reached an impasse, for once Epps declared blacks inferior to
whites there was no coming to terms. What is significant is not that
Epps justified slavery on racial grounds, but that black inferiority was

not his first line of defense. For his argument to hold, his assumptions had to be racist, but his defense of slavery was primarily one of economics and property rights: he had bought his slaves and paid for them. A South Carolina master agreed. The slave's earnings "belong to *me,* because I bought him; and in return for this I give him maintenance, and make a handsome profit besides." That was the way most slaveholders preferred to look at it.[25]

Thus, the slaveholders' chief defense of bondage focused upon the profitability of slavery and the white man's right to make money and accumulate property. "As an owner of slaves (and one whose income is derived almost entirely from their labor)," one master wrote, "I assert an unquestionable right to my property, and protest against every attempt to deprive me of it without my consent." A southern congressman sought out the philosophical origins of the right of property in man. "We go out of a state of nature into a state of society, to render certain our personal liberty, our personal security, and the right to acquire and enjoy private property," William O. Goode explained. Because "the right of property exists before society. . . . The Legislature cannot deprive a citizen of his property in his slave. It cannot abolish slavery in a State. It could not delegate to Congress a power greater than its own."[26] Here was a philosophical defense of slavery which was at once consistent with traditional American principles, amenable to the values of slaveholders, and directly relevant to the issues in the sectional crisis.

Yet in practical terms, property rights represented little more than the slaveholders' assertion of their intent to make as much money as possible from the labor of their slaves. Whereas white labor was difficult to hire, troublesome, and costly, "the slave can be well and plentifully fed for twenty-five dollars a year, and clothed for fifteen dollars." If the initial price was exorbitant, the slave was still a profitable investment as far as slaveholders were concerned. Fifteen hundred dollars for a man "was fully worth it," one slaveholder confidently asserted, "because he could earn a handsome income."[27]

Slaveholders simply imbued this defense with their racist assumptions. "Slave labour is more valuable than free labour," one writer declared, because the "white cannot endure heat and labour so well as the negro." White men "don't like the work, and won't do it unless they are compelled to," a western ironmaker reasoned. "You can't depend on 'em. You can't drive 'em like you can a nigger."[28]

This defense of slavery was largely pragmatic, even though it rested heavily on the slaveholders' racism and the principles of private property. In fact, many masters expressed impatience with philosophical arguments about the benefits of bondage. "Slavery was justified by its results," a Louisiana master who owned one slave declared. "It was nonsense to say that Slavery was sustained for the benefit of the negro." To the argument that slavery uplifted and enlightened blacks one master responded by admitting that "our slaves is kept in Ignorance as much as possible." Another "advocate of slavery" declared that if bondage was a "blessing" to blacks, "the sentence of slavery upon the descendants of Ham would not have been accompanied by a curse." To the assertion that slavery was a positive good, one slaveholder answered that it was "a moral evil" made necessary by the "condition of the negroes."[29]

Those who were familiar with and amenable to the growing body of literature in defense of slavery found countless arguments at their disposal, but the more common themes revealed a reticence bordering on defensiveness. This was certainly true of the frequent claim that slavery was milder here and now than in older times or other places. "With regard to the situation of slaves here, I am of the opinion that there is no country where they are better treated than in the Mississippi Territory," William Dunbar wrote in 1800. At the other end of the South, just three years earlier, Maryland slaveholders were accusing others of particularly harsh treatment of bondsmen. Though the "blacks of Maryland are slaves forever," a French traveler wrote, "they have nevertheless, according to what I was told in Baltimore, some advantages over those of Virginia and the southern states."[30] In the nineteenth century, slaves in Virginia were said to fare better than those elsewhere; slaves in the border states were better off than those in the Deep South; bondsmen in the East, it was said, had an easier life than those in the West. No slaveholder was willing to acknowledge that the slaves were worse off where they were than elsewhere, for such comparisons were designed as defenses in the first place.

Equally self-serving was the assertion that slavery was milder than previously. In 1836 the *Farmers' Register* claimed that in Virginia "the condition of negroes . . . has been greatly ameliorated." In 1849 *DeBow's Review* insisted that slaves "are better treated now than formerly." While it is probably true that antebellum slavery was generally less harsh than colonial bondage, there is no evidence that by 1849 the "improvement" in the slaves' condition was "progressing." If anything, slavery became more oppressive in the 1850's.[31] And while there were certainly variations in the treatment of slaves, they had less to do with the state or region in which the slaves worked than many slaveholders claimed. The structure of slavery implied and required repression everywhere it existed. A cruel master or a difficult crop like sugar cane simply made matters worse for the slave.

When slaveholders pointed an accusing finger at other times and places, it was most often aimed toward England. Southerners had been blaming their problems on England since the earliest years of settlement. In 1676, Thomas Glover complained that Virginians were "so intent on their *Tobacco Plantations* that they neglect all other and more Noble improvements. . . . From their planting Tobacco they find the greatest encouragement from England, by reason of the vast revenue it brings into the Exchequer." The Reverend Peter Fontaine of Westover Church, who in 1757 bequeathed nineteen slaves to his heirs, defended black bondage to his inquisitive European relatives by noting that Africans enslaved and sold each other, and by asserting that the Virginia assembly had repeatedly tried to discourage the slave trade but was always overruled by Parliament. But mostly Fontaine blamed slavery on "that stinking and, in itself useless weed tobacco." By the revolutionary period many slaveholders had convinced themselves that England was responsible for foisting slavery on the colonies in the first place, and so were doubly offended by Lord Dunmore's threat to turn the slaves against rebellious Americans. During the early national period, British interference with United States commerce was resented by slaveholders as much as by other Americans. "We are too submissive to Tyrants!" one Virginia master wrote to his father. "Let us wage eternal war with all the enemies of our heavenly Country. . . . If our slaves attempt to make an insurrection, we must make awful examples."[32]

England led the world—or so antebellum slaveholders believed —in the fight against slavery. The British patrolled the seas against the slave trade. England's emancipation movement had a strong influence on abolitionism in the North. The emancipation of British slaves in the 1830's affected areas relatively close to the southern states, and it coincided with a tense period in the history of southern politics. It also coincided with the British debate over the reform of the Poor Law, a debate that conveniently provided slaveholders with substantial evidence that free workers in England were often as miserable as southern bondsmen. By the antebellum era, then, slaveholders had a lengthy indictment of Great Britain, which they employed in defense of slavery. If bondage was criminal, as the Englishman said it was, one Southerner wrote, "the crime was long ago committed by his country and the necessity and evil (if any evil) has been put upon the South, not by themselves, but by his country." A British traveler in South Carolina was told that the English had "abolished slavery in the West Indies, for the sake of encouraging a negro revolt in the Southern States, and thus, revenging yourselves on America."[33]

Post-Civil War romantics often depicted the Old South as a chivalrous society strongly influenced by the example of the English aristocracy. In reality, slaveholders frequently looked upon England with contempt. Any natural feelings of association Southerners had with Britain were "neutralized by a dislike of the abolitionist party in England," Charles Lyell observed. England's recognition of Texan independence was seen as an abolitionist ploy that "had done much to alienate the planters, and increase the anti-English feeling in the south." Indeed, "hatred of England" was a source of political capital for southern office seekers. The Richmond *Enquirer* accused "the aristocracy of England" with "abetting the anti-slavery movement in this country." Similarly, a candidate in Warrenton, Virginia, told his listeners, "We want no English liberty here, we are not indebted to kings and emperors for our rights. They were earned not granted."[34]

Many slaveholders apparently believed that if it could be shown that British workers were oppressed then somehow southern slavery was justified. They would print an article on "Infant Labour in English Factories," one visiting Briton noticed, "and because this blot stains the picture of English humanity, therefore it is sought to be inferred that slavery in America is no blot at all! Such are the delusions which prejudice leads men to practice." Because they were reluctant to attack the North for historical and patriotic reasons, much of the slaveholders' anti-English rhetoric was a diversion thrown down in frustration. As a defense of slavery the argument certainly came to little, unless it was raised to a theoretical attack on free society in general, and even at that it was still not much of a defense of bondage. Few slaveholders took the argument very far, however. A northern traveler listened as one slaveholder expressed his satisfaction "that our slaves are better off, as they are, than the majority of your free laboring classes at the North." When the Northerner voiced his doubts, the slaveholder quickly retreated to a safer position. "Well," he said, "they certainly are better off than the English agricultural laborers." Unwilling to attack the North, most slaveholders reverted to the more comfortable and familiar assault on Great Britain.[35]

Yet anti-English rhetoric, like assertions of slavery's continuing amelioration, went beyond the needs of the typical master. Most tended to think of black bondage as a means to various ends, including racial subordination, individual advancement, southern prosperity, and American greatness. It was in the repeated expressions of the gospel of prosperity, not the abstract ruminations of southern intellectuals, that most slaveholders implicitly defended their peculiar institution.

RACISM AND THE GOSPEL of prosperity fused to form the prevailing ideology of the slaveholding class, but their pragmatic cast of mind hindered most slaveholders from committing their world view to print. It was in the arena of southern politics that their implicit defense of slavery received its clearest expression. In this way another major historical tradition—political democracy—became inextricably linked to the slaveholders' defense of bondage.

One of the things that most impressed and disturbed Sir Charles Lyell about antebellum southern politics was its assertive anti-elitism. "I can scarcely conceive of the ostracism of wealth or superior attainments being carried farther," he wrote from Alabama. In one election the favored candidate conceded all of his opponent's qualifications but suggested that the man was simply too wealthy to be elected. "A rich man," the candidate said, "cannot sympathize with the poor." Henry Watson was surprised that politics was so much more democratic in the South than in his hometown of East Windsor, Connecticut, where only the most successful and talented citizens were awarded political leadership. "None of the *candidates* are men of talents. . . . They feel about to *ascertain* public opinion, and *follow* on," Watson complained. "They would consider it madness to attempt to *lead,* and never do it in anything, whether of consequence or not."[36]

In New Orleans, a lawyer complained that the capital of Mississippi had been moved away from Natchez, the city "to which the richest and best informed citizens resorted, representing both the landed and monied interests of the state." "[T]he democratic party," he explained, "could not be expected to put up, for so many years, with an arrangement of affairs so reasonable and advantageous." So they decided to move the capital to Jackson, a "wilderness . . . in the middle of a swamp, accessible only by canoe. . . . This was welcome news; all might now be placed on a footing of equality, the spot being equally inaccessible and inconvenient for all."[37] There were similar decisions in other southern states to move the capital away from the centers of wealth, decisions that likewise aroused indignation along with broad popular approval. In actual fact, the motives for these moves were less than populistic; they were not gestures to placate the crowd. Nonetheless, their symbolism indicates the nature of the slaveholders' politics.

In the nationwide movement to democratize state constitutions in the 1820's and 1830's, the southern states held their own and in some cases took the lead. The Alabama constitution of 1819, for example, was one of the most progressive in the United States, and it was not changed significantly in the reforms of the following decades. In the 1830's new constitutions in Arkansas, Virginia, Mississippi, and Tennessee, and amendments to the constitutions of Maryland and North Carolina all tended away from property qualifications and toward universal white manhood suffrage. The reforms were slower in reaching the older eastern states, but by the end of the antebellum era even the constitutions of Virginia and South Carolina became more democratic. In most southern states there was persistent debate over the replacement of appointed officials with popularly elected representatives. "The interest of the people will always make the masses honest in the exercise of their civil rights," an Alabama politician said in 1853, arguing for the election of circuit court judges. "Misplaced confidence in demagogues and politicians by profession, may cause them to be deceived; but they are generally prompt to repair their errors."[38]

All of these democratic trends resist simple analysis. There is no pattern of slaveholder support for or opposition to the reforms. In the Atlantic coast states from Virginia to Georgia large planters along the eastern seaboard openly resisted democratization, indicating a deliberate unwillingness to compromise with the majority to maintain their historic domination. Yet even here the democratic opposition was composed largely of slaveholders. In some of the largest slave states, Mississippi and Alabama for example, slaveholding politicians led the nation in instituting democratic reforms. Yet the state with the highest concentration of slaveholders, South Carolina, retained the least democratic constitution throughout the antebellum period. It is clear that slaveholding itself was not an indication of a conservative or democratic political outlook. Most slaveholders, like most Americans, supported democratic reforms that reduced the power of the oldest and wealthiest regions, if for no other reason than that most slaveholders did not live in those areas.

The slaveholders' adherence to the principles of representative democracy was established by the early national period and was reinforced by the conflicts of that age. In 1796 a Virginia slaveholder wrote of his fear that the "Aristocrats . . . would deprive the popular branch of the Government of its essential advantages" should the details of the Jay Treaty negotiations be kept from Congress. In the mid-1820's Edward Harden looked back to the philosophical conflict between Thomas Jefferson and John Adams. Where Jefferson "administered the government for the good of the people and to fix deeper and deeper the principles upon which it was founded," the Georgia slaveholder wrote, Adams "seemed to think his own and his family's consequence was entirely identified with and dependent upon a magnificent and powerful government and according to those selfish principles were his principles and practices regulated and controlled." Thus were the lessons of democracy and tyranny taught to the children of slaveholders from their earliest years. At the age of thirteen William Lawrence already understood that "Tyranny is the mother of injustice."[39]

The fear of strong, centralized political authority was widespread among slaveholders; they tended therefore to put their faith in the most democratic branches of government. More than one slaveholding legislator felt "strongly impressed with a sense of the duties owing by the representatives of a free people elected by their free suffrages." Increasingly, the South's elected representatives came to accept this view. Governor John M. Gregory told the Virginia legislature in 1842 that the only duty of elected officials was to carry out the wishes of the people. "If any other theory than this be adopted, all proper restraint over the representative is destroyed, and the people instead of being sovereign become the mere tools of political aspirants."[40]

Slaveholding politicians paid constant homage to popular democracy. "Let the slaves of Europe and Asia bow the knee, and raise the timid glance to executive supremacy," the governor of Louisiana declared in 1820. "Here, in this great American democracy, the people respect first themselves, then their legislators, and afterwards bestow on their executive, judicial and ministerial agents, that countenance which their talents and virtues may entitle them to receive." A slaveholding politician in Kentucky told the state's elected representatives that they were "more honorable than Princes or Potentates. *You* act for the people with their consent; *they* oppress the people, in contempt of all rightful authority."[41]

The racist subjugation of blacks helped open the way to universal white manhood suffrage by silencing a potentially rebellious underclass of black workers. "In this country alone does perfect equality of civil and social privilege exist among the white population, and it exists solely because we have black slaves," the Richmond *Enquirer* declared. "Freedom is not possible without slavery." The editor framed his remarkable analysis as an assault on the English upper class: "The spectacle of Republican freedom and Democratic equality in this country, is an eye-sore to an aristocracy whose system of exclusive privilege and arbitrary distinctions rests upon the false assumption of a right to degrade and oppress men whom God has made as good as themselves. The abolition of negro slavery in the South," he concluded, "would inevitably end in the ruin of the political constitution of the country."[42] Thus, when they considered the relationship between American liberal democracy and black slavery, masters saw not conflict and contradiction but harmony and mutual reinforcement.

Newspapers throughout the South illustrated this symbiosis. "The more democratic the papers are in their general politics," James Silk Buckingham observed, "the more indignant are they at all attempts to make their coloured brethren as free as themselves." White democracy freed slaveholders to pursue their goals without political interference just as capitalism freed them from economic restraints. Most slaveholders could not separate their own material success from the freedom and opportunity afforded by their country. They clung tenaciously to America's revolutionary heritage, made heroes of its statesmen, and often cited their nation's history as the ultimate defense of slavery.[43]

In this spirit James Monette named one of his slaves "America," while John Houston Bills named slaves after two of his favorite presidents, Polk and Jefferson—"that great apostle of liberty." Henry Marston was not the only slaveholder to see the hand of God in the workings of American democracy. On the anniversary of the battle of Bunker Hill in 1822, Marston spoke of the inability of Britain's "corrupt ministry" to resist divine ordinance. "The only free government on earth was about to be brought into existence by an enlightened and free people, —How dark and intricate are the ways of *Providence?*" Slaveholders frequently made the Fourth of July a holiday for their slaves. In 1827, John Nevitt, a Mississippi planter, celebrated Independence Day by relieving his slaves of their work at noon before going off to a barbecue with his friends. An Alabama master gave his bondsmen "a barbecue and a Holiday" on July 4, 1846.[44]

Even as the sectional crisis intensified in the 1850's, many slaveholders continued to display their confident patriotism by celebrating Independence Day with their slaves. In 1856 the celebration lasted several days on Mary Bateman's Mississippi plantation because it coincided with the marriages of two slave couples. A Louisiana master released his slaves from work on July 4 in 1856, 1859, and 1860. The erosion of unionist sentiment in both the North and the South did cause some slaveholders to bemoan the lack of patriotic "Spirit" among the people. But if the sectional conflict made it difficult for them to continue to celebrate the Fourth of July, it was not because slaveholders had abandoned their devotion to the principles of liberal democracy. Nor had slaveholders become aware of any glaring inconsistency between their political principles and their practices.[45]

Most slaveholders had long since rationalized their devotion to slavery and freedom in the same way that Northerners justified their own discriminatory practices against blacks. When asked if all men were created "free and equal as the Declaration of Independence holds they are," a Louisiana slaveholder answered confidently: "Yes. But all men, niggers, and monkeys *aint.*" A Virginia congressman was less crude but no less adamant. To say that the Declaration of Independence was implicitly antislavery "virtually brands Washington a hypocrite," he declared. In fact, the document was written and signed by slaveholders who were among the great revolutionary heroes and who represented Virginia's "noblest and most gifted sons." There was, he concluded, "no ingenuity which could torture the Declaration of Independence into having the remotest allusion to the institution of domestic slavery." Alexander Stephens did not disagree. Indeed, because he recognized that slavery in a democratic society represented "a peculiar phase of republican civilization and constitutional liberty," Stephens was all the more impressed by the legacy of the Founders. They had established, he declared, "the first great principles of self-government by the governing race."[46]

THE MAJORITY of southern politicians were aspiring non-slaveholders and upwardly mobile masters whose success was earned rather than bequeathed, and who transformed their personal histories into a middle-class politics that was as devoted to liberal democracy as it was to black slavery. From the humblest county courtroom to the most impressive statehouse, slaveholders dominated southern politics in numbers well beyond their proportion in the population. The nature of that domination and the tone it imparted to antebellum politics reveals how traditional American values sustained the authority of the slaveholding class.

One of the most powerful political officials in the Old South was the magistrate of the county court. Although persistent reform efforts weakened their authority in many states, county courts in some areas remained, as one Southerner wrote, "the most powerful branch of the judiciary, capable of exerting a greater influence than all others." The county courts in Kentucky controlled local patronage appointments, adjudicated probate conflicts, disposed of orphans, administered poor laws, granted ferry franchises, levied and collected taxes to build roads and canals, and tried slave manumission cases. Nearly three out of four of these judges were slaveholders in Kentucky counties where only one out of three heads of families held slaves. The political power of the slaveholders was reflected among southern governors as well. Between 1850 and 1860 every southern governor for whom adequate biographical information can be obtained was a slaveholder.[47]

In the wake of democratic reform, however, southern governors had little real power, and the authority of the local courts was checked. The focus of politics was concentrated on the state legislatures. In 1860, slaveholders held the majority of seats in every southern legislature except those of Missouri and Arkansas. In Alabama and the Carolinas over seventy-five percent of the legislators owned slaves.[48] Even though a majority of Southerners in most Deep South states probably had a material interest in slavery, masters still held political office in unrepresentatively large numbers. Nevertheless, it is significant that in 1860 large slaveholders—planters with more than twenty bondsmen—held the majority of the seats in only one state legislature, South Carolina's. The slaveholding legislators held more bondsmen on average than their slaveholding constituents, but most were not planters. In fact, small slaveholders together with non-slaveholders held clear and sometimes overwhelming majorities in all but one southern legislature in the 1850's.

The middle-class orientation of southern politics is indicated by the inordinate power of slaveholding lawyers. They dominated the county courts in every southern state. In the upper South, twenty-three out of thirty governors were lawyers as well as slaveholders. Though less conspicuous in the more democratic state legislatures, lawyers and other slaveholding professionals were still over-represented. In Alabama, where less than one percent of the free white males were practicing attorneys, twelve percent of the men in the House of Representatives were lawyers.[49] If slaveholders dominated southern politics, slaveholding lawyers epitomized its tone.

Benjamin Fitzpatrick was typical. Born near the Indian territory in Georgia in 1802, with "but few advantages of education," Fitzpatrick nevertheless was trained in the law and admitted to the Alabama bar. He settled in Autauga (later Elmore) County when the area was barely more than a frontier. He prospered and in the 1830's began making regular purchases of land and slaves. Fitzpatrick became one of the wealthiest planters in the state and spent the rest of his life enhancing his already substantial wealth. Inevitably his politics were shaped by his experience. In 1843, in his second inaugural address as Governor of Alabama, Fitzpatrick recited a philosophy that incorporated the slaveholders' gospel of prosperity within the principles of enlightened liberalism. "Reflection and experience" had confirmed Fitzpatrick's devotion to the republican tradition of state sovereignty "as the great bulwark of popular liberty [and] equality of rights and privileges among all free citizens. . . . Freedom of trade, freedom of opinion, and freedom of industry, are the birthright of our free institutions."[50]

If one man can be said to have represented the mainstream of slaveholding politics it was Andrew Jackson. He inspired more admiration among antebellum slaveholders than any living politician; in death his memory was cherished. As the British traveler, Charles Lyell, observed, Jackson's popularity stemmed in large measure from "his having risen from a very humble origin." This made Jackson not only seem more typical than his enormous wealth implied, it made him a symbol of the slaveholding culture of upward mobility. Jackson did nothing to discourage that image. He never once questioned the morality of slavery (he attacked abolitionists vehemently), even as he articulated a profound conviction that in a democratic society all men should be afforded every opportunity for individual advancement unhindered by the arbitrary restraint of concentrated economic and political power.[51]

Jackson's influence on southern politics was overwhelming. In 1828 he received over eighty-one percent of the popular presidential vote in the eleven southern states, and four years later he was supported for re-election in the same states by an astonishing eighty-eight percent of the electorate. "D—n him," Robert R. Reid, a Florida slaveholder, wrote of Jackson in 1832. "He frocks and unfrocks at pleasure, but he is a magnificent fellow and the best constitutional President since the days of Jefferson." Slaveholders who disliked Jackson could not deny his popularity. "The Old General has . . . been on to see us," an Alabama slaveholder complained to a friend in 1833, "and you would have been disgusted and sick at heart to have seen the adoration paid him by all classes." On June 13, 1845, the Tennessee planter J. H. Bills recorded in his diary "the Death of Genl. Andrew Jackson, one of the greatest and best men." The following month Bills visited the grave of "the immortal Jefferson," George Washington's home at Mt. Vernon, the nation's capital, and the Bunker Hill monument at Boston. After fourteen years, on the eve of the Civil War, the patriotic slaveholder was still inspired by Andrew Jackson's legacy. His memory "is fresh and green in the minds of all classes—his faults are all forgotten and his great virtues lauded by all classes of the community."[52]

Among slaveholders, Jackson's most ardent opponents came largely from a small group of wealthy planters in the oldest areas of the South—eastern Virginia, lowcountry South Carolina, Natchez, Mississippi. Inspired by their distaste for democracy, they supported the Whig party or none at all. It is symptomatic of their minority standing within the slaveholding class that anti-Jackson planters found refuge in a political organization that seemed more a coalition of the disgruntled than an ideologically unified party. The Whigs in the South survived on the strength of local issues and local personalities; they appealed to an unlikely constituency of established planters, city dwellers, and nonslaveholders, all for different reasons. Through the 1830's and 1840's, this coalition proved strong enough to sustain a potent opposition to the Democratic party across the South. Yet it was altogether fitting that the Whig party, born in a blaze of states' rights rhetoric, should die in the name of unionism twenty years later. For the only Whig principle that consistently attracted anti-Jackson planters was a studied resistance to the democratic impulse. Most slaveholders, including the majority of planters, had no need for such a philosophy.[53]

In Jackson's wake, southern politicians quickly learned to connect their devotion to freedom to the defense of slavery. As he scanned the newspapers of Athens, Georgia, James Silk Buckingham noticed that "here, as elsewhere, the Democrats accuse the Whigs of being favourable to Abolition; and take especial merit to themselves, as the champions of liberty, though they are the exclusive advocates and defenders of the institution of domestic slavery!" What was doubly surprising to the English visitor was the fact that the Whig and Democratic newspapers were both strongly antiabolition. He concluded that the "literary taste of the South" revealed "a singular admixture of the most opposite principles; especially of the most unbridled democracy, and an earnest defense of the institution of slavery."[54] By the mid-1830's, slavery was the only unifying theme of southern politics. Whigs and Democrats who disagreed on such powerful issues as the Bank, internal improvements, and democratic reform virtually tripped over one another pledging eternal devotion to slavery, each charging the other with identical heresies on the subject. Under the circumstances, few slaveholders found anything in the American political tradition that required repudiation for the sake of slavery.

JUST AS THEY HAD COME to view political democracy and the capitalist economy as essential safeguards of slavery, masters believed that expansionism was in their own and their nation's best interests. Their position followed logically from the principle of private property and individual accumulation. "A man's slave is his property, so recognized by the constitution," A. G. Brown said in 1848, "and a citizen of Mississippi may settle with his slave property in the territory of the United States, with as little constitutional hindrance as a citizen from any other state may settle with any other species of property." In a society that viewed westward migration as an essential element of upward mobility, expansionism became a central theme of slaveholding politics. At a local meeting in Tennessee called to discuss the Texas question, one slaveholder learned "that both Van Buren and Clay are opposed to Annexation. I say away with both of them." Like most masters, Bennet Barrow saw that expansionism was closely related to slavery. He believed that anyone who supported Henry Clay was a "traitor" to the South. "God grant he may be defeated," Barrow wrote privately. "The main question is slavery & anti slavery & Texas."[55]

Expansionist sentiment had a long history among slaveholding politicians, and it was not simply the byproduct of crude economic materialism. Some of the Founders favored the expansion of slavery, hoping to dilute black influence on the developing white society. During the Missouri controversy, a Virginia editor echoed this position when he asked how proposals to restrict the expansion of slavery would remedy "the evil" of bondage. "Crowd our slaves into a smaller compass; increase their relative proportion to the whites; enlarge this kind of property in the hands of fewer masters—is this the way to encourage abolition . . . ? You only coop more of them into a smaller compass; and is this the way to insure their better treatment?" Through the last decades of the antebellum era some slaveholders continued to argue, with diminishing credibility, that diffusion of the black population was in the slaves' best interests.[56]

Nationalist sentiment was as strong among slaveholders as any other group of Americans, and they viewed physical expansion as genuine evidence of the progress of freedom. The acquisition of Louisiana, a Virginia congressman told his constituents in 1804, opened to the territories "new prospects of increasing wealth, importance and national strength. . . . With the incorporation of that country into the union, they extend the principles of their own benign institutions of government to those spacious regions, where the mild and equal laws of a republic will thenceforward succeed to the rigid maxims of arbitrary power." The patriotic outbursts that appear regularly in the papers of slaveholders reveal the sincerity of their motivations. "The crushed Eagle of Liberty has found an asylum in this western Hemisphere, in America, the grand nucleus around which the mighty affairs of the future must transpire," a Mississippi slaveholder declared in 1849.[57]

Slaveholders were fascinated by the phenomenal growth and prosperity of America, and they connected it in their minds to the expansion and protection of slavery. One of the most forthright proslavery periodicals in the Old South, *DeBow's Review,* was also the most aggressively expansionist. "Westward is the tide of progress, and it is rolling onward like the triumphant Roman chariot, bearing the eagle of the republic or the empire, victorious ever in its steady but bloodless advances." It did not escape the attention of proslavery writers that the great mobility of slaveholders was largely responsible for America's remarkable expansion. "While the North has not extended her limits northward a single degree since the birth of the Constitution," D. R. Hundley wrote in 1860, "the South has already seized on Florida, Louisiana, and Texas, and her eagle eye is now burning with a desire to make a swoop on Cuba, Central America, and Mexico."[58]

By the 1850's, slaveholding politicians were so accustomed to resting the greatness of American society upon the protection and expansion of the slave economy that the prospect of abolition provoked images of unparalleled horror. The purity of white society was jeopardized, the very basis of individual advancement was threatened, national greatness would be subverted. The consummate defense of slavery, then, was the one that assumed the highest place and the broadest significance of black bondage. Its destruction foreshadowed nothing less than global economic calamity. "So great has become the necessities of the world for cotton alone—which can only be produced, to any considerable extent, by slave labor, and in Southern climes," John Winston of Alabama warned in 1857, "that the suspension of involuntary servitude for a single year only, would cause convulsions in all the governments of the civilized world, the disastrous results of which, it would be beyond human ken to foresee." Few carried the slaveholders' logic further than James D. B. DeBow. The profits of cotton, he declared, have "gradually enveloped the commercial world, and bound the fortunes of American slaves so firmly to human progress, that civiliza-

tion itself may almost be said to depend upon the continual servitude of blacks in America."[59]

FROM THEIR FEAR of failure and their pride of accomplishment,
from their psychological ambivalence and the contradictions of
their culture, slaveholders fashioned a spacious vision that put
human bondage at the center of their private worlds. As if to overcome their own uncertainty, they expanded that vision into a political outlook that defended slavery as a bulwark of southern prosperity, American democracy, and even the world economy. "I
think the United States fulfills a higher destiny," Adam McChesney
explained in a veiled attack on abolitionists, "and can do more for
freedom and suffering humanity in being an Asylum for the oppressed and home for exiles than in drawing the sword for abstract
principles and against institutions that have existed in the old world
for ages."[60] Thus did every expression of the slaveholders' gospel of
prosperity become an implicit defense of slavery.

PART III

~

Plantations,
Plebeians, and
Patricians

~

Chapter 6

~

Factories in the Fields: The Managerial Ideal and Plantation Realities

Such was the diversity among slaveholders that no single theory of master-slave relations emerged in the antebellum South. Yet if there was an ideal to which slaveholders aspired, it took form in the literature of plantation management that flourished in the South in the three or four decades before the Civil War. Articles appeared in the agricultural press advocating the systematic management of everything from hogs and cattle to overseers and slaves. The ideal plantation was a model of efficiency. Its premise was black inferiority, its organizing principle was the absolute control of the master, its structure was bureaucratic. It was governed by rules that were enforced by persuasion if possible, by force if necessary. The ideal plantation perfectly harmonized the material interests of the slaveholder with the humane treatment of the slave. "No more beautiful picture of human society can be drawn," the *Southern Cultivator* boasted in 1846, "than a well organized plantation, thus governed by the humane principles of reason."[1] What emerges from this literature reveals more about how the authors felt than how slaveholders behaved. At some points the ideal merged with prevailing practice, but for the most part there were gaps between the real and the ideal that could never be bridged.

BEFORE ALL ELSE, the advocates of plantation management assumed the inferiority of their labor force. "We believe the negro to belong to an inferior race," one planter wrote. "We teach them they are slaves . . . that to the white face belongs control, and to the black obedience." Because blacks "have very inferior minds and brains . . . , tangible punishments and rewards, which act at once on their senses, are the only sort most of them can appreciate." As a race, "Negroes . . . can neither do as much work nor continue at it as long as the whites," thus a system of distribution of labor was advisable. So thriftless and thoughtless was the black man, *DeBow's Review* insisted, that he "requires government even in his meat and drink, his clothing, and hours of repose."[2] Naturally unclean, slaves had to be made to wash themselves. Naturally lazy, they had to be kept busy. Naturally licentious, their morals had to be checked. There were few principles of plantation management that strayed far from the assumption of black inferiority.

Plantation management theory was developed around the concept of "obedience." The most important thing about managing slaves was "always to keep them under proper subjection," the *Farmers' Register* advised. "They must obey at all times, and under all circumstances. . . . Unconditional submission is the only footing upon which slavery should be placed." There should be a "perfect understanding" between the master and the slave, one planter wrote. "The slave should know that his master is to govern absolutely," he explained, and the slave "to obey implicitly."[3]

On the ideal plantation, obedience was maintained through a bureaucratic chain of command. All were subservient to those immediately above them, and at each level of the bureaucracy, duties and responsibilities were explicitly defined. On large, highly organized plantations, there might be separate rules for watchmen, truckminders, nurses, cooks, as well as drivers, overseers, and field hands. The chain of command went upward from drivers to overseers to masters. Always there was obedience. "An order from a driver is to be as implicitly obeyed as if it came from myself," one master declared. The function of the overseer, another planter wrote, was "to teach the slave subordination . . . , to teach him obedience at every hazard." By the same principle, "no overseer, however high his standing, should hesitate to obey implicitly the orders of his employer."[4]

The construction of a plantation bureaucracy was part of a conscious effort to create social distance between management and labor. "The more the driver is kept aloof from the negroes, the better," an enterprising overseer declared. "Once let them believe that they are his equals, and all control is lost." The same rule applied to overseers. They were "required not to chat with the negroes, except on business." An overseer would "be immediately discharged, if it is ascertained he is too intimate with any of the negro women." On the ideal plantation, even the interaction between master and slave was minimal. "All conversation with a negro is forbid[den], except about his work," R. S. Blackburn wrote. "This is important; he should be kept as far from his master as possible, but with no accompanying *harshness.*" The "uncompromising discipline" of slaves required a "line of distinction between master and servant," a young South Carolina planter concluded, "prohibiting entirely the association of any and all white persons from intercourse with them who do not observe the same rule rigidly."[5] Bureaucracy thus served the needs of the slaveholders by enhancing their authority and at the same time reinforcing the racial basis of slavery.

Many large slaveholders, leery of the competence of their own employees, explicitly permitted their slaves to bring complaints directly to them. Joseph Acklen barred punishment of slaves who brought grievances to him. Some slaveholders suggested, however, that the integrity of the plantation bureaucracy was so essential to the maintenance of absolute control that the slaves should occasionally be denied access to their masters. "Too much familiarity with negroes ought never to be indulged in by the master or overseer, as it causes them to lose the proper respect for them," one master warned. He concluded that "Negroes soon discover any little jarring between the master and overseer, and are sure to take advantage of it." To avoid this possibility, many slaveholders insisted that their overseers discourage "tale-bearing, nor is any tale to be told to him or the employer, by any negro, unless he has a witness to his statements."

An angry Tennessee slaveholder asserted that "it has always been a rule with me to whip any negro that tries to tell me anything about the overseer."[6]

There was of course a larger purpose to the hierarchy beyond the physical control of slaves. The bureaucracy served to initiate and implement the rules of the plantation. Like all good businessmen, effective plantation managers understood the importance of rules. Nothing seemed as conducive to profitable enterprise as the systematization of the workplace. Before persuasion and punishment, rules were the primary means of maintaining order on the ideal plantation. They served first "to reduce every thing to system," and so enhance efficiency and, second, "to introduce a daily accountability in every department," and so check the bureaucracy itself.[7]

In the bureaucratic setting of the well-managed plantation, rules were not devised only for the slaves. Masters set rules for themselves, mostly general propositions warning against undue harshness or leniency, excessive familiarity with slaves, or general neglect of detail. More specific rules were developed for overseers and drivers. Overseers were enjoined to keep constant check on the slaves' whereabouts, particularly at night. They were to remain on the plantation, seeing to it that there was always work for the slaves and that the bondsmen understood their duties. Overseers had to check on the sick, inspect the tools, maintain the livestock, and be in the field beside the slaves, although they were not to do field work themselves. Ultimately overseers were held responsible for the health and well-being of the slaves as well as the profitability of the plantation. This was a great deal to ask. One writer, for example, argued from the premise that good overseers were devoted to *"one object*— to carry out the orders of your employer." He held overseers responsible for an increase in the number, condition, and value of the slaves; an abundance of provisions so that the plantation could feed itself; the home manufacture of all slave clothing; an improvement in the plantation's productive capacity; the condition of the livestock, buildings, and tools; *"then,* as heavy a crop of cotton, sugar, or rice, as could possibly be made under the circumstances."[8] Such broad responsibilities made it all but impossible for overseers to satisfy their employers.

Directly or indirectly, however, most rules were aimed at the slaves. Work was to be distributed equitably, according to the skills and abilities of each bondsman. For this reason, many masters rated their slaves in fractions: full-hand, three-quarters, half, or quarter. There were general rules of the plantation; special rules for field hands, children, and women, particularly "breeders" and "sucklers." There were different rules for winter and summer, and rules for different days of the week. There were even rules requiring that rules be uniformly enforced. Slaves were to wake up and go to sleep according to the rules, and rules determined when they ate, how much they ate, and how their meals were prepared. Rules governed the slaves' intercourse with other slaves as well as with whites, on and off the plantation. Additional instructions described in detail how each job was to be performed, how far apart rows should be planted, how many bales should be picked by each hand, and how quickly slave songs should be sung in the field. On the ideal plantation, rules outlined every aspect of the slaves' behavior, from the details of the daily work routine to the personal relations of husband and wife.[9] By 1860 the accumulated list of suggested rules published in the dozens of articles on plantation management could have filled volumes.

It was up to the bureaucracy to see that these rules were implemented, and to that end the maintenance of detailed records was widely advised. On a model Georgia plantation the instructions for record-keeping were a labyrinth of detail: "Every evening the drivers and heads of classes make a report to the overseer in my presence of the employment of their respective hands. The drivers report the number of hands and their rates employed in the field, the quantity and kind of work they have done, and the field in which it is done —the number and rates of the sick—the number and rates of such hands as may have been employed in jobbing, and how they have been employed. The heads of classes report the quantity of work done by that class. These reports are taken on a slate, and are copied into the 'Journal of Plantation work,' which forms a minute and daily record of the occupation and quantity of work done by the different gangs." By analysis of these reports and "daily inspection" of the work performed, "constant check is had on the fidelity of the reports as to the quantity of work done."[10] The rhetoric of proslavery ideologues and postwar romantics notwithstanding, this was hardly the ideal of a society that prided itself on the personal rule of the master.

The point of such detail was to impress upon the slaves an automatic sense of place and duty that could bypass the rational process of human thought. Rules became their own justification. "Habit is every thing," a Louisiana planter wrote in his diary. "The negro who is accustomed to Remain constantly at Home, is just as satisfied with the society on the plantation as that which he would find elsewhere, and the verry restrictions laid upon him being equally imposed on others, he does not feel them, for society is kept at Home for them." One large slaveholder argued that the black man, "subjected to constant employment without the labor of thought . . . , is by far happier than he would be if emancipated, and left to think, and act, and provide for himself."[11]

Nevertheless, the advocates of efficient plantation management developed two basic means of enforcing rules, the first of which was persuasion. If rules alone did not adequately impress the slaves, perhaps they could be made to understand their duties as bondsmen. "I treat them as rational beings," one master wrote of his slaves, "to stimulate their pride and cultivate a feeling of self-respect, without which the negro can only be prompted to his duties by the fear of the lash and the presence of the overseer." Another slaveholder recommended sending the bondsmen to church to learn "the reasons which sanction the master to exact of him his respective duties." Others suggested slaves be taught by example. "Preserve order yourself, in all your actions, and your negroes will imitate you," one planter wrote in 1836.[12]

Yet in a huge body of literature based on the presentation of successful examples, no one was able to cite a single instance of a slave who was genuinely convinced by the sheer force of the master's logic. What persuasion really meant was either indoctrination—as with the master who sent the slaves to church—or, more commonly, bribery. Various forms of material reward were held out to slaves to win their loyalty as well as their labor. To "impress on their minds the advantage of holding property, and the disgrace attached to idleness," one master recommended that slaves be given their own patches of land to cultivate. "Surely, if industrious for themselves," he reasoned, "they will be so for their masters."[13]

It was at the point where persuasion failed that effective plantation managers resorted to punishment, the most decisive means of maintaining control of the slaves. "After reason and persuasion have been exhausted," a Georgia agricultural society concluded, "punishment of some sort must be resorted to." W. W. Hazzard applied the rule to his driver. If reasoning "fails to excite his pride," Hazzard wrote, "I then appeal to his passions, and rouse his fears by moderate punishment." Experts on the management of slaves often disagreed about how, when, and how much punishment should be administered. Even who should punish the slaves was an open question. Most suggested that overseers be given limited discretion to punish certain offenses with a given number of lashes. Others insisted that masters administer all punishment, though frequently warning that they should never do so "when in a passion." A similar concern with their own dignity led some slaveholders to suggest avoiding administration of punishment wherever possible. "I rarely punish myself," one slaveholder wrote, "but make my driver virtually an executive officer to inflict punishments."[14] Most argued for immediate punishment, but some suggested masters wait a day or so. Some recommended that punishments be administered privately and with discretion, others preferred public humiliation as a deterrent.

When punishment was necessary on the ideal plantation, not all slaveholders resorted first to the lash. R. S. Blackburn preferred "a mixed system of rewards and punishments." He suggested that masters establish a *"code* of laws, in writing, stating the offenses to be punished—classify them, and affix to them the penalty in dollars and cents." One "small farmer" advised his fellow slaveholders to build jails on the plantations. "The first negro that steals, or runs away, or fights, or who is hard to manage . . . must be locked up."[15] But no one repudiated the use of punishment, and for most that meant whipping.

On the well-managed plantation, whipping could be kept to a minimum and was usually justified by the violation of rules. "Negroes must be made to obey and to work," one slaveholder insisted, but the attentive overseer could achieve this result with very little whipping. Most would have agreed with W. W. Gilmer that "a great deal of whipping is not necessary; *some is.*" It was an important distinction. For once the unavoidable necessity of whipping was acknowledged, the emphasis was shifted to what was really a different issue, the certainty of punishment. According to the *Farmers' Register,* "real faults will not go unpunished; but at the same time, moderate punishment, with a certainty of its succeeding a fault, is much more efficient in producing good conduct, than severe punishment irregularly inflicted." Joseph Acklen's well-publicized rules reflected this common opinion. "It is the *certainty,* more than the *severity,* of punishment that prevents crime," Acklen believed. "Never fail, therefore, to notice the breach of an established rule."[16]

Testimonials of praise to efficient management practices poured forth from the agricultural press like the oaths of the converted at a faith healer's revival. On the ideal plantation, "contented and profitable" slaves were clean in appearance, respectful in manner, and vigorously obedient. Well-fed slaves rarely got sick; they did their work quickly and efficiently. "Tractable, obedient and trust-worthy," the slaves produced what every master hoped for, the "good crop." All slaveholders organized their work force and established rules to suit their own needs and temperaments, but few disagreed with the widely repeated definition of a good crop as "one that is good, taking into consideration *every* thing." To most writers, "everything" included slaves, land, horses, stock, fences, and farming utensils of all sorts. The good crop, all agreed, meant an abundant harvest "as well as the steady increase in the value of the rest of the property."[17] It was the certain reward of the well-managed plantation.

THE ALMOST RELIGIOUS ZEAL with which the advocates of managerial expertise advertised their "system" exposed their conception of themselves as reformers. Although most of the authors were slaveholders writing from "experience and observation," they wrote also out of frustration with prevailing practices. As reformers, they proposed efficient management as an alternative to the wastrel ways of their contemporaries. Indeed their most frequent complaint was that not even the agricultural press seemed adequately interested in such a vital topic. "There is no one subject, which our planters so much neglect, as that of the management of their negroes," the *Southern Agriculturist* warned in 1832. Too few of the contributors to the *Farmers' Register* were interested in such "important topics as slavery and the management and treatment of slaves," one reader complained. "Most planters fall far short of what they are able to perform," one writer insisted, "arising in most cases, from negligence, and a want of energy, or a divided business incompatible with their planting interest."[18] If they were justified in their frustration, the managerial practices they held up as examples must be regarded as atypical.

Ironically, the reformist mold into which these writers cast themselves had as its byproduct the most damning indictment of the slave system drawn up in the antebellum South. Charles Woodson declared the internal slave trade "an evil" that was "too generally practiced" by white Southerners. Efficiently managed plantations were stable, Woodson implied, while the slave trade encouraged roving, debauchery, and "severe treatment, which would otherwise be unnecessary." Although few masters starved their bondsmen, a Virginia slaveholder wrote in 1837, "I have no doubt that the slow motion, and thin expression of countenance, of many slaves, are owing to a want of a sufficiency of nourishing food." A young South Carolina planter complained that some large slaveholders who fed and clothed their slaves adequately nevertheless exacted labor from them well into the night and on Sundays, the only day "in which they may recover from the exhaustion and fatigue" of plantation labor. Slave houses were generally put up in a "very careless, bungling manner," one reformer complained, "always *too small* and *too low*. No attention is paid to ventilation and shading, nor anything else with reference to the health and comfort of the occupant."[19]

The Barbour County Agricultural Society of Georgia complained that because their "only aim in general is the mere crop results," overseers had a "strong inducement" to overwork their slaves. Punishments were inflicted more "from private pique, than from a neglect of duty," the *Southern Agriculturist* asserted. "The lash is, unfortunately, too much used." A Mississippi slaveholder wrote that "some of us resort too much to the simple and low principle of fear in the government of our slaves." The planter who hired an overseer usually cared for little besides a large crop, one writer complained. "To him it is of no consequence that the old hands are worked down, or the young ones overstrained; that the breeding women miscarry, and the sucklers lose their children." A Louisiana planter attacked the bad management practices that left "thousands of acres lying useless, or badly cultivated, yielding no profit to the owner."[20]

On the ideal plantation there was "perfect understanding" between a benevolent master and his contented slaves. In practice, the reformers complained, licentious, incorrigible, and lazy blacks ran about inadequately managed. On the ideal plantation, slaves were well fed and decently clothed, while in practice they were overworked, underfed, and dirty. The reformers held out the vision of an efficient bureaucracy with the master in complete control, and contrasted it with the prevalence of unwatched overseers, absentee landlords, and brutalized bondsmen. As a rhetorical device, such logic was an effective and revealing weapon, but with the emergence of the sectional conflict, it was an increasingly dangerous one.

Around 1850 the advocates of plantation management began to shy away from their reformist stance as pressure to defend their institution mounted. With no discernible shift in prevailing practices, with their reformist origins distorted by current events, the advocates of plantation management joined forces with the proslavery ideologues. Abolitionism replaced widespread inefficiency as the chief justification for publishing case studies of individual farms. On Colonel W. H. Huntingdon's "model southern plantation" in Louisiana, fantastic profits were reported because the slaves were so marvelously treated. "All the abolitionists in the world," it was suggested, could not persuade the colonel's slaves "to quit their old master or his family."[21]

The antislavery movement had occasionally been derided in earlier articles on plantation management, but the ideal itself was rarely presented as typical before the 1850's. Thereafter articles on plantation management stressed the great humanity of slavery. Attempting to separate their system from those of more industrialized societies, reformers now minimized the extent to which efficient management depended upon detailed rules, bureaucratically enforced. Attempting also to deny the decisive role of physical punishment in maintaining plantation discipline, they were left with no explanation for the successful planter other than the effective use of persuasion. Reformers began to describe as primarily benevolent and singularly humane the same system they had spent years trying to change.[22]

There had always been slaveholders concerned that bondsmen look to the master as "their great arbiter and protector." But recognizing that a system that demanded strict obedience to rules could not avoid the use of punishment, earlier reformers took pains to counsel moderation, fairness, and restraint of passion. Because they were "compelled to use coercive measures for their good discipline," one writer had encouraged slaveholders in 1830 to "avoid the whip as much as possible, and let other modes of punishment be substituted in lieu." Before 1850 it was frequently suggested that bad management had led to too much whipping; after 1850 such sentiments were rarely voiced. "Some few persons are too strict with servants," W. W. Gilmer wrote in 1852, "but for every one who errs in this way, one hundred may be found who go to the opposite extreme." Four years later another writer insisted that "strict rule has to be held over every plantation," because discipline among slaves was breaking down all across the South. The principal cause for these "outrages" was "a too lenient mode of government among the slave owners." By 1860, one frustrated master declared that the whole effort to "try to *persuade* a negro to work" was like "casting pearls before swine." Grounding his argument on the primary assumption of plantation management—that "negroes are weak-minded, unprincipled creatures"—he insisted that the slave "must be *made* to work, and should always be given to understand that if he fails to perform his duty he will be punished for it."[23]

As they affirmed the humanity of the slave system, management experts recommended reforms that would deny to the bondsmen many of the small privileges they had enjoyed. Many began to justify increased repression on paternalistic grounds. "Slaves have no respect or affection for a master who indulges them over much," Robert

Collins wrote. He recommended that slaves no longer be permitted to grow small crops of their own. "It gives an excuse for trading," Collins explained, "and encourages a traffic on their own account." Another slaveholder saw even worse implications in the practice, for besides causing the slaves to roam about trading and visiting other plantations, besides encouraging theft, selling their own crops gave slaves money. "Money is power," the writer observed, and giving that to slaves is "fraught with evil." Even the smallest privileges, such as the traditional "strolling about of negroes" at Christmas, should be stopped, one writer insisted. There were increasingly vehement denunciations of those who fomented "insubordination and rebellion" by teaching slaves to read. And more and more slaveholders publicly repudiated the practice of allowing slaves to marry off the plantation on the grounds that bondsmen used it as an excuse to leave the workplace. In plantation management theory at least, the more slavery was defended as benevolent and humane, the more repressive it became.[24]

THE IMPACT of this management literature is not easy to assess. It was written by slaveholders, and there is scattered evidence that some masters did pay close attention to it. In 1829, Robert Leslie left a Virginia estate of some twenty-five slaves and a library that included such titles as *Farmer's Magazine, Farmer's Manual,* and *Management of Slaves.* In 1850, E. G. Baker subscribed to the *Southern Cultivator* in order "to make my plantation a self sustaining operation." The influence of the reform proposals could be very direct. Slaveholders frequently wrote down rules of the plantation or instructions to overseers whose wording was virtually identical to the published recommendations. The handwritten rules for Andrew Flinn's Green Valley Plantation began with the familiar definition of a good crop as "one that is good taking into consideration everything." Flinn instructed his overseer to keep the interests of his employer first in his mind. He established rules for when and how slaves were to be fed in both winter and summer. Flinn was careful to see that the black children were properly attended to, "for rearing them is not only a duty, but also the most profitable part of plantation business." In an equally familiar refrain, Flinn instructed that the slaves "be flogged as seldom as possible yet always when necessary." Finally, he listed ten specific offenses for which he permitted his overseer to inflict a maximum of fifty lashes a day.[25]

The popularity of rules alone suggests the representativeness if not the influence of reformers, even though slaveholders rarely emphasized more than a few basic regulations. William Ervin had four: Quarrels were to be settled by arbitration; husband and wife were to live together and fulfill their respective duties; no one was to leave the plantation without permission; all slaves were to retire at the nine o'clock horn. Violation of any of Ervin's rules made the slave "liable to stripes." Some slaveholders chose rules that stressed the daily work routine, others emphasized maintaining order and discipline. Haller Nutt was particularly concerned that his overseer "avoid all intercourse with negro women," whereas George Kollock's rules seemed designed to check the slaves' sloppy work habits.[26] Of all the suggestions that reformers had to offer, the elaboration of plantation rules was the one that slaveholders took most to heart.

Long before the reformers had suggested it, however, slaveholders learned the value of detailed record-keeping. In the 1760's the Jerdone family of Virginia maintained records of its slave holdings under a "list of tithes." After the Revolution, it simply became a "list of taxable property." Even the smallest slaveholders maintained such records. John Brown of North Carolina kept yearly accounts of his taxable holdings, which in 1783 included five hundred acres of uncultivated land, "2 Negroes Fellow, between the age of twenty or thirty; 1 Negro girl about eleven years old," and seventeen head of cattle. Sixty years later a South Carolina planter calculated his slaves to be worth $33,000 by listing all ninety-three of them with a brief description of their usefulness or work—"good cotton picker," "cook," "seamstress," and so on. John Francis Page catalogued the actively breeding slave women on his farm, with the names of the children born and those who died, plus tallies of the yearly totals. Henry Pinckney's plantation book registered 113 slaves by name along with his cows, sheep, hogs, wagons, and acres. An Alabama slaveholder listed his thirty-one blacks according to where he got them and how much they cost.[27]

The slaveholders' fondness for lists and numbers was often excessive. Ivey Lewis's accounts from his Alabama plantations in the late
1850's are minutely detailed. He recorded the productivity and
whereabouts of each of his slaves, exact information on the number
of bushels harvested daily by each worker, weekly totals, combined
totals, descriptive locations of the whereabouts of slaves employed
elsewhere, and exact formulations of the time lost to poor weather.
Some slaveholders used such records to enhance the efficient operation
of their plantations. In 1827 William Jemison announced to his slaves
that an account of all lost time would be maintained and "those that
earn most shall have most. What comes off the lazy shall be added
to the industrious." To all slaves on his plantation Jemison promised
rewards "in fair proportion for their labor." You will be whipped
for violating the rules, he added, "as many times as you are guilty."[28]
The smallest slaveholders could establish the simplest rules and keep
the scantiest records. That so many did suggests their attraction to the
managerial ideal.

But, despite these bare indications, it is unlikely that most slaveholders saw the ideal plantation as anything other than an abstraction.
Plantations were more than heartless bureaucratic structures. On most
of them there was a human dimension and human relationships that
somehow got lost in the impersonal managerial machinery reformers
described. Furthermore, most of the principles of comprehensive
management were worthless to the great majority of slaveholders
who owned fewer than ten bondsmen. Because only a relatively small
number of masters hired overseers, the bureaucratic chain of command central to efficient management was all but absent on most
farms with slaves. Masters with one or two slaves could not divide
their labor as efficiently as could large slaveholders. Indeed, for the
majority of masters, the very idea of systematization was impractical.
"Owning but few slaves," a small farmer wrote, "I am probably able
to do a better part by them than if there were one or two hundred.
But I think I could do better if I had enough to permit me to
systematize better." One visitor was amazed by the "utter want of
system and order" on Virginia farms.[29]

Although there is no way of knowing for sure, most slaveholders were probably unfamiliar with plantation management theory. The circulation figures for agricultural periodicals were fairly low, and most slaveholders never read such journals at all. Judging from their letters, thousands of masters were barely literate, and many were illiterate altogether. Among those who were exposed to articles on plantation management, many dismissed them as impractical anyway. "There is in fact little or no *'system'* of management in regard to our slaves," one master argued, for "they are insubordinate and *unmanageable.*"[30] The ideal plantation was an unrealistically stable enterprise in a world of restless slaveholders continually on the move. It is no coincidence that most of the journals that proselytized for efficient management took the lead in attacking westward migration. Indeed, they argued for agricultural reform in the older states precisely in order to make slavery so profitable in the East as to discourage migration to the West. They were fighting a losing battle.

The reformers were similarly frustrated in their efforts to promote a system of management so perfectly rationalized that the physical punishment of slaves was all but eliminated. In theory, whipping was a last resort; in practice, it was the disciplinary centerpiece of plantation slavery. "If the law was to forbid whipping altogether," a Louisiana slaveholder said, "the authority of the master would be at an end." According to one Virginia master, "a slave does not do half the work he easily might; and which, by being harsh enough with him, he can be made to do." The truth is, one forthright slaveholder asserted, only compulsion causes men to work. "This compulsion is more readily and fully applied to the black than the white laborer," he argued, "and consequently more work is obtained from the former than the latter." Masters who felt compelled to whip a slave, particularly for the first time, often reacted squeamishly. "Unpleasant disturbance with my negroes," William Moseley wrote in his diary, "found it indispensably necessary to flog a favorite servant." Others took such responsibilities in stride. "Whiped all the hoe hands," James Torbert wrote in 1856, "whiped Spencer the first time I ever whiped him. Alls well."[31]

The public denunciations of "lenient" slave management that appear in the rhetoric of the 1850's may have pushed otherwise kind masters toward cruelty. Austin Steward recalled his Virginia owner as "kind, humane, and indulgent," yet pressured by neighbors who thought his slaves pampered and spoiled by misguided benevolence. "The more tyrannical a master is, the more will he be favorably regarded by his neighboring planters," Steward concluded, "and from the day that he acquires the reputation of a kind and indulgent master, he is looked upon with suspicion." Blatant, excessive cruelty was always condemned publicly, but as Frederick Douglass noted, the same people who were appalled by one mistress's "disgraceful and shocking" treatment of her slaves "would have condemned and promptly punished any attempt to interfere with Mrs. Hamilton's *right* to cut and slash her slaves to pieces." Bennet Barrow repeatedly beat, caned, imprisoned, and even shot his own slaves, yet professed in his diary to be shocked by a fellow master who whipped a slave to death.[32] Such contradictions went to the heart of management theory.

Reformers deplored the use of threats by slaveholders, yet proposed a system in which the threat of punishment was institutionalized. Most masters understood that slavery depended upon the threat of violence. Even in theory slaves were to be informed of the specific punishments that would follow the violation of a rule. Whatever the theoretical rationale for not threatening slaves, humanity was rarely the motive in practice. Confronted by the problem of a "disorderly" bondsman, the wealthy Georgia planter, Charles Manigault, cautioned his overseer to "keep in mind the important old plantation maxim—viz., 'never to *threaten* a negro' or he will do as you & I would when at school, *he will run.*" Masters often argued that the use of threats made whipping unnecessary. A Louisiana slaveholder wrote that he governed his slaves "without the whip" simply by threatening to sell them "if they do not concern themselves as I wish." A Virginia master boasted that when he took possession of his plantation he got his slaves to double the amount of wood they chopped each day by threatening them: "You have two cords of wood cut tonight," he warned an old man, "or tomorrow morning you shall get two hundred lashes." In one extreme case a South Carolina man held a group of disputed slaves in his possession and ordered them to obey him and no one else. "He did not know if they would obey him," a witness recalled, but knew that if he had them in his possession a little longer "they would obey him at the risk of their lives."[33]

ADVOCATES of scientific management were wrong to assume that slaveholders would always behave rationally. But to ignore economic instability was simply naive. The ideal plantation seemed never to come up against the forces of nature or the disruptions of the marketplace. In practice, battling the elements caused slaveholders constant grief. M. W. Philips ought to have understood this, for his diary reveals what his numerous articles on plantation management never even hint at. As a planter in Hinds County, Mississippi, Philips was undoubtedly a spectacular success. He had moved with his family from Columbia, South Carolina, in the early 1830's, and before the decade was out his twenty-one field hands were producing nearly a hundred bales of cotton yearly. He seems to have run his farm as closely as possible to his managerial ideals, but he was periodically bothered by foul weather, bad overseers, and high rates of sickness and death among his slaves. Eighteen-forty was a particularly difficult year for Philips. His cattle were killed by disease, his corn was "destroyed by bugs and cut worms," sickness set him "back in my cotton picking very much." It rained so hard the cotton was "washed up and died out." At year's end none of Philips's crops met his expectations, and debt forced him to sell some of his slaves.[34]

Yet Philips was among the most successful slaveholders, a diligent planter, and better able than most to withstand such periodic setbacks. Others were less fortunate. "I am not making anything this year," Joseph Thompson wrote to his uncle in 1849. Heavy rains had caused the weeds to grow thicker than usual in the cotton fields of his Alabama plantation. Then the boll worm destroyed most of his crop. After that, Thompson's fields were attacked by caterpillars. "They have been in my cotton about a month and just got through and have hardly left a leaf." A severe drought in 1856 cost one planter a hundred bushels of corn for every dry day. In 1833, a dry season in parts of Tennessee burned most of the crops, Thomas Gale reported. "The farmers will be nearly ruined," Gale wrote to his brother, "and many are determined to remove to Mississippi next winter, indeed the spirit of emigration seems almost general." If reformers failed to note such disruptions, slaveholders often grew accustomed to them. H. C. Anderson of Louisiana complained in 1860 that "the cotton crop has the appearance of Rust generally all over—It will be a very poor one—You can scarcely see a Bloom on any Stalk—What a Bad ending for such a good beginning—It was nothing more than I expected, & I thank God if it be his will."[35]

But it was the normal fluctuation of prices on the market that most bothered the slaveholders. Cotton prices jumped up and down throughout the first half of the nineteenth century, from over thirty cents to as low as five cents a pound, although they were relatively stable in the decade before the Civil War. Nonetheless, the letters of the slaveholders reveal an obsession with the price fluctuations on the various commodity exchanges. In 1840 Bennet Barrow recorded a typical entry in his diary: "bad news from N. Orleans, impression their, that there is enoughf Cotten made this year to answer for the next two—now selling from 4 to 11 ct—Money market very tight evry Where—negros have fallen from $1200 to 8 & 900 'men'—Pork prime $11. mess $12.50 & 13 pr barrel. Molasses lower than usual."[36] Like most people, slaveholders stood helpless before the vagaries of the free market. Its daily intrusion into their lives had the effect of directing their attention toward the best price, away from the good crop.

Political disruptions could be just as unsettling. In 1810 William Berkeley in Hanover County, Virginia, was trying to find a market for his tobacco, but the Napoleonic wars had disrupted international commerce. France had closed off the continent to trade, Berkeley was told, and England's market "will be so glutted—that Tob. must go down to almost nothing."[37]

To some degree or another, most slaveholders tried to use their work force efficiently so as to minimize the impact of such disruptions. When the ground was too hard for plowing, for instance, Hugh Minor had his slaves cut and haul wood for sale and thus clear land for future use. Similarly, most slaveholders tried to produce provisions for home consumption, although the larger plantations were more successful in this than small farms. At Mulberry Grove, A. M. Reed's slaves planted citron and strawberry melons, figs, potatoes, pecans, and corn, as well as cotton. But the question was never whether self-sustaining farms were feasible, as the *Farmers' Register* pointed out, but whether they were expedient. Every slaveholding farmer had to decide how worthwhile it was to plant crops for home consumption that diminished the production of cash crops. Most compromised by planting foodstuffs and raising livestock that only minimally interfered with the planting cycle of the cash crop. But when there was a conflict, the cash crop nearly always won out. "I never want to sow any more wheat in Ala.," Philip Pitts wrote in 1852. "It comes in during such pressing times. . . . Cotton & Wheat do not go well together." From then on Pitts would be "practical" and not grow wheat.[38]

It was inevitable that slaveholders would come to speak of their bondsmen in the language of the marketplace. "A nigger that wouldn't bring over $300, seven years ago, will fetch $1000, cash, quick, this year," one speculative slaveholder declared, "but now, hogs, they aint worth so much as they used to be." I "purchased the negro property of C. R. Jordan," William Ervin wrote in 1848. The next day he "closed the settlement with Jordan" and "Gave him an indemnifying Bond of 5000 Dollars to secure him against loss should there arise any." The North Carolina Mutual Life Insurance Company instructed its agents that when estimating the value of the slave, "reference should be had to what the slave would sell for in the Market." In 1858 a Tennessee master "exchanged Ben for George . . . [and] received cash 'to boot' $50." When one of his slaves got frostbitten toes, J. H. Bills considered his loss and declared the bondsman "ruined." On his model plantation in Mississippi, M. W. Philips wrote in 1840 that "Dick died last night, curse such luck." On his way from Alabama to Texas, one master's slave ran away and died. "It comes kinder hard on me," he said. "I bought the nigger up, counting I should make a speculation on him. . . . As niggers is goin' here now, I expect 'twas a dead loss of eight hundred dollars, right out of pocket."[39]

Such language was underscored by the slaveholders' behavior. Property that valuable was worth taking relatives to court for. In 1787 John Brown sued his brother-in-law for possession of a slave left to his wife. Indeed, for a society that is said to have prided itself on

a strong sense of family, the court records of the Old South are
literally filled with cases of relatives who brought suit against each
other over the issue of slave property. This was inevitable in a society
where slaves and their "increase" were distributed through wills,
given away as gifts, or sold to raise cash. "I have got tired of mandy
and sold her for eight hundred dollars in gold," one Texas master
wrote in 1854. "I need a boy." As capital, slaves were often accepted
as payment in lieu of cash. J. L. Watkins put up three lots for sale
in 1829 and asked "for likely young negros of any kind," rather than
money. A Louisiana planter "took 4 negroes of George Joor 2 women
2 men—for $2000. part of money due me." Austin Steward recalled
how his master once lost a game of cards and paid the winner in cash,
a horse, a watch, and a slave.[40]

Slaveholders frequently pointed to breeding as an example of
how interest and humanity could be served at once in slavery. The
better care they took of their slave women and children, masters
reasoned, the more likely they were to profit from their "increase."
Frederick Olmsted paraphrased a Mississippian who explained the
system: "A man might not raise a nigger with a well-considered plan
to sell him eighteen years after he was born; he might never sell a
nigger, but for all that, it was the readiness with which he could
command a thousand dollars for every likely boy he had, if he should
ever need it, that made him stay here and be bothered with taking
care of a gang of niggers who barely earned enough to enable his
family to live decently."[41]

When slaveholders talked of breeding they did not mean miscegenation and they did not imply sexual abuse. They generally
expected that slaves would bear children within the context of mo-
nogamous relationships. Nevertheless, the high value placed on fertile
black women—"breeders"—made sexual abuse inevitable, and reduced slave marriages, in many masters' eyes, to a functional convenience. "The rearing of slaves in Lower Virginia has so generally been
considered a source of profit to their owners," the *Farmers' Register*
admitted, "that it has scarcely been questioned or doubted." To
achieve success in "negro raising," one writer recommended that it
"be conducted as a business separate from, and unconnected with the
market crop." The ability to bear children helped determine the

market value of female slaves, and various incentives were offered them to encourage reproduction.[42]

In the spring of 1857, in Cooper County, Missouri, Thomas Houston was visited by a generous benefactor who offered him as a gift three thousand dollars in cash, or a family of slaves valued at four thousand dollars. "We concluded to take the *money,*" Houston explained, to "invest it in negro boys, from 12 to 16 years old." The slaves offered to Houston were much like those he already owned, women and girls. "If I can succeed buying boys to suit it will increase my male force to 10 or 12 hands, & in a few years, as they & the girls grow up, we may be able to pair them all off in families *at home.*" Perhaps slaveholders were foolish to view breeding as economically profitable, but the fact is that most of them did. They boasted of their achievements in this respect. Archibald Arrington spoke anxiously of the four or five slaves whose chances of giving birth one year looked "promising." In addition, "there may be a few others who may comply with or obey that scriptural injunction which commands us 'to multiply and replenish the earth,' " Arrington told his wife. A Charleston planter claimed that keeping the slave cabins whitewashed *"makes the slave prolific.* I have, at this time, a hundred and fifty of these people; and their *annual increase* may be estimated as *adding as much to my income* as arises from all other sources." Frederick Douglass recalled that the most valuable part of his master's property was his thirty slaves, "of whom he could afford to sell one every year." A Florida planter defended his management practices by pointing to his slaves' "natural increase which in the last year has been over ten percent, in a gang of 120." A Georgia overseer informed his employer that with good management his plantation could produce much more cotton. "The increase of your negroes," he added, "(& they increase like rabbits) would soon carry the figures much higher."[43]

The pecuniary nature of the master-slave relationship did little to encourage close emotional bonds. Public officials complained that slaves convicted of capital crimes could not count on their masters' intercession because many states indemnified owners for bondsmen who were put to death. As far as the material interest of the master was concerned, one governor warned, he was "perfectly indifferent, for if his slave is condemned, he is entitled to his full value." The "feelings of humanity" were not enough to protect the slaves.[44]

Because of the slave's status as property, masters had to deal with their bondsmen in accordance with the requirements of the market. By their consistent failure to recognize this fact, reformers constructed an ideal plantation that virtually ignored its own economic context. It was not sadism that made life so difficult for most slaves, although there certainly were cruel masters. Nor did kindness necessarily make slave life bearable. Every time a slaveholder went into debt, or died, or moved, the stability of slave life was disrupted. Every time a slaveholder looked for ways to cut costs, raise cash, or reinvest profits, the slaves were affected, and frequently they suffered. It was simply not possible to separate the commercial market in which antebellum slavery functioned from the day-to-day relationship of master and slave. The reformers conceded as much when they tied the humanity of slavery to the material interests of the master.

Occasionally, the masters' interests did protect the bondsmen. A Virginia slaveholder hired Irish workers to drain his swamps because the labor was dangerously unhealthy. "A negro's life is too valuable to be risked at it," he said. "If a negro dies, it's a considerable loss, you know." To the dismay of many overseers, masters frequently intervened to stop excessively harsh treatment. When the overseer on George Kollock's plantation flogged a single slave twice in one day, cutting her near the eye, Kollock stepped in and reproached him. "The first thing I tell a man when I hire him, is, 'if there's any whippin' to be done on this place I want to do it myself,' " an Alabama slaveholder declared. "If I saw a man rappin' my niggers with a hoe-handle, as I see him, durned if I wouldn't rap him—the lazy whelp." A Florida overseer complained that his employer failed to sympathize with his fear that a slave would kill him. "Your Negros behave badly behind my back and then Run to you," he wrote, "and you appear to beleave what they say."[45]

Largely because of their excessive harshness, overseers were widely considered a "worthless set of vagabonds." "I hope the time will come When every Overseer will be compelled to addopt some other mode of making a living," Bennet Barrow wrote. "They are a perfect nuisance." A North Carolina slaveholder hired an overseer to care for his slaves, but considered the man "as much of a negro in principle as is a one of them." Overseers, he thought, "require little less oversight from their employers than the negroes require from *them* and . . . in point of *fidelity*, there is not so much *Difference* between *white* and *black* as our natural partiality for the former would persuade us." Yet when overseers wrote to their employers about the plantation, most references to the slaves' health indicated that the master's chief interest in such news was its effect on the farm's productivity. From the distance of absentee ownership, masters could not have helped their slaves anyway. "Overseers in Alabama prefer living with me to anyone else in that vicinity for two reasons," Archibald Arrington wrote from his other farm in North Carolina, "one is that my negroes are obedient and work well and the other is that I am away and cant find fault 'till the end of the year."[46]

There was more than a little disingenuousness in the masters' protests over the cruelty of overseers. For, in holding them to intrinsically contradictory standards of behavior, masters virtually assured their own dissatisfaction. If they preferred that their slaves be well treated, they also insisted that the overseer produce the maximum in profits. "The future of the overseer depends altogether on the quantity of cotton he is able to make for the market," one Mississippi slaveholder wrote. Even M. W. Philips, a staunch advocate of scientific plantation management, hired an overseer on terms which practically ensured that the slaves would be overworked. The overseer's salary for 1856 would be "$500 per year with an addition of $3 per bale for all over 240 bales." James Torbert was appalled when one of his slaves was "badly bruised" by the overseer. "He can whip them if he wishes when he does wrong but to beat them up with Sticks and his fist Must not be," Torbert wrote. Yet within months he was "Mad as the devil" that the same overseer had "only Sent 5 bales Cotton the last load."[47]

Slaves victimized by cruel overseers or hired out to severe masters could not normally expect the plantation bureaucracy to check itself. Jacob Stroyer was repeatedly whipped by an overseer who forced the slave to work in the cotton field against his master's orders. Stroyer complained to his mistress, and she sent him to be trained as a carpenter, as her husband had promised. But the overseer paid no attention to her orders and instead forced Stroyer to return to the field. Once again the slave was severely whipped. When he finished planting the cotton and returned to the carpenter's shop, the overseer followed, "gave me another severe whipping," and again put Stroyer to work in the field. He was not the only slave with such recollections. William Wells Brown complained to his master of the severe treatment he had received from Major Freeland, to whom Brown had been hired. "But it made no difference," Brown later wrote. His master "cared nothing about it, so long as he received the money for my labor." Frederick Douglass was so abused by Edward Covey, the "negro breaker" to whom Douglass had been hired, that he went to his master and begged to be taken back. But Douglass's master dismissed the slave's claims as "nonsense," and told him that if he left Covey with his year "but half expired, I should lose your wages for the entire year."[48]

Slaveholders who spent every cent they could to enhance their property holdings, who endured great personal deprivation to buy one more slave or a few more acres of land, and who lived in a style not much different from their poorer, non-slaveholding neighbors could not be expected to shower their bondsmen with worldly luxuries. Well into the nineteenth century, slaveholders continued to provide their slaves with so little clothing that "when they wear them out, they go without." Travelers confirmed the numerous claims by former slaves that they were "kept almost in a state of nudity" all year long. Slaveholders practiced frugality at the expense of their bondsmen. "Now that molasses can be obtained so cheap," one writer suggested, "planters would find it decidedly advantageous to use it to considerable extent, as food for their negroes." Slaves "relish" molasses, he continued. They find it "highly nutritious and do with half their usual quantity of meat when they are supplied with it." On a Florida plantation the meat "gave out" periodically, and the overseers reported that the slaves were "eating dirt" uncontrollably.[49]

In the entrepreneurial economy of the antebellum South, the threat of depression, tight money, or debt drove the kindest masters to neglect or sell their bondsmen. Most indebted slaveholders could not afford to be so humanely inclined as the Natchez master who tried to sell his slaves in a single lot to an "excellent" owner. Slaveholders simply accepted the need to sell slaves in order to pay their bills. Thus

most of the blacks sent to the slave market in Louisiana were sold
not because they were incorrigible but because their masters had gone
bankrupt or died in debt. In 1830, John Nevitt sold a slave woman
and her daughter "for 900 Dollars in payment of Anthony Smith."
Thomas Sparks was anxious to repay his debts as quickly as possible,
but Sparks could see no good opportunity "as all Negro trading is
done" for the season. A Virginia master purchased the winter supply
of hogs only to find he did not have the money to pay for them. "To
escape from his embarrassment," Elizabeth Keckley wrote, "it was
necessary to sell one of the slaves." The cook was ordered to dress
her son and send him to the master's house, where he was "placed in
the scales, and was sold, like the hogs, as so much per pound."[50]

One of the most common disruptions of slave life came with the
death of the master. The evaluation and division of the bondsmen
among contending heirs was a frightening prospect for most slaves.
"The character and tendencies of the heirs, are generally well understood among the slaves who are to be divided," Frederick Douglass
noted. "But neither their aversions nor their preferences avail them
anything." Slaveholders occasionally used their wills to reward a
particularly faithful servant with anything from manumission to
money. Mary Houston bequeathed to her slave, Matty, "what she
may choose out of my apparel," as well as the right to hire herself
out. More often, individual slaves were diversely distributed among
white friends and relatives "in consideration of the natural love and
affection which I have to bear unto my beloved." Because so many
slaveholders died with debts to their name, not even their stated
preferences to have their slaves kept together could always be honored. "I should rather wish that the person who takes the Land had
the Negroes," John Brownrigg wrote in 1789 on the death of his
father. But because he wanted to have the debts paid and the estate
settled as "soon as possible," Brownrigg asked "to have the Land and
negroes Hired . . . either together or separate as I and the rest of my
Friends and Attornies shall think most to my advantage & Interest."[51]

The sale and hire of slaves upon the death, movement, or indebtedness of the slaveholders made the bondsman's life inherently unstable. Born in 1832 near Charlottesville, Virginia, Louis Hughes was
separated from his white father and transferred, with his mother, to

a new owner who died when Hughes was eleven. He and his mother were then bought by Washington Fitzpatrick of Scottsville, Virginia. Shortly thereafter, Hughes was taken to Richmond and purchased from his mother by George Reid. Because Hughes was sickly, Reid sold him in 1844 to Edward McGee, one of the largest cotton planters of Pontotoc, Mississippi. In 1850 McGee moved his whole plantation to a huge new estate in Memphis. By the time he was eighteen years old, Louis Hughes had been owned by five masters and had moved six times. Henry Clay Bruce's master, Jack Perkinson, was a restless man. Born in 1836, in Prince Edward County, Virginia, Bruce was moved to Missouri in 1844, back to Virginia in 1847, to Mississippi in 1849, and to Missouri again in 1850. There Bruce was hired out year after year to a succession of masters. In 1856 his owner bought a plantation and worked his five slaves on it, but the following year he sold it and moved closer to his brother-in-law. Frederick Douglass was moved about to several different masters in Maryland. When his original owner died, he was taken from Anthony Lloyd's daughter in Baltimore, with whom he had been living, and was given to his owner's son. From there Douglass was sent to a "breaker" for a year. Implicated in an escape plot, Douglass was returned to Baltimore and rented to several different masters.[52]

An incessant compulsion to move on the part of owners was the most frequent cause of the breakup of slave families. It was not uncommon for planters to sell all their slaves before a major move. In 1846 William Shepard of Elizabeth City, North Carolina, offered a 1300-acre estate for sale as a "desirable investment to both capitalists and farmers." There were sixty slaves on the plantation, all of whom Shepard was willing to sell with the land "if desired." Elizabeth Keckley and her mother served a cruel master in North Carolina until they were separated from her father and returned to Virginia to work. But her new master was not prosperous in Virginia, and so after several hard years he moved to St. Louis, "hoping to improve his fortune in the West." He fared no better in Missouri. "The necessities of the white family were so great," Keckley later wrote, "that it was proposed to place my mother out at service." Olmsted met an old slave in Texas who had been born on the Eastern Shore of Maryland. "My mass'r sold me to go in a drove when I was a little boy," the slave explained, "and I was bought out of the drove in South Carolina, and when I was most a man grown my mass'r moved to Tennessee. Thar I got my old woman, and we raised thirteen chil'en. Then we was sold to go to Arkansaw." Only one of his children was sold to Arkansas with him, and from there he was sold to Texas, where the slave moved around hiring himself out until the master found a place to "suit him."[53]

THERE WAS NO GREATER FLAW in the theory of plantation management than its failure to recognize the extent to which the slaves themselves altered the conditions under which they lived. They deeply resented their enslavement and made constant complaint to their masters. They demanded a variety of privileges that eased their burdens, successfully forcing the hands of their owners. By resorting to any number of sophisticated mechanisms of physical and psychological manipulation, the slaves denied their masters the absolute control that was the goal of good plantation management. In all of this, the slaves responded to their bondage as workers might logically be expected to respond to an oppressive system of labor exploitation. Indeed, the history of slavery is in many ways a chapter in the larger history of American workers.[54]

Short of overt rebellion, little of the slaves' behavior represented a frontal assault on the system of slavery itself, and in this sense even pervasive resistance may be properly termed "accommodationist." But to define accommodation so broadly is to overlook the diversity of the slave experience, for it makes the most loyal house servant fundamentally indistinguishable from the most troublesome runaway. It mattered to both master and slave that large numbers of bondsmen openly and persistently resisted, that the slave community —with its powerful religious traditions, its rich folk culture, its adaptive family structure—sustained and encouraged that resistance. Granted that all of this behavior represented the slaves' adaptation to the system, it remains an open question whether day-to-day resistance is usefully understood within the framework of accommodation. For that framework divorces behavior from context by rendering the slave's motivation irrelevant. If the bondsmen consciously resented and deliberately resisted enslavement, if the masters spent a good deal of time thwarting resistance by the sheer use of force and violence —pervasive, institutionalized violence sanctioned by the highest court in America and extending down to the most isolated overseer's whip—can the term "accommodation" convey the substance and meaning of daily life in the slave South?[55]

Loyal house servants and faithful mammies did not disturb the workings of the slave system; hostile slave laborers did, and there can be no question that in terms of the master's perceptions, hostility prevailed. The painful ambivalence of the house servant's existence could manifest itself in behavior that ranged from the murder of a master to the devoted protection of the white family in the face of an invading Union Army. But for the mass of field hands, daily life was a perpetual grind of hard work characterized by nearly universal hatred of the slave system and punctuated by periodic and often sustained acts of resistance. It was the resistance that made its mark.

Slaveholders complained that their bondsmen were impudent because they *were* impudent; masters complained that their slaves were lazy because they frequently would not work. By deliberate lassitude, by running away, by sabotage, slaves withheld their labor from the master. In effect they were striking, and to some degree every master succumbed to the slaves' demands. By planning their individual and collective acts of day-to-day resistance as deliberate responses to particular grievances, the slaves were punishing their masters for mistreatment, neglect, or overwork. The experiences of the large slaveholders who could and did systematize reveals that there could be no ideal plantation without the cooperation of the slaves.

At Highland Plantation in southern Louisiana, Bennet Barrow copied a typical set of rules into his diary in 1838. They emphasized the importance of keeping the slaves from leaving the plantation, prohibiting marriage to bondsmen from neighboring farms, and denying the slaves the right to sell anything away from home. "The verry security of the plantation requires that a general and uniform control over the people of it should be exercised," Barrow reasoned. Because the slaves could not leave, they should be made "as comfortable at Home as possible." In this way the master provided all that was "essentially necessary" for the slave's happiness, creating in the bondsman "a habit of perfect dependence" on the master. All of Barrow's rules were designed with this in mind. He even preferred to give the slaves money at Christmas "thereby creating an interest with you and yours." Barrow believed that he should be "uniform in his own habits" because, he said, "the general conduct of master has a verry considerable influence on the character and habits of his slave." He considered his plantation "a piece of machinery" whose successful operation depended upon the steady force of the master, and whose "different departments" were the responsibility of individual subordinates. Once the slaves were disciplined, Barrow concluded, "planting is a pleasure."[56]

But life at Highland was anything but pleasurable, for the slaves or for Barrow. He complained repeatedly that money was tight, cotton prices were low, loans were not repaid. His crops suffered from droughts and floods; if they were not "eaten by bugs," he "never saw crab grass as thick." Barrow also complained that his slaves picked cotton "verry trashy" or that he was never "more dissatisfied with my hands."[57] His slaves were not contented either. Some ran away repeatedly, and when Barrow whipped them they ran away again. Others put rocks in their cotton to fool the master, or they hid out in the woods and killed hogs for food.

So annoyed was Barrow by the slaves' behavior that in a diary entry in 1840 he virtually reformulated all of his rules, reducing them to one simple proposition: "The best plan is to give them every thing they require for their comfort and never that they will do without Whipping or some punishment." In fact, this had been Barrow's practice all along, though the slaves seemed to disagree with the master's assessment of their requirements. Barrow's punishments were notorious. He jailed slaves for months at a time, until they escaped. One year he chained some slaves up "during Christmass" for "general bad conduct." At other times he chained them "till I think they are broke in—to behave." But the slaves would not behave, so Barrow beat them. And when they ran away he sent dogs after them. In one case the dogs caught a runaway and "nearly et his legs off—near Killing him." Another runaway was *"treed,"* so Barrow "made the dogs pull him out of the tree, Bit him very badly." When one slave ran away after shirking his duties, Barrow got his gun and went on a chase, "found him in the Bayou behind the Quarter, shot him in his thigh."[58] It is difficult to escape the impression that the status quo at Highland Plantation was less "perfect dependence" than perpetual warfare between angry bondsmen and their frustrated master.

On poorly organized plantations the situation could approach anarchy. John Nevitt was a well-to-do slaveholder in the Mississippi cotton belt with a plantation near Natchez. He lived on his farm but paid relatively little heed to its daily operations. Indeed, he was very fond of going off to town and "doing nothing." Perhaps it was because of his lackadaisical management that Nevitt seemed unable to control his slaves. He whipped them regularly and casually. Sometimes individuals were a problem—Maria, for example. She ran away in 1827, was captured and "lightly whiped." A few months later, in October, she ran away with another slave, was brought back and given a "severe whiping." The following May, Maria was caught sneaking about the kitchen, was "whiped lightly and put to work." In December she ran away again, and when returned she was sent by her frustrated owner to the Natchez jail. She was not Nevitt's only rebellious slave. Sam ran away and Nevitt "had him whiped and put in Irons." John was flogged for "ill treating his oxen." One spring night in 1830 "Jerry and one or two others got a flogging for misconduct," and the next day "Rubin runaway [for] nothing perticular." Later that summer Nevitt rode to Natchez and discovered that one of his slaves, Kate, was in jail for stealing meat. Kate got the meat from Bill, "who after a little flogging confessed" to the act. Bill, it turned out, had joined up with Sandy, one of the neighbor's slaves, to take bacon and liquor from a local warehouse. Kate was brought home. Sandy testified against Bill, who was convicted of larceny and sentenced to thirty-nine lashes. Several months later, when Bill was found stealing molasses regularly, Nevitt gave him a "good whiping and sent him to jail," and a few weeks later had him sold.[59]

The slaves made perpetual turmoil on John Nevitt's plantation, ostentatiously violating rules, seemingly impervious to their owner's liberal use of the lash. Yet the specific violations for which Nevitt's slaves were whipped were common to most large plantations. Masters often complained that their slaves would not perform adequately. To a North Carolina woman, "making others work" was "the most disagreeable labour in the world." Bennet Barrow did not doubt that his slaves were deliberately rebellious. During a prolonged illness, he discovered a "number of hands pretending to be sick. knowing I am not able to go out as yet." It was a cliché among slaveholders that "if you give a nigger an inch, he will take an ell." A Virginia master asserted that slaves "never would lay out their strength freely, and it was impossible to make them do it." Most attributed such behavior to the blacks' alleged racial inferiority. "I assure you that these negroes are the laziest creatures in the world," a wealthy Georgia planter claimed, "and would never work but by compulsion." A Northerner who moved to Texas complained that her "yankee" experience had left her unprepared "for ordering people who are not accustomed to use, for their owners good, the small capacities they possess." James Bailey's wife wished she "could trust more" to her servants. "I suppose it must be my own fault that they seldom do a thing as I want it unless I am looking at them," she lamented. They "seldom think for themselves."[60]

In fact, the slaves often thought deeply about their bondage. When a traveler asked a Louisiana slave if the bondsmen talked among themselves about being free, there was no hesitation in the response. "Yes, sir," the slave declared, "dat's all dey talk" about. Indeed, slaves often revealed a complex understanding of the nature of their oppression. "It is not the fault of the slaveholder that he is cruel," Solomon Northup wrote after twelve years of servitude, "so much as it is the fault of the system under which he lives." According to James Pennington, the "chattel principle" was responsible for the cruelties of slavery. "Talk not then about kind and Christian masters," the former slave wrote. "They are not masters of the system. The system is master of them; and the slaves are their vassals." Many slaves acknowledged the existence of "good masters" but dismissed them as almost irrelevant in a system that was intrinsically oppressive. Certainly they preferred kindness to cruelty, but much more than that they preferred freedom to slavery. Thus Mary Anderson recalled her master as a kind and benevolent man who apparently viewed his slaves' well-being as a reflection on his own dignity. Yet when freedom came, the slaves on his plantation rejoiced that their prayers had finally been answered. A traveler asked a Virginia slave if her mistress treated her well. "Yes," the slave answered, "but I could take better care of myself. What is to become of me when she is gone?" Kind treatment did not affect the slaves' desire to be free from a system that oppressed them, regardless of the master's benevolence.[61]

Because so many slaves understood this, the master's success depended less upon scientific management than on the good will of the bondsmen. No struggling young slaveholder could easily anger or abuse his few bondsmen. In the Spartan life of the southern frontier a crude egalitarianism was often a prerequisite to survival. Nor could the established slaveholder entirely disregard the will of the bondsmen without jeopardizing the plantation's efficiency, not to mention security. Insightful masters recognized this by leaving their slaves alone to do their work, by rewarding slaves for good work, and occasionally by freeing one or more bondsmen whose service was particularly faithful. In North Carolina, Nathaniel Macon's slave, Natt, was such an "Extraordinary Shoemaker" and was so industrious that Macon entrusted to him "an abundance of business." When Natt's free wife could afford it, Macon sold him to her "for but trifling."[62]

Masters relied on their slaves not only to produce the cash crops and maintain the farms, but in dozens of smaller ways. Individual slaves became expert craftsmen, herdsmen, or cooks, making themselves indispensable to their owners. Alexander Telfair instructed his overseer that "Elsey is allowed to act as midwife, to black and white in the neighborhood, who send for her." She was, the Georgia planter explained, "the Doctoress of the Plantation. In case of extraordinary illness, when she thinks she can do no more for the sick, you will employ a physician." As a young boy, James Pennington was hired out to a stonemason, and his brother to a pumpmaker. "In this way," Pennington recalled, masters not only saved money but in addition "they got among their slaves useful trades." Thomas Trotter was establishing a light machinery and construction business near Washington, D. C., when he wrote that "my Negros seem to understand the business so well I hope I shall be able to carry the business on to perfection by my close attention." David Ross's slaves acquired an impressive array of industrial skills, and Ross recognized his dependence upon them: "Many of my Servants . . . have double trades some of them treble," he wrote. "The Servants belonging to the Estate are sufficient in number, well qualified by experience and practice and properly arranged to the various departments of the business," Ross boasted, "to execute every branch without the assistance of any other mechanic."[63]

But it was on farms and plantations that the slaves most often made themselves sufficiently valuable that their labor could become a bargaining chip in conflicts with their masters. A visitor to a Georgia plantation who thought slaves "dumb" by nature was nonetheless "agreeably surprised to see the rank held here by the black mechanics. One day I observed a set of carpenters putting up sluices, and a lock in a canal of a kind unknown in this part of the world." The black foreman and the slaves were following the plans that their master had brought over from Europe. When the various mechanics on the plantation consulted their master, Charles Lyell recorded, "their manner of speaking to him is quite as independent as that of English artisans to their employers." One of Isaac Mason's owners purchased a sixty-acre plot of very poor land and put Mason and an older slave to work on it by themselves. For five years Mason and his partner worked alone, building up the productivity of the land from five to thirty bushels of corn and wheat to the acre. In the last three years the farm was under Mason's charge and in all that time, he recalled, "I was never struck a blow. There was no one to find fault with my work."[64]

Frederick Olmsted correctly perceived that the most productive plantations throughout the seaboard slave states were those where the slaves had the most autonomy. Charles Pettigrew found that the slaves on his plantation "have commonly done better by themselves with a little direction than with such overseers as we have had." Pettigrew's grandson, William, regularly left control of his plantations with black managers. In northern Mississippi, Olmsted visited a farm where the slaves were never whipped, were fed all the meat they wanted, were permitted to leave to visit wives and friends, and worked by themselves. According to the owner, "my niggers never want no lookin' arter; they jus tek ker o' themselves." His slaves taught themselves how to read, and one of his bondsmen learned carpentry so quickly that his master concluded that "niggers is somehow nat'rally ingenious; more so'n white folks." Unlike most slaveholders, he would "rather have a rascally nigger than any other—they's so smart." So averse to the use of force was he that "if I ever notice one of 'em getting a little slack, I just talk to him; tell him we must get out of the grass and, I want to hev him stir himself a little more, an then, maybe, I slip a dollar into his hand."[65] The striking success of his antimanagerial approach eluded those masters who did not recognize their own dependence upon the slaves.

For service to their owners, slaves came to expect assistance in times of need. They asked to be sold to their spouses, or to be purchased back from unsatisfactory owners. May Brown begged her former master to "receive mee back home" from a man whom "I Cannot please." When Benajah Nicholls's slave, Sam, expressed "a great wish to be with his wife," Nicholls told him to ask his wife's owner, Thomas Purdie, to buy him. Short of cash, Purdie offered instead either a four-hundred dollar note, or two hundred and fifty dollars in notes plus "a negro girl about nine or ten years old for one hundred and fifty." It was, Purdie explained, "the Best I can do." Slaves came to expect certain holidays, and masters frequently met resistance if some free time was not forthcoming. Haller Nutt's overseer tried to wait until the owner arrived at his Louisiana plantation before celebrating Christmas, "but the negros being very anxious for the frolicks," the overseer was forced to begin the celebration the next day.[66]

When they were dissatisfied, slaves openly complained. At a Washington, D.C., hotel, a harried bondsman asked a guest, "Don't you tink I'se too ole a man for to be knock roun at dis kind of work, massa?" A Florida overseer dismissed a slave's report that on a nearby plantation the "Negroes . . . Looked bad," arguing that blacks "will in a General way report things worst then they Realy are." Moses Grandy went to his master and told him that he was unaccustomed to field work and "that his overseer was the worst that had ever been on the plantation, and that I could not stand it."[67]

When conditions became intolerable, some slaves simply decided not to serve their masters and went elsewhere. "Scott has run away," an Alabama master complained. "I had determined to send him to the plantation, to work in the crop, rather than be troubled by his laziness and rascality. This mortified him exceedingly, and he tried to induce several persons to buy him, failing in which, he decamped." A Florida slave was sent to a different plantation because the overseer "could not get her to work. I have not had the Cause to strike her a Lick," the new overseer reported. "I wish he would let her stay hear She will work for me without any trouble." Clarissa Town was less fortunate with her slaves. Determined to mend the ways of an intractable house servant, Town complained from her Louisiana plantation in 1853 that it was "quite out of my power unless I had a whip in my hand all the time. . . . She takes advantage of every indulgence. It grieves us to think we have so little influence over her." Another plantation mistress complained that when she ordered her servants to perform a task "I never can be sure I am obeyed. . . . And, when I reprimand them, they only say they don't mean to do anything wrong, or they wont do it again, all the time laughing as though it was all a joke."[68]

Bondsmen who laughed at their masters understood that the slave's ambiguous legal status as both labor and property allowed them to manipulate the owner's material interests. They withheld labor by slowing down or shirking duties; they deprived the master of his property by simply running away. The same indemnification laws that left them defenseless in capital cases, also left them "without any legal restraints in all minor offences." As if to recognize this, many slaves openly defied their masters. "Mr Turnbulls negros are cutting up a great many shines," a Louisiana slaveholder reported. "16 ran off & have defied him—are well armed killed two of his dogs while in pursuite of them." When Frederick Douglass's master forbade the slave to continue visiting a priest, Douglass was infuriated, and vowed that he *"would* go to Father Lawson's, notwithstanding the threat." One slave told her mulatto daughter not to wait upon the overseer's family. The overseer whipped the insubordinate girl and then went after her mother, who "got the Devil in her and walked off."[69]

The history of slave labor is rife with instances of primitive rebellion by bondsmen determined to exert some control over their own workplace. Employing a technique that would become familiar to later generations of factory laborers, slaves often initiated work slowdowns. A wealthy Maryland slaveholder implemented the principles of scientific management carefully and successfully. Yet his slaves moved so "slowly" in obeying his orders that the master frequently had to complete their tasks himself. In Virginia, the slaves on a construction site seemed to a northern observer to move "so indolently" that they must have been "trying to see how long they could be in mounting the ladder without actually stopping." When the slaves were ordered to perform a task "they undertake it in such a way that the desired result is sure not to be accomplished," Olmsted thought. "The negroes require such constant watching to have things done well," a Louisiana mistress complained, "that it is almost as easy to do ourselves."[70]

Similarly, running away for any reason effectively deprived the master of the slave's labor. Even leaving the workplace to see one's spouse required the repudiation of the master's rules. Barbarous owners were particularly troubled by runaways. William Dunbar could not understand his slaves' behavior. He "condemned" two runaways "to receive 500 lashes Each at 5 Dift. times, and to carry a chain & log fixt to the ancle—Poor Ignorant Devils; for what do they run away? They are well cloathed, work easy, and have all kinds of Plantation produce at no alowance." In 1851 William Hamilton wrote to his father explaining the circumstances of a recent escape from his Louisiana plantation. "My Pet John has taken to the woods and I am afraid for good. I have punished him very severely lately for his rascality, and on last Saturday night, my negroes gave a supper party at my place above, just about the time they were ready to set down to tea I waked them up with the contents of my gun—such scampering you never did see, running over cordwood, tree tops, in ditches etc. I saved only one of the flock, a boy belonging to a Dr. Smith; he is very badly wounded and may in all probability be disabled for life, the same boy has been shot twice this year, and once before by me. I only regret that it was not John." In 1856 a Virginia master offered "a reward of six cents for the apprehension of his boy 'Sam,' who absconded some time in the month of March. . . . He has a down look, and, on his back, wears the stripes of a recent whipping.

One tooth is knocked out, and I believe he has a scar under the left eye."[71]

Slaves sometimes threatened, even plotted, to run away if the master or overseer mistreated them. Calculating his owner's thwarted efforts to beat him, Isaac Mason recalled that "I knew my man, and I felt he was on the watch and only waiting for a chance to pounce down upon me." On one plantation, the overseer threatened to flog a slave who had run away for a few days. "He told me he would take it [the whipping] and run off," which he did. A Louisiana cotton planter "whiped near half the hands to day for picking badly & trashy. Tom Beauf came up to the scales and put his Basket down and it is the last I've seen of him." Dennis "ran off yesterday," Bennet Barrow wrote, "& after I had Whiped him." One slave claimed to have lost his eyesight and refused to work for months until Barrow "gave him 25 cuts yesterday morning & ordered him to work Blind or not." The next day the slave "run off."[72]

"They are deceived," a former bondsman warned, "who flatter themselves that the ignorant and debased slave has no conception of the magnitude of his wrongs." Indeed, the depth of the slaves' consciousness is suggested by their behavior, for despite the relative paucity of large, organized slave rebellions, it was quite common for slaves to assist one another in their resistance. When Isaac Mason hid from his cruel and abusive master, a fellow slave brought him food for several days. When a Florida slave ran away, the overseer expected him to "Stay out for Sometime, for the people has incurged it all they can." On George Jones's two plantations, the slaves were highly organized. In 1854, three of them "made a plot to Leave if I should attempt to Flog them for picking Cotton," the overseer wrote. They persuaded two others to join, and the two ran away and were flogged along with the three plotters who "acknowledge they had done wrong." In one case Jones got into trouble because his slaves plotted to run away and go to jail if the overseer tried to "whip enny more about thar craps." A group of slaves left the plantation and "went Strait to Talahassee and was put in jail." A lawyer who examined them "Reported about town that they was badly Whiped." Clearly embarrassed by his slaves, Jones was forced to defend his planting practices in a letter to the lawyer. Moses Grandy's parsimoni-

ous master allowed his slaves "very few clothes and but little to eat."
Dissatisfied with the work he was getting in return, the master went
into the field and demanded an explanation. Grandy bluntly announced that the slaves were too hungry to do their work. "From
that time," Grandy recalled, "we had food enough, and he soon found
that he had a great deal more work done."[73]

Slave autonomy and resistance altered the shape and course of
slaveholding in America. For all the masters who took up the lash
to suppress the bondsman's "insolence," there were others who were
compelled to recognize the dignity of their slaves as workers. Still
others came to a standoff. One traveler found the slaveholders so
afraid of their bondsmen that they were prevented from inflicting
punishment "lest the slave should abscond, or take a sulky fit and not
work, or poison some of the family, or set fire to the dwelling, or
have recourse to any other mode of avenging himself." A Texas
family would not send a slave out into a storm to get wood because
the bondsman had been hired out beginning the following week.
They "were afraid if they didn't treat him well, he'd run away." A
Virginia slaveholder whose bondsmen frequently feigned illness was
so afraid of punishing slaves who were not really ill that he never
questioned their claims, "ill or not."[74]

In various ways, the slaves frustrated, infuriated, and manipulated
their owners. The bondsmen never took control of the farms on
which they worked, but neither did they permit their masters to take
complete control. By their ceaseless complaints about the difficulty
of managing bondsmen, masters recognized what reformers never
saw: that the slaves were determined against all odds to make their
own history. In the process, they shaped the history of slaveholders
as well. Perhaps that is why, when asked by a traveler if she belonged
to a nearby master, a Georgia slave replied without hesitation. "Yes,
I belong to them," she said, "and they belong to me."[75]

AGRICULTURAL REFORMERS never came to terms with those features of
the slave system that precluded the existence of the ideal plantation.
In large measure this was because they were influenced by a paternalistic tradition that had disappeared in most parts of the South by the

end of the colonial era. If the reformers' vision of a rationalized bureaucracy looked forward to advanced forms of industrial organization, it also recalled paternalistic conceptions in its evocation of a harmoniously integrated social world. But the paternalistic elements were overshadowed by the reformers' need to appeal to the prevailing entrepreneurial ethos. Thus they actively embraced the capitalistic economy, arguing that sheer material interest, properly understood, would prove both economically profitable and socially stabilizing. But this intense devotion to the capitalistic spirit of accumulation had done much to diminish the influence of paternalistic ideals within the slaveholding class, and that spirit was never successfully reconciled with the conflicting devotion to stability and social harmony. This was the contradiction that rendered paternalism so anachronistic to the nineteenth-century South.

Chapter 7

❧

Masters of Tradition

PATERNALISM WAS DEBILITATED but not destroyed by the slave-holding experience of colonial America. The same forces that diminished its influence in the seventeenth and eighteenth centuries —the rise of the commercial market, the broad distribution of slave wealth, the diversity of the master class, and the spread of economic and political liberalism—continued to operate against the effective-ness of paternalistic ideology in the antebellum South. Yet the nine-teenth century witnessed a dramatic rise in the rhetoric of paternalism in both England and America, and there was more than coincidence in these simultaneous developments. For despite many differences, British and slaveholding paternalism shared the same historical origins and suffered similar fates in the modern age.[1]

Although it was the reigning theory of human social relations from the medieval through the Tudor ages in Britain, paternalism received its first clear theoretical expression in the Tudor humanist tracts of the sixteenth century. But the traditional bases of a paternal-istic society—church, monarchy, and aristocracy—lost much of their authority in the late Stuart era. With the rise of Newtonian physics and Lockean philosophy, and the emergence of capitalistic economic and democratic political structures, paternalism was rendered increas-ingly irrelevant. Even in Britain there had always been a chasm between paternalistic ideals and practices, most visible in the tendency to preach the economics of the "just price" while acting on the principles of laissez faire. With the rise of the capitalist economy the chasm widened to the point where it could not be bridged without altering fundamental paternalistic assumptions.

Tudor ideas were revived in nineteenth-century Britain, but not in their original form. The re-emergence of paternalist thought was characterized by a theoretical acceptance of the free market economy, coupled with the principle that all property—whether land or factory —bestowed paternalistic authority. In practical terms, nineteenth-century English paternalists opposed "meddling" government, preferring to exercise their power locally. Yet they supported authoritarian rule, advocating monarchy and reviling democracy. Not surprisingly, they were devoted to a powerful hierarchy within the Anglican Church.

By the nineteenth century, these conservatives were no longer defending a society under attack but a form of social organization that had disappeared a century earlier. Paternalism in early Victorian England drew its strength as a response to the social disruptions wrought by industrialization, urbanization, and population expansion. Paternalists were enchanted by their nostalgic vision of an older and better age when social relations were stable and harmonious. Such images proliferated in the romantic novels and Tory magazines of the day. Yet it was a perennial complaint that Britain's patriarchs were not meeting their paternal responsibilities. Thus British paternalism suffered the inevitable fate of an anachronistic world view: as its advocates grew more vocal, its impotence became more apparent.

In all of this, English and southern paternalism bore striking resemblances. With the added impetus of an emerging abolitionist movement, slaveholding paternalism by the nineteenth century had become both conservative and reactionary—it sought to preserve an older tradition, and it moved aggressively to bring southern society back to a patriarchal ideal. As an ideology of opposition it can be understood best by how it differed from the mainstream of slaveholding thought. Where most masters preached the ethos of individualism, paternalists adhered to an organic conception of a society bound by interdependent human relations and reciprocal obligations. Where most slaveholders believed in upward mobility and physical movement in pursuit of their goal of material advancement, paternalists preferred stasis and were appalled by the prevailing urge to move.

Most slaveholders accepted social equality and political democracy as mainstays of southern white society. But paternalists assumed humanity's inherent inequality and tended to be suspicious of, if not hostile to, democracy.

The anachronistic tone of slaveholding conservatism derived primarily from its colonial origins. Its political rhetoric was reminiscent of the seventeenth century. David Gavin, a South Carolina slaveholder, spoke favorably of "free" government but opposed "mob-o-cratic" rule and supported property restrictions on the franchise. "Times are sadly different now to what they were when I was a boy," he wrote. There were "few popular elections" then, and the *"Sovereign* people, alias mob" did not rule. Alfred Huger was another nineteenth-century slaveholder with a seventeenth-century mind. He was more concerned with "liberty" and "freedom" than with equality and democracy. Huger was as deeply loyal to the United States as to the principles of aristocracy, for although America tended to be too democratic for him, it was the freest nation in the world.[2]

Paternalists stood with the slaveholding majority in their embrace of the free-market economy and of white supremacist values, and in this they rendered paternalism useless as a description of slavery itself. They had always insisted that paternalism tied the master and slave together so closely that the dehumanization of the free labor system was avoided in the master-slave relationship. Yet it was the racial basis of slavery, coupled with the bondsman's dual function as laborer and capital asset within a commercial market economy, that tended to dehumanize slaves. Paternalism could not alleviate these tendencies.

Thus, even as articulated by its most persuasive spokesmen, slaveholding paternalism carried no implications of especially kind treatment of the slaves. The patriarchal ideal alone furnished a model of oppression capable of sustaining the rationalizations of the most inhumane master. The added burdens of racism and the profit motive only heightened paternalism's intrinsic cruelty. Benevolent masters were often motivated by religious, ideological, or pecuniary considerations that carried no necessary suggestion of paternalism. The "good master" need not have adhered to the paternalistic ideology, just as the paternalist need not have been a benevolent master. Yet the point is not that paternalists were worse masters than most, but that, having accepted the racist assumptions and commercial structure of slavery, they were in practice no different.

If benevolence did not necessarily imply paternalism, neither did familial rhetoric. To a large extent, slaveholders who spoke of their black "family" were employing colloquial speech patterns that were common throughout antebellum America, for theirs was an age obsessed with the family. At a time when Americans were unusually sensitive to such issues, slaveholders were particularly stung by an abolitionist literature that stressed slavery's disruption of the black family. Indeed, the theme of familial disruption dominated the most influential antislavery novel of the period, *Uncle Tom's Cabin* by Harriet Beecher Stowe. If slaveholders responded by exaggerating the close, familylike atmosphere of the plantation, their defensiveness should not be mistaken for a genuinely paternalistic world view. Thus, one Virginia planter went so far as to distinguish the offspring he had fathered by his slave Rachel from his "legitimate" children. "I do not feel for these poor children the affection which a father should feel for his legitimate child," Benjamin Watkins explained, for although the slave's children were also his own, they were not "the fruit of his love & of his care, the object of his constant anxiety and attention, and the inheritor of his name & fortune." For the slaves in the master's "family" who were not related to their owners, there was even less affection.[3]

Reinforcing the racist ideology that cast blacks as "childlike" were structural forces that encouraged masters to assume a fatherly pose before their slave "children"—forces that, again, carried no necessary suggestion of paternalism. Because slaveholding was the life goal of ambitious white Southerners before the Civil War, the master class was composed of relatively old men. The average age of the slaveholder in 1850 was over forty-three years, a year older than the average life expectancy for Americans in general. By contrast, slavery encouraged reproduction among blacks while discouraging their longevity. With an average life expectancy of less than forty years, most slaves were dead before they reached the age of the average master. The majority of slaves were children eighteen years of age or under. Demographically, therefore, the most common master-slave relationship was between a middle-aged white man and a black child. If slaveholders spoke of their bondsmen as children, we need go no further than population statistics and racist assumptions for an explanation.[4]

Nevertheless, paternalism was an articulate ideology in the antebellum South. It persisted most strongly among three small groups of masters whose political and social traditions were, in significant ways, distinct from the typical patterns of slaveholding: those reared under the influence of the military; those born in the Northeast and influenced by federalism; and some of those in the oldest areas of settlement around the South's perimeter. Paternalism served the needs of this small but vocal minority of masters whose sense of isolation was soothed only by their pride in the patriarchal ideal. Ultimately these masters of tradition were united not so much by similar historical circumstances—for some were wealthy planters from old southern families while others were northern-born entrepreneurs—as by their traditional, conservative world view.

The great irony is that, whether they were the objects of derision or were themselves the critics of southern society, paternalistic slaveholders were increasingly alienated from the world they are widely thought to have represented in its ideal form. In fact, the sense of displacement stands out as the most dramatic theme in the biographies of conservative slaveholders. Deeply interested in antebellum politics, they were disgusted by its democratic excesses. Fiercely devoted to America, many openly rejected Jeffersonian liberalism. Intensely religious, they were often repelled by evangelical Protestantism. And the more they felt themselves rejected by their fellow Southerners, the more strident they became, for theirs was a dying philosophy, not an emerging one.

THE BACKGROUNDS and circumstances of paternalistic masters indicate that conservatism derived less from the material imperatives of the plantation than from specific historical traditions originally unrelated to slavery. The first slaveholding tradition that sustained paternalism most effectively grew out of a pattern of settlement that was established in the colonial era. Before 1800 a unique slaveholding culture had coalesced in the oldest and wealthiest sections of the South. This culture was most evident in the perimeter that extended down the Atlantic Coast, across the Gulf Coast and up the Mississippi River. The English traveler James Silk Buckingham recognized this region's distinctiveness in a series of unconnected observations. Though offended by the lowly habits of most slaveholders, Buckingham found the "manners and customs" of Charleston and Savannah more "polished" and "hospitable" than those of the inland town of Augusta. In the Gulf Coast port of Mobile "the higher orders partake much of the hospitality and elegance of Charleston and Savannah." Likewise "in New Orleans and other places on the banks of the Mississippi, the sugar and cotton planters live in splendid edifices, and enjoy all the luxury that wealth can impart." At inland towns like Attakapas and Opelousas, Buckingham noted, "the glare of expensive luxury vanishes."[5]

The slaveholders in this perimeter were set off from the majority of masters not simply by their extraordinary wealth but by the physical and social stability that wealth produced. To a large extent this was because they grew crops that were consistently profitable and could not be grown elsewhere: rice in the South Carolina lowlands, sea-island cotton off the Georgia coast, sugar in southern Louisiana. Or else they held the most fertile land, along the James River in Virginia or around Natchez, which grew the best crops in soil that was continually and naturally replenished. The outstanding wealth of these regions allowed many slaveholding families to pass their holdings from one generation to the next, shielding them from the disruptive effects of the westward migration just as their distinctive crops protected them from the speculative instability of the cotton economy. Within this perimeter a conservative, paternalistic slaveholding ideology survived long after most masters, even those in the perimeter itself, had adopted the prevailing principles of political liberalism and free-market commercialism.

Settled by the end of the colonial period or shortly thereafter, many slaveholders in these unusually stable regions managed to retain much of the traditional emphasis on social stratification that was inherited from the slaveholders' seventeenth-century forbears. As "King Cotton" assumed its near-monarchical domination of the antebellum economy, this traditional slaveholding culture became, for all its wealth and pretensions, increasingly isolated and exclusive. Yet its proximity to urban centers and its alliance with the southern intelligentsia helped produce a powerful consciousness of class and a volume of conservative rhetoric that far exceeded its representativeness. Because paternalists were most prominent at the major points of entrance into the South, observers often came away with a deceptive sense of conservative predominance.

The South's perimeter was not, however, the exclusive domain of slaveholding paternalists. Even in the wealthiest plantation districts, small slaveholders who did not share the conservative ethos lived in close proximity to the wealthy planters, most of whom were not paternalistic anyway. Nor were conservatives absent from the interior regions of the cotton belt. There were paternalistic masters in the Upper South states of Kentucky and Tennessee and in the frontier regions of Texas. But if they were not reared in the traditional culture of the South's perimeter, their paternalism most likely derived from a northeastern federalist heritage or a strong military background.

The persistence of conservative values was often distinct in slaveholding families with ancestors who fought in the Revolutionary War. Isaac Guion, a Mississippi planter and graduate of West Point, encouraged his sons to follow him in a military career. His strictures emphasized not so much prudence and hard work as "Virtue, honor and honest fame." George Washington Sargent, son of a Revolutionary War hero, inherited a great estate and became territorial governor of Mississippi. But he was deeply disturbed by the democratic course of southern politics and was strongly opposed to secession.[6] Like Isaac Guion, Sargent paid unusually close attention to the careers of his sons; both fathers openly encouraged the maintenance of deferential relations between elder and younger siblings, and both made their homes at the wealthiest point on the southern perimeter, Natchez. Thus the military mind, hierarchical by nature, became indistinguishable from the paternalistic mentality of the conservative slaveholder.

The ranks of conservatives in the southern perimeter and from military families were enhanced by a third group of paternalistic masters and proslavery writers who were northern-born. Many of them traced their ideological roots to northeastern federalism. Born in New York City, John G. Winter moved to the South to pursue his mercantile business and eventually settled in Columbus, Georgia, having become a wealthy slaveholder. Thoroughly disgusted with political democracy, Winter lashed out at "the People" and their elected representatives, convinced that private property could never be protected under such anarchistic conditions. Elijah Fletcher was born in New England and trained as a teacher. But after moving south, he married a Virginia heiress, lived on a plantation near Lynchburg, and set up a newspaper. Appalled by the spread of Jacksonian Democracy, Fletcher devoted his publishing career to the advancement of Whig political principles.[7]

It was from this tradition that Henry Watson, Jr., received most of his ideas about the world around him. Watson was born in 1810 in the town of East Windsor, Connecticut, the eldest of Henry and Julia Watson's twelve children. After completing college in 1831, Henry Jr.'s health forced him to move to a more salubrious climate. He settled in Greensborough, Alabama, but found the job of teaching so unrewarding and unprofitable that in 1833 he returned to Connecticut to take a law degree. The following year, back in Greensborough, Watson settled down to the task of building a practice. But for him the law was merely a stepping stone to a more noble profession. "My ambition has been for years to be able to own a farm," he assured his father in 1839, "and whenever able to do so I shall resort to that business as a permanent pursuit. I think it is the *most reputable,* the *most* healthy and the *most* honest; in this country, with a sufficient capital, the most safe."[8] Taking advantage of the unstable economy of early Alabama, Watson collected his reserves and in the late 1830's began buying land and slaves. In 1845 he married and moved to his plantation. Within a year his farm was producing 124 bales of cotton annually. He continued to practice law, however, and in 1854 he formed the Planters Insurance Company with six partners, becoming its president in 1860.

Whatever else he was, Watson was no landed aristocrat carrying on a prestigious family tradition. Little in his biography distinguishes him from the pattern of the middle-class slaveholders who combined careers to reap their fortunes. Yet from the day he arrived in Alabama until the state seceded from the Union, Watson felt out of place in the South. Virtually everything about it annoyed him; he had not even wanted to leave Connecticut in the first place. "*I* was *driven* from home to this distant land by sheer, absolute necessity," he complained to his mother, more than a decade after his arrival in Alabama. "Emigration or starvation seemed the only alternative." He was put off by the unsettled ways of southern life. "Though many about me salute me with the endearing application of friend, my Northern habits & feelings do not permit me to acknowledge their claims upon so short an acquaintance." Long after having established a place for himself in Greensborough society, Watson told his father that "I am in a wilderness, cut off from all mankind, and dependant upon the kindness of others for information relative to all those I hold most dear."[9]

What is significant about Henry Watson's career is that despite its representativeness he felt profoundly alienated from the world around him and that the source of that alienation was the conservative ideology he carried with him from New England. Watson's world view was classically paternalistic. All his life he was impressed by wealth and status. He spoke of society in terms of the "high and low" orders. Though he served in local government offices and took an active interest in politics as a Whig and a Unionist, Watson was repelled by the "thorough going democratic notions" of Alabama cotton farmers. He was scandalized by the election of "ordinary" men to high office, writing at one point that "neither in the Senate or the House of Representatives at Washington have we a man but what disgraces us." He had yet to buy a single slave when he concluded that "the people in a state where *universal* suffrage is allowed are proverbially fickle." Above all others, he loathed Andrew Jackson.[10]

Watson was no less offended by the religious habits of his fellow Alabamians. "I myself am an Episcopalian and should wish that we might have a clergyman among us," he wrote in 1835. But after attending the state's Episcopal convention the year before he "could not give a very good account of the *Church* here. We could not get a quorum in the convention, and two parishes only were represented." Watson was forced to endure the evangelical services of the Baptists, Methodists, and Presbyterians, "all of them in the ranting, methodist, vulgar style, infinitely worse than *any* we ever heard at the East Windsor Baptist house."[11]

His traditionalism, his conservatism, his alienation from the mainstream of American life, were all products of a small-town New England upbringing, yet they served Watson well in his formulation of the paternalistic defense of slavery. "Most people here feel an attachment to their servants similar, in some respects, to that we feel for our children," Watson assured a northern friend in 1861. "We feed them, clothe them, nurse them when sick and in all things provide for them. How can we do this and not love them? They too feel an affection for their master, his wife and children, and they are proud of his and their successes. There seems to be a charm in the name of 'master'—they look upon and to their master with the same feeling that a child looks to his father. It is a lovely trait in them. This being the case, how can we fear them?"[12]

It was not alienation that led Henry Watson—and most conservative slaveholders—to a paternalistic defense of slavery. Rather, the sense of isolation was the inevitable fate of paternalistic masters in a society that had long since rejected their principles. So anachronistic were their ideals, even to the dominant slaveholding culture of the antebellum South, that it is necessary to reconstruct the ideological framework of paternalism, as it was understood by conservative slaveholders, before a true understanding of their alienation can be achieved.

Slaveholding paternalism was firmly grounded in the patriarchal family. While it was not at all unusual for slaveholding parents to take anxious interest in their children's careers, the concern of paternalistic parents was unusually intense, with subtle but significant differences of emphasis from that of most slaveholders. Where prudence and sobriety were normally encouraged as the pathway to success, material reward was not stressed heavily in conservative households. "Everything bends to the pursuit of the dollar where anyone can obtain social position by means of money," Samuel Walker, a Louisiana master, complained. "Where money can be so easily made, the citizen forgets his duty to his country in what he conceived to be his duty to himself and his children."[13]

Paternalistic parents saw their responsibilities differently. Justifying his concern with their education by explicitly invoking his patriarchal authority, Clement C. Clay encouraged his sons "to qualify themselves, by learning, to be useful to yourselves, and others; and, in the meantime, respectable in the world." The concern with respectability over material success was common; it passed from one generation of conservative slaveholders to the next in strict accordance with the rules of family and tradition. In the case of the Clays, that tradition was strong, for Clement's own father was no less interested in the progress of his grandchildren than he had been in his son's. "We congratulate you on the proficiency & progress our dear little grande Sons are making in their studies," William Clay informed Clement, "& sincerely hope that they will persevere & acquire that knowledge that will qualify them for the future duties and business of life, and do honor to our dust when we are no more."[14]

Thus, the distinguishing characteristics of the patriarchal slaveholding family included a deep respect for the wisdom of the elders, an entrenched concern with the family's image, an extraordinary interest in posterity manifested in a close attention to the rearing of children, particularly male children. Paternalistic fathers encouraged the maintenance of deference toward elders, be they grandparents, parents, or siblings. In keeping with their traditional devotion to the family, conservative parents also encouraged their children to maintain physical proximity to one another, if only to preserve the hierarchical relations. In 1851, for example, G. W. Sargent, a Natchez slaveholder, encouraged his son to stay close to his older brother and sister-in-law. "Love them and let them see it and by this means make them love you. Defer to their opinion, and when you can not agree try and be silent."[15]

The emphasis on honor and respectability within the context of a patriarchal family left the children of paternalists with a strong sense of obligation to their parents' legacy. Ten years after arriving in Alabama, Henry Watson assured his mother that his parents "have been solely in my thoughts since I left Connecticut. I have lived for them, thought I was accumulating property for them, and always thought of the comfort I could be to him & you & the family hereafter." William Withers was paying the highest compliment when he assured his nephew that because of his good education he "will one day repay his parents by the rank he will hold in society."[16]

Most of the legendary virtues of the planter aristocracy can be traced to the relations of the patriarchal family: the graciousness and hospitality born of the concern for a decent public image; the sense of honor arising from the emphasis on respectability; the subordination of materialism to the pursuit of virtue and the fulfillment of duty; the reticence implicit in the devotion to dignity; the privatism demanded by loyalty to family. These were the themes of the paternalistic ideal, principles grounded firmly in an institution so basic as the family that they imparted a tone of inevitability to the ideology of conservative slaveholders. For the paternalistic master, slaveholding was not simply a duty, it was a destiny. *"Gentleman,"* a Louisiana slaveholder observed by way of definition: "No education can make one of a man who is not a gent. at heart; for whether his station in life be that of a plow boy or an Earl, the gentleman, like the poet, is born and not made."[17]

The patriarchal family thus shielded conservative slaveholders from the outside world by reinforcing traditional values within the home. Yet, in its function as guardian of a dying tradition, the patriarchal family served ultimately to highlight and exaggerate the isolation of conservatives from the entrepreneurial slaveholding culture of the antebellum South. From the pens of paternalistic slaveholders came wildly unrealistic descriptions of the plantation as a haven of Edenic ease and regal abundance. "What can be more honorable employment for a Southern gentleman than occupation such as this?" Samuel Walker asked rhetorically. "All admit that a good and wise despotism is the wisest of earthly governments and why then are the slaveholders of the South caviled at by Monarch and by subject? . . . Let a Southern gentleman abide at home or let his absences be seldom and short. With his business, his library, his reviews from all parts of the earth, his crops and his garden, his fruits and his flowers and periodicals and proper idea of his responsibility to his God and he has within his grasp as near an approach to earthly contentment as is usually within the reach of mortal!"[18]

NOTHING SEPARATED the conservative master from the slaveholding mainstream more dramatically than the obsession with stability that arose in reaction to the apparently pointless mobility of the majority. Conservatives needed only to draw on the lessons of their own experience. Where the life history of most planters showed a pattern of steady accumulation, conservative slaveholders, like Dr. Louis M. DeSaussurre of Beaufort, South Carolina, often maintained a steady, albeit substantial, slave force over several decades. Because of the economic basis of their stability, conservative planters like Zephaniah Kingsley occasionally directed—with some assurance of success— that upon their death their slave families were not to be broken up. White children reared in this unusually stable environment were rarely encouraged to seek their fortunes on the frontier. If they left home, it was not usually by choice. When J. M. C. Breaker was offered a ministry in "my dear old native State" of South Carolina, he viewed as "highly satisfactory" the prospect of living in aristocratic Beaufort, close to his family, "near the seaboard, and among a people whose social characteristics are identical with my own." On a visit to his father's farm in North Carolina, David Witherspoon wrote that the "old Plantation looks quite natural. I feel as if I never wanted to leave it again & would not if I could stay."[19]

Endeared to stability, conservative slaveholders were reluctant to change. "I am so old, am so happy and contented, am so hard to please and fear that I might make my condition worse," a thirty-four-year-old master wrote, "that I shall hesitate long before I change it." For some conservatives, the slaveholders' penchant for movement defied explanation. On a trip across the Blue Ridge in 1827, Juliana Conner found "a great spirit of emigration and adventure" among the people. "So many of them have grants or claims of lands that [migration] becomes a matter of necessity or speculation," she noted. "I cannot conceive of its being *choice.*" These were the sentiments that informed the conservative assault on emigration that filled the pages of antebellum agricultural periodicals. "Every virtuous and patriotic citizen should feel himself bound to the soil which gave him birth, which has been the home of his father, and which contains the bones of his ancestors," one speaker told the Greenville, South Carolina, Agricultural Society. "This miserable, selfish, avaricious and dastardly spirit of emigration, not only paralyzes the energy of improvement of our country, but it destroys all local attachments and all love of country!"[20]

Conservative slaveholders felt no less out of place in their rejection of prevailing religious practices. If the violent freneticism of evangelical Protestantism satisfied the emotional needs of most slaveholders, the calm orthodoxy of the conservatives seemed equally appropriate to their own situation. Thus orthodox religious worship in the Old South corresponded with the perimeter that sustained the most entrenched conservatism. Nowhere in the southern states were Episcopal worshipers more concentrated than in the South Carolina lowcountry and in Chesapeake Maryland; nowhere were Roman Catholic churches more numerous than in southern Louisiana, and again in Chesapeake Maryland and the South Carolina lowcountry. In 1855, a slaveholder near Natchez wrote in his diary that the recent Methodist revival in the area "met with no success."[21]

Not surprisingly, conservative slaveholders seemed as concerned with the institutions of the church and the rituals of worship as they were with their actual religious convictions. While most slaveholding nonbelievers bemoaned their lack of faith, irreligious conservatives complained about " 'the Church, the Church!' by which they meant standing up and sitting down, & gowns & reading prayers out of books & a great observance of *form.*" While evangelicals spoke of their worthiness in accepting Christ, Sarah Guion, the Episcopal wife of a Natchez slaveholder, told her son not to "feel any scruples about not being worthy to become a christian; but remember it is your duty to do so."[22] Conservative slaveholders were scandalized by the vulgar enthusiasm of the camp meeting. They preferred the more hierarchical forms of religious practice, paralleling a social outlook that emphasized the duties and responsibilities of superiors and inferiors.

Distressed by demographic instability, unmoved by evangelical fervor, conservative slaveholders—with the possible exception of

those in South Carolina—were increasingly alienated from southern politics as well. For a social class bred to a sense of public duty,
the emerging irrelevance of conservative ideals frequently led to
embittered disillusionment. Edmund Ruffin typified this pattern. A
well-born Virginia planter now remembered as a great agricultural
reformer, Ruffin turned his attention to soil preservation in a stubborn determination to reverse the course of southern development.
Before his thirtieth birthday Ruffin had been elected to a four-year
term in the Virginia Senate. But he entered politics just as Jacksonian Democracy was beginning to transform popular conceptions
about the nature of representative government, and Ruffin was unwilling to change with the times. "I reached this position [in the
Senate] almost without seeking either public favor or any of its
reward and certainly without my using any electioneering arts,
which I always despised. . . . But I soon found that my views of
duty were very different from those usually acted upon by other
representatives." Unable to agree that politicians should be judged
by the electorate according to the positions they made known during a campaign, repelled by the idea that a representative's first duty
was to carry out the wishes of the constituents, Ruffin left politics
"tired and disgusted with being a servant of the people."[23]

Conservative slaveholders felt least uncomfortable among the
Whig nationalists, represented by Henry Clay. Long before the secession crisis, however, many of them had begun to assume the disdain-
ful attitude toward politics that was one of the hallmarks of the
English gentry they so admired. "Politicians consider men, pieces
upon a chess board," a Louisiana planter complained, "to be moved,
advanced, or sacrificed, as best suits their scheme." Samuel Walker
dismissed all United States congressmen as "a set of demagogues."
The pursuit of wealth, he complained, "has absorbed almost all the
better talent of the country . . . , and the unprincipled demagogue
whose life and time are valueless to himself, his family, this country,
packs the preliminary political meetings and drinks and sniggles
himself into office to the great disgrace of the land and injury of his
country's character." Indeed, Walker concluded, "it is to my mind
something derogatory to character to be known as a professed politician or an office holder."[24]

Disdain became anger in one Virginia planter who retained an affinity for the New England federalism of his upbringing. He violently denounced Andrew Jackson's northern supporters. "I am sorry to see any of the New England states worshipping Jackson," Elijah Fletcher wrote. "Such people are fit for nothing but slaves. If the northern states have not the sense to stick together and protect their own interest, they ought to suffer and they will." With the collapse of the Whig party in the 1850's, conservative slaveholders who remained politically active were increasingly drawn to third-party efforts based on nativism or unionism. In the 1856 elections, David Gavin saw no fundamental distinction between the major parties. "I do not consider the democratic candidate much better than the abolition candidate, nor his party," the disgruntled South Carolina slaveholder declared in his diary. The candidate and "his party do not advocate abolition openly, but many of them profess or pretend to be opposed to it, yet they advocate a doctrine which will lead to abolition if carried out."[25]

Edmund Ruffin's short-lived political career demonstrates that conservative hostility to democracy preceded the sectional crisis by decades. As early as 1823 a proslavery tract by Frederick Dalcho, a South Carolina minister, recommended that slaves be kept away from Fourth of July celebrations "lest they imbibe false notions of their personal rights and give reality in their minds to what has no real existence." In fact, conservative slaveholders never rejected the democratic tradition, because they never had one to reject. Their open hostility to democracy, which reached its climax in the 1850's, thus reflected the conservatives' nearly complete alienation from American and southern society—which many viewed as indistinguishable. "The theory of universal human freedom is the mad offspring of delusion and passion, and not the result of enlightened reason," a Florida slaveholder concluded. "Democracy abolished slavery in St. Domingo during the French Revolution in 1789," David Gavin declared. "It abolished slavery in the British West Indies in 1836 or about that time and has been gradually abolishing slavery in the U. States."[26]

Throughout the antebellum era the most conservative slaveholders demonstrated a persistent unwillingness to compromise their antipathy toward democracy for the sake of political expediency. As the gap between their presumed social status and their actual political influence widened, many stood firm or even hardened their convictions to the point of extreme reaction. Edmund Ruffin became convinced that Thomas Jefferson had been an abolitionist, "covertly & cunningly." Those conservatives who did not reject America's revolutionary legacy out of hand acted on the assumption that either the United States was an exception or else the Declaration of Independence was irrelevant, since human societies were only held together by organic rules of order. "I fear that other nations are being deluded by our success and will pay in tears of blood for the unhappy belief that a 'Declaration of Independence' can make a people free!" a South Carolina master concluded. Alfred Huger remained impressed that a society could survive in which "those who are Governed dictate those who govern! and yet the *Public* Peace is undisturbed and Private rights are not invaded!!" David Gavin was not so sanguine. On July 4, 1856, he refused to "rejoice for a freedom which allows every bankrupt, swindler, thief, and scoundrel, traitor and seller of his vote to be placed on an equality with myself."[27]

None of this anti-democratic rhetoric would have seemed out of place among the earliest settlers of the colonial South, for theirs was the ideal echoed by conservative slaveholders of the antebellum era. In eastern Virginia, in Charleston, South Carolina, and in Savannah, Georgia, haughty masters boasted of their age-old traditions. And rightly so. For whether their ancestral ties to the colonial elite were direct or not, the legacy of the seventeenth century was strong among those slaveholders who continued to view society as a complex organism in which reciprocal obligations defined the relations between the upper and lower classes. Antebellum conservatives struggled not to establish a new orthodoxy but to retrieve an old one.

CLASS CONSCIOUSNESS was nothing new to conservatives; it was one of their ancient hallmarks. Indeed, this was the ideological tradition that led Henry Watson, Jr., to look upon many of his Alabama neighbors with contempt. "The more recently settled the more crude and barbarous are the people," Watson declared. "The first settlers are always the offscourings of the community." Disdain for the lower classes, combined with their traditional nationalism, made conservative slaveholders particularly hostile to poor Irish immigrants. "Let Aliens and Papists rule the country awhile and we will see the consequences," David Gavin assured himself in a vituperative defense of the Know-Nothing Party. An Alabama slaveholder vowed never to rent his home to an Irishman. "I prefer it should *rot* down to being pulled to pieces and defiled."[28]

But if the conservatives' class consciousness intensified their hostility to poor immigrants, it also had the potential to soften the intense racism that characterized the slaveholding class in general. Because paternalistic masters accepted social inequality as inevitable, they sometimes felt less need to deny the humanity of their slaves. For them, blacks simply occupied the lowest stratum of a hierarchical social order. Ideally, slaves fulfilled their reciprocal obligations and so benefitted from the paternalistic affection of a benevolent master. When the Connecticut legislature banned unlicensed private schools in a deliberate effort to prevent the education of blacks, Henry Watson, Jr., objected to the law as "unconstitutional . . . cruel and unjust." Fifteen years later, as an Alabama planter, Watson spoke of his slaves with unusual affection while he was away on a trip. "I find that I care more for them than I was aware and look upon them as an important and interesting portion of our family."[29]

Few conservatives carried the logic of their class perspective further than did Zephaniah Kingsley, a Florida planter. He believed that while whites were unfit to work in hot climates, that did not make them superior to blacks. Under a "just and prudent system of management," Kingsley argued, blacks "are not naturally desirous of change but are sober, discreet, honest and obliging, are less troublesome, and possess a much better moral character than the ordinary class of corrupted whites of similar condition." Kingsley was so convinced that race should play no part in the justification of slavery that he recommended that free black Southerners be permitted to vote and be admitted with full rights and privileges to southern society. Thus slavery would be shown to be patriarchal rather than racial. To speed up the process, Kingsley espoused widespread miscegenation. "The intermediate grades of color are not only healthy, but when condition is favorable, they improve in shape, strength and beauty, & are susceptible of every amelioration. Daily experience shows that there is no natural antipathy between the castes on account of color," the slaveholder concluded, "and it only requires to repeal laws as impolitic as they are unjust and unnatural." Kingsley personally advanced his own ideals by fathering children by his slaves.[30]

If this was the tendency of paternalistic theory, Kingsley's very unorthodoxy suggests how far his conclusions strayed from most conservative slaveholders' practices. "To accomplish these objects," he wrote, "will require a considerable sacrifice of local prejudice to the shrine of self-interest." His own frustration with the prevailing racism of the South was revealed in his last will and testament. There he asked that his mulatto children be taken to "some land of liberty and equal rights where the conditions of society are governed by some law less absurd than that of color." In fact, racism was so much a part of the southern tradition that even the most paternalistic slaveholders rarely rejected it completely. If racism was less virulent in conservative rhetoric, it was by no means absent. In his most generous moments, Edmund Ruffin "would not deny the possibility of one negro in a hundred thousand cases being capable of receiving a college education, & being competent to write a commonplace address." Like most conservative slaveholders, Ruffin believed that "the negro will not work, nor take care for his support, unless when compelled by a master of the white race."[31]

Thus there was really no significant repudiation of racism among conservative slaveholders. At most they denied the relevance of race to their justification of a stratified social order, thereby reinforcing the distinction between their own world view and that of most slaveholders. It was in this context of profound isolation that conservative masters and southern intellectuals joined to produce a paternalistic defense of bondage. Yet in its pervasive theme of alienation, the conservative proslavery ideology exposed its own distance from the thinking of the slaveholding class at large.

CONSERVATIVES SPENT relatively little time outlining the basics of the paternalistic system and extolling its virtues. Instead they concentrated on criticism of the theoretical foundations of free society, for they all agreed that the roots of social upheaval in the nineteenth century were planted in the preceding age of democratic revolution. George Fitzhugh's "chief object," for example, was not to write an abstract defense of slavery so much as a general critique of free society. When Chancellor Harper considered the proposition that "all men are born free and equal," he wondered whether it was not "nearer the truth to say, that no man was ever born free, and that no two men were ever born equal?" Another ideologue insisted that Thomas Jefferson's "doctrine of [equality] . . . is the dream of an enthusiast or visionary, and was never intended for a practical principle in government."[32] Thus conservatives began their defense of slavery with assumptions far different from those of most slaveholders.

For Fitzhugh, the rejection of democracy and equality necessarily entailed the repudiation of free trade as well, but few conservatives agreed. After all, the hierarchical ideal was never entirely antithetical to the principles of the marketplace. Nor were paternalists in Britain concerned any longer with distinguishing themselves from the rising capitalist class. Thus Edmund Ruffin dismissed Fitzhugh's logic out of hand. Though he rejected the doctrine of human equality, Chancellor Harper believed that "every one should be left at liberty to obtain all the advantages of society which he can by the free exertion of his faculties, unimpeded by civil restraints." Others went so far as to defend the South's unique form of capitalism. "We are the only capitalists whose system embraces humanity to the laborer consistently with economy of investment," William C. Daniel argued. In a speech to the Alabama State Agricultural Association, Henry W. Hilliard explained that "with us there is a Union between capital and labor, and there is much less friction in the working of a social system."[33] Conservative proslavery rhetoric thus consisted of a series of propositions establishing the differences between free and slave society, but within the context of a capitalist economy.

Despite efforts to be distinct, however, conservatives drew heavily on one of the most common prejudices in the Old South, the distrust of Great Britain. British paternalists only served to reinforce the conservative slaveholders' prejudices, for English conservatives made constant complaint about their society's failure to behave according to paternalistic principles. Because conservative slaveholders were as nationalistic as they were anti-democratic, they were more than usually concerned to separate free society in the Old World—particularly England—from that of the antebellum North. As their patience with abolitionism waned, the bounds of restraint were occasionally broken. In 1859, a writer for *Cotton Planter and Soil of the South* asked if a system of free labor would not be more suited to the slaveholders' needs. "Let England answer! let the North answer!" the pundit proclaimed. "They have *cheap labor* there, and a half-starved, half-clad, vicious, pick-pocket, degraded population are some of the legitimate fruits."[34]

For the most part, however, the "free society" that was the nemesis of slaveholding conservatives was strictly European. "The little experiment of universal liberty that has been tried for a little while in a little corner of Europe, has resulted in disastrous and appalling failure," George Fitzhugh declared. When he considered "the condition of the laborious poor" in England, Ireland, France, and Germany, one writer found that "They earn hardly coarse food, wretched clothing and lodging; and little indeed remains of their wages to bring up their children, or to maintain themselves in sickness, in age or when out of work." But it was England that proslavery writers most commonly used to contrast the free and slave labor systems. In his "Memoirs on Slavery," Chancellor Harper extolled the benefits of bondage as a social system, comparing it favorably with the poverty that was rampant in England under the Poor Laws. It was not paternalism's "mutual love and good will and spirit of mutual protection, binding southern masters and slaves together, that keeps English *freemen* in submission to a system inconceivably worse than any system of negro slavery in the United States," another writer claimed. "It is want, absolute want, and perfect inability to escape from it." Under the circumstances, conservative slaveholders were especially galled by English leadership in the abolition movement. "There never was more unblushing hypocrisy than in this pretense," Edmund Ruffin declared.[35]

The antebellum North did not lack its own social critics to provide conservative Southerners with the same evidence of social decay that they drew from English reformers. But rather than reiterate the critiques of Northerners, conservative ideologues instead pointed to the mere existence of northern reformers as evidence of the weakness of free society. In effect, proslavery intellectuals defended the North against its own critics. Conservative intellectuals thus felt compelled to construct a theoretical justification for their refusal to repudiate free society in the North.

Many conservatives declared America a great exception to the iron laws of political economy. Alfred Huger feared the "spirit of democracy" in both England and America would be artificially sustained "for ages" owing to the "cheapness of land and the facility of earning property" in a society where taxpayers "control the developments." While they disagreed on how long the exceptional American democracy could survive, most conservatives at least acknowledged its existence. "As long as there is an outlet for the excess of population; as now in this country," Ruffin argued, "all the evils of the corruption of 'free labor'" would be avoided. In 1859, Ruffin asserted that those evils would be manifest "hereafter, in our northern states," but in the same year George Fitzhugh saw continued hope. Responding to a critic who had misread Fitzhugh's book, *Cannibals All!*, wrongly attributing to the author the desire to enslave poor white Northerners as well as blacks, Fitzhugh reiterated his position by quoting himself: "The social forms of the North and South are each excellent, and should not be changed or tampered with. The social condition of the South is normal, natural, historical, and biblical; that of the North exceptional, but admirably adapted to a new country where lands are cheap and abundant, population sparse, capital but little power to tyrannize over labor, and wages good. And that until the continent is densely peopled, which may never occur, this free and *exceptional* form of society will answer well."[36]

Fitzhugh and other proslavery conservatives did draw invidious distinctions between the North and South, but they criticized the former less for its oppression of free laborers than for nurturing fanaticism. "Strange to tell," Fitzhugh wrote, "in the free states of America too, Socialism and every other heresy that can be invoked to make war on existing institutions, prevail to an alarming extent." Because subversive ideas were said to arise from the miseries of free society—miseries that Fitzhugh claimed did not exist in the North —he acknowledged that "even according to our own theory" the prevalence of "isms" outside the South was difficult to explain. Nevertheless, he found no shortage of dreadful tendencies in the free states, among them "anarchy," "infidelity," and "wife-murder, [which] has become a mere holiday pastime" among northern husbands. The women's movement came under sharp attack by the patriarchs of the Old South, among whom the cult of masculinity was especially influential. Paternalistic masters professed to be shocked by "the grossness of dissipated intercourse." David Gavin was so fearful of "libertinism" that he "sternly condemned all sexual intercourse" until, in his mid-forties, he decided he had made a mistake in remaining celibate for so long. Traditional sexual mores thus account in large part for the repeated conservative attacks on alleged northern "Freelovism . . . , Incest . . . , and Polygamy," which Fitzhugh fit into his general critique of free society. "Women fare worst when thrown into this warfare of competition," he wrote. "The delicacy of her sex and her nature prevents her exercising those coarse arts which men do in the vulgar and promiscuous jostle of life."[37]

Whatever else these arguments came to, they did not amount to an abstract defense of slavery. Although their paternalistic ideals provided conservatives with the materials for such an argument, their equally traditional devotion to America prevented them from rejecting northern society in general. Having repudiated the suggestion that all poor people in America ought to be enslaved, conservatives argued instead that slavery, as practiced in the South, represented the fulfillment of destiny and their acquiescence in it. "Destiny is a hard taskmaster, even when quietly and philosophically obeyed," a South Carolina planter assured his daughter, "but when resisted and denounced it becomes a Tyrant that tramples under foot." Shall we turn the slave "loose upon the desert sands to root there for a living?" one proslavery writer asked. "No! our destiny is linked with his. . . . Bound are we to him, and wisdom should teach us not to cut him loose."[38]

Yet this position tended to contradict the conservative distaste for the principles of higher law. Fitzhugh had compellingly argued that "no two men are agreed as to what the higher law, alias 'fundamental principles,' is."[39] The problem with "destiny" was really no different: How does one decide who is destined to rule and who to submit? In need of a better argument, conservatives finally resorted to racism.

Convinced of the superiority of a stratified social order but unwilling to propose the enslavement of lower-class whites, conservatives resisted the logic of paternalism and argued instead for the specific enslavement of blacks on the basis of white supremacy. It is not surprising, therefore, that conservative slaveholders rarely repudiated racist dogma. The writings of the proslavery ideologues are littered with crude racial stereotypes depicting blacks as bumbling, docile, "with that broad grin of greasy delight which now spreads his teeth from ear to ear." The same antebellum publications that featured the arguments of proslavery conservatives also printed articles by the Old South's most popular racialist, Dr. Samuel Cartwright. All of the doctor's works were directed toward proving "that the Negro is under different physiological laws from the white man," and that therefore "domestic slavery is not a blot or excrescence" upon southern institutions "but a component part of their structure."[40]

The conservatives' inability to resolve the conflict between their class and race perspectives is revealed most clearly in the rambling, cranky, but nonetheless paternalistic theories of George Fitzhugh. He professed to "abhor the doctrine of the 'Types of Mankind'; first because it is at war with scripture . . . and, secondly, because it encourages and incites brutal masters to treat negroes . . . as wicked beasts, without the pale of humanity." Yet, as the writings of countless proslavery apologists demonstrated, the rejection of the theory that blacks were a different "type" of human never implied a corresponding rejection of the idea that blacks were inferior. Thus, Fitzhugh declared again and again that blacks were "weak . . . , ignorant . . . , improvident . . . , wholly unequal to whites." A few short pages before he revealed his abhorrence of racial typing, Fitzhugh flatly declared that "the negro race is inferior to the white race." In fact, Fitzhugh could not repudiate his racist convictions, for his entire thesis rested on their validity.[41]

In George Fitzhugh's ideal America, only blacks were to be

enslaved, and their condition would proceed directly from their alleged inferiority. He realized that this reasoning conflicted with the abstract defense of slavery. "As a general and abstract question, negro slavery has no other claims over other forms of slavery, except that from inferiority, or rather peculiarity, of race, almost all negroes require masters, whilst only the children, the women, the very weak, poor, and ignorant, &c., among the whites need some protective and governing relation of this kind." The patriarchal family already provided for the "protective governing" of white women and children. As for the rest, "Educate all Southern whites," Fitzhugh urged, "employ them, not as cooks, lacqueys, ploughmen, and menials, but as independent freemen should be employed, and let negroes be strictly tied down to such callings as are unbecoming white men."[42]

At times Fitzhugh seemed annoyed by the distorting effect racism had on paternalistic ideology, but he freely acknowledged that as long as whites in America remained equal—as he believed they were —and as long as blacks were inferior, or racially "peculiar," which he also believed, there could be no popularly accepted abstract defense of southern slavery. Black inferiority had led the South "to defend negro slavery as an exceptional institution," Fitzhugh wrote, "admitting, nay asserting, that slavery, in the general or in the abstract, is morally wrong, and against common right."[43] In addition, Fitzhugh admitted that as long as slavery functioned within the free market, capitalism would stretch its influence from the far corners of the Western world down into "every recess of domestic life." In all of this, Fitzhugh was conceding more than he would have liked: that the material conditions and racial values of most slaveholders rendered paternalism irrelevant to their needs.

Conservative ideology was forever revealing its own unpopularity by contrasting itself with the thinking of the masses. For every Fitzhugh who announced the failure of free society there were innumerable southern critics who dismissed such remarks as "a great deal of twaddle." Intellectually oriented slaveholders frequently complained that the "current taste is . . . physically utilitarian" rather than philosophically abstract. "I find that all people in the country are something of practical engineers," Samuel Walker confided in his diary. So concerned were his neighbors with making money, the

Louisiana planter complained, that they could "recite from memory . . . like a talking field book" long lists of statistics on land and slave holdings. They had amassed a great deal of wealth, the planter conceded, but "they seem to be mean, utterly ignorant [of] how to use it. Thinking that the great object in life is to add to it," slaveholders deprive themselves "of any accessory which can render fortune valuable." In reviewing a biography of Thomas Jefferson, one southern conservative lamented the third president's "extensive and continued control over the popular mind. His opinions have gradually pervaded every corner of the Republic. The universal democracy, unrestrained by class, orders, customs or usage, is the work of his hands. Whether it be for good or evil, his influence has shaped or modified the existing polity of the United States."[44] If conservatives rejected America's revolutionary legacy or its traditionaly materialistic individualism, their complaint was that most slaveholders would not reject them as well.

Conservative proslavery intellectuals sensed this isolation more acutely than most. "I have never known what was cordial sympathy in any of my pursuits among men," William Gilmore Simms complained. "I have been an exile from my birth." Similarly, George Frederick Holmes described himself as "an alien on a desert shore." Nathaniel Tucker suggested that Robinson Crusoe had been "hardly more completely isolated than I." Such laments accord with the general sense of displacement among conservative slaveholders.[45] Indeed, the alienation of the proslavery intellectuals would be of no historical consequence were their writings not so commonly mistaken for the mainstream of slaveholding thought.

THE CONSERVATIVE PROSLAVERY DEFENSE embraced the paternalist's conviction that the principles that held together the traditional family could be profitably applied to the relations of master and slave. "A patriarchal feeling of affection is due to every slave from his owner, who should consider the slave as a member of his family, whose happiness and protection is identified with that of his own family, of which his slave constitutes a part," a Florida planter argued. "This affection creates confidence which becomes reciprocal," he added, "and is attended with the most beneficial consequences to both. It is certainly humiliating to a proud master to reflect that he depends on his slave even for bread to eat. But such is the fact." For conservatives like George Fitzhugh, "Slavery without domestic affection would be a curse, and so would marriage and parental authority."[46]

In their reactions to the realities of slavery, however, conservatives revealed how far the paternalistic vision strayed from everyday practices. "Our people do not live right," a Georgia master complained. "In granting us the inestimable boon of African slavery, the Almighty has coupled with it a responsibility that is too much overlooked by slaveholders. It is not enough, to exercise one's intellect in the law, medicine or merchandise, until the means are acquired, then to purchase lands and negroes, to be managed by an overseer, away off yonder, whilst the dronish proprietor vegetates *in town* upon the proceeds of their labor. This is not meeting the responsibility." The Georgian was not simply attacking the prevailing practices of middle-class slaveholders. He was admitting that paternalism had broken down in the market culture of the slaveholding majority. "The reciprocal duty of *protecting* those who owe us *obedience* cannot be complied with under these circumstances," the writer continued. "This practice cannot strengthen 'the institution.' It is no pro-slavery argument. It removes it too far, from the patriarchal idea."[47]

But the patriarchal "idea" may have left conservative slaveholders less equipped than most to deal with the realities of bondage. The master-slave relationship had rarely exhibited the mutual interdependence of reciprocal obligations that paternalists cited in their defense. A volatile personality could rupture all feelings of paternal affection; the exigencies of the market consistently prevailed over human relations; racism poisoned the atmosphere of the plantation, and the slaves demonstrated a clear and consistent capacity for separating whatever feelings of affection they had for a good master from their overriding hostility to slavery in general.

In structure and practice, slavery allowed only limited room for the intrusion of personal feelings into the master-slave relationship, and such feelings were not invariably benevolent. But paternalistic masters believed otherwise, and so were most perplexed by rebellious bondsmen. When a runaway slave returned to Alfred Huger's South

Carolina plantation, the master protested that the slave's behavior was "without a shade of provocation that I know of. I never said an unkind word to her in my life—until this morning—& she has never swept a chamber or turned down a bed for me, without being doubly or trebly paid." But the slave was no less intransigent upon her return. "She seems to be entirely ignorant that there is any difference between her grade and mine," the master complained. Edmund Ruffin also found it difficult to believe that slaves could be rebellious. He was convinced, along with many others, that "negro plots" could only be the work of "northern agents of mischief." Only after repeated cases of arson on nearby plantations would Ruffin entertain the possibility that the slaves were responsible. He considered the mere fact of such behavior "worse than the pecuniary loss by fire."[48]

But there was little reason for a slave to submit to a paternalistic master any more than to a typical master, and of all proslavery ideologues, Edmund Ruffin should have understood why. For despite the wealth and stability of many of the plantations owned by conservative masters, Ruffin correctly insisted that the chief goal of all slaveholders was profit. "I do not think that in any country, unless for transient times, & peculiar conditions, free labor is so cheap as slave labor," he wrote. The suggestions that masters free themselves from the burdensome expense of slaveholding by shipping American blacks to Liberia struck Ruffin as "absurd," an act of "mere benevolence . . . and disputed expediency." As the Virginia planter acknowledged, even paternalistic masters were motivated by material considerations. When Henry Watson, Jr., who spoke so affectionately of his slaves, purchased a black nurse for his child, he callously announced his intention to "dispense with her however as soon as the child gets old enough to go about." G. W. Sargent, the Natchez planter who repeatedly stressed to his sons the virtues of duty and honor, nevertheless spoke proudly of his slaves' reproductive capacities. "In a few years if the Women go on as they have we shall have a fine lot of children," he wrote.[49] Conservatives could not logically endorse the capitalistic framework and racist assumptions of slavery and argue at the same time that paternalism somehow made a difference to the slaves.

Even if most of the great plantations of southern legend were indeed ruled by paternalistic masters, the slaves would not have been affected in most cases. The townhouses that to this day grace the narrow streets of Charleston's battery, the elegant residences of New Orleans's Garden District, the surviving antebellum homes of Savannah and Natchez, stand as testimony to a great tradition of absentee proprietorship among the Old South's wealthiest citizens. Paternalists were often better able than most slaveholders to leave their bondsmen in the care of overseers. Thus fatherly affection made little difference to the slaves owned by Clement C. Clay, who prided himself on his patriarchal dignity. "I was at the plantation last saturday and the crop was in fine order," Clay's son wrote in 1832, "but the negroes are most brutally scarred & several have run off."[50]

PATERNALISTIC MASTERS were the South's most vocal unionists. The continuity between the Southern Whigs of the 1830's and the Constitutional Unionists of the late 1850's was provided by the sustained allegiance of conservative slaveholders. An underlying philosophical consistency marked conservative Whigs, despite their party's superficially erratic stance on many issues. From the very beginning, the Whig Party merged the nationalist's faith in American progress with the conservative's disdain for excessive democracy. Paternalistic masters who accepted the capitalistic economy while resisting the trend toward democratization were among the party's logical constituents. In the late 1850's the Constitutional Unionists based their opposition to secession on traditionally Whig principles: nationalism to defend the Union, anti-democracy to attack secession.[51]

No single event so exposed the ideological divisions within the slaveholding class as did the secession crisis. Slaveholders had never disagreed among themselves about the threat of northern antislavery sentiment. But conservatives viewed the threat differently from others. A Florida planter believed that abolitionism would destroy the paternalistic relationship of master and slave by breaking the "tie of sympathy and kindness" between them. "Let the attempt to incite insurrection in the South be placed on the same footing with maliciously casting a fire brand into a neighbor's dwelling," Robert Reid declared in 1835, "and let him that is guilty of such offense be punished with perpetual imprisonment." Yet Reid reacted harshly to those who would have the South separate from the North in retaliation. "No, no—let us cling together and preserve the Union. Let us so manage it as to put down the Abolitionists . . . rather than the Union be endangered for a single moment." In 1850, when some politicians called for a convention of the southern states at Nashville, a conservative slaveholder denounced the move as "revolutionary in its tendency. I most solemnly protest against it."[52] By 1850 the pattern was set. Conservative masters distinguished themselves from the slaveholding majority by using all of their traditional arguments to denounce the secessionist impulse and, in one last futile effort, to restrain the South from blustering its way into a suicidal war.

Conservatives were not optimistic. "It is dreadful to me to think of it," a Natchez planter wrote in late 1860, "but so sure as you and I live, in less than six Months we shall have two Governments here each bitterly antagonistic to the other." The breakdown of American society's organic unity—the source of conservative nationalism—was particularly distressing to paternalistic masters. An Alabama planter believed that the *"people* of the two sections cannot be made to understand each other. I much fear that the days of the union are numbered."[53]

As the crisis of the Union approached, conservative slaveholders called up their traditional patriotism. "My soul is afflicted with anxiety for the country," one Virginian proclaimed. "The bonds of the American Union, the work of Washington, of Franklin, of Madison, and other great sages and statesmen of a glorious age, have been rent and snapped like cobwebs," Richard Keith Call declared, "and the greatest fabric of human government . . . has been destroyed in a few months—madly and rashly destroyed." Robert E. Lee agreed. "The framers of our Constitution never exhausted so much labour, wisdom & forbearance in its formation & surrounded it with so many guards & securities, if it was intended to be broken by every member of the confederacy at will."[54]

Conservative opposition to secession was motivated as much by hostility to democracy as by patriotism. Many viewed the sectional crisis as the logical outcome of democratic government. To John G. Winter, a Georgia master, "the theory that man is smart enough to govern himself has culminated in a most stupendous and magnificent humbug." Democracy was a "delusion," Winter declared, leading to the "diabolical heresy of Secession." Another Georgian wrote that he was "one of the few who ever dared to think that Republicanism was a failure from its inception. . . . I have never wished to see this Union disrupted, but if it must be, then I raise my voice for a return to a Constitutional monarchy."[55]

Like many conservative slaveholders, H. C. Anderson held popularly elected representatives, northern and southern, responsible for the crisis. "There is a class of men in the south, ambitious to set up a separate government or Confederacy they call it. These men are backed by the fanatical abolition party of the north (but for a different object) [and] are doing all they can to dissolve this Union." To Edward Taylor, it was "sad [that] such a 'Union' should be victimized by traitors and trading politicians of the North and the South." John Winter dismissed all politicians as "the hangers on of the public teat . . . [who] excited my most intense disgust." He was no less offended by the "folly of the People in allowing themselves to be deluded by the base rebels."[56]

As the prospect of secession became certain, the conservatives reacted caustically to its revolutionary implications. Both the southern secessionists and the northern Republicans were working for the "*overthrow* of the government," H. C. Anderson complained. Not surprisingly, conservatives were strongest in their denunciation of "the people," whom they often held responsible for the success of the secession movement. "The feelings of even the most moderate here are above bloodheat," a Mississippi planter wrote privately, "and a majority at the boiling point."[57]

There was a pervasive sense among conservatives that they were being overwhelmed by the popular will. In a series of letters in 1860, Henry Watson, Jr., declared that "the people are almost to a man for secession. . . . They do not realize the consequence of the changes." Anti-secessionists in Georgia were equally virulent. "The people [are] mad, drunken, and crazy," one of them declared. "Lawlessness runs riot, liberty is but another name for licentiousness, and patriotism is swallowed up in partyism." In Virginia "madness, literal frenzy seems to me to possess our Countrymen." Thus Robert E. Lee was not alone when he told his son that "Secession is nothing but revolution," and likened it to anarchy. Henry Watson, Jr., likewise feared that "we are on the verge of dissolution and anarchy." William J. Minor, who lived in Natchez and owned three sugar plantations in Louisiana, thought in 1856 that secession was "perfect madness." He opposed it four years later, "apprehensive it would lead to war and war to emancipation." Even before the 1860 presidential election the slaves on G. W. Sargent's Mississippi plantation were "prophesying freedom for themselves," the frightened planter wrote his son. In the wake of Lincoln's election, H. C. Anderson wrote that "the negroes are expecting to be made free & they are not far from being right about it."[58]

Not all conservative slaveholders opposed secession. For Edmund Ruffin, it was the fulfilment of a lifelong dream. But like George Fitzhugh's rejection of capitalism, or Zephaniah Kingsley's advocacy of miscegenation, or David Gavin's self-imposed celibacy, Ruffin's zealous hatred of the Union was but another personal idiosyncrasy in a group that seemed to attract a disproportionate share of the Old South's misfits. For the overwhelming majority of southern conservatives, secession symbolized all that had gone wrong with America and with the South in the preceding generations. Gentility had given way to crass materialism; paternalist ideology was distorted by racism; the rule of the elite succumbed to the age of the "common man"; a stable slaveholding culture was displaced by a mobile one. With their political base seriously eroded, conservatives tried desperately to stem the tide of revolution. "The most that the most staunch Union man can now do," Henry Watson, Jr., wrote, "with any hope of doing the least good, is to advise delay till a sufficiency of the states may agree to secede together to make the new government a respectable one."[59] This was the "cooperationist" position, and it was the one conservative slaveholders adopted all across the Deep South in their efforts to restrain the most anarchistic tendencies of the secessionist revolution.

It was the conservatives' final and most humiliating defeat. Cooperationist resolutions were submitted to the secession conventions across the Deep South, and every one was easily defeated. Faced with the fact of secession, conservatives could do nothing more than submit. "What the result is to be God only knows," G. W. Sargent lamented, "but I shall go with my section of the Country." A Union "that can only be maintained by swords and bayonets, & in which strife and civil war are to take the place of brotherly love & kindness, has no charm for me," Robert E. Lee wrote. "I shall mourn for my country, & for the welfare and progress of mankind."[60]

Epilogue

~

The Slaveholders'
Revolution

TIMELESS STABILITY never really characterized the slaveholding experience in America. The remarkable expansion of the slave South provided continuing evidence of the vitality of the master class. From its confused and uncertain beginnings in a small settlement in eastern Virginia, slaveholding society spread to cover a million square miles of the North American continent. The twenty blacks of ambiguous status brought to Jamestown on a Dutch trading ship in 1619 grew to a strictly defined class of nearly four million slave laborers. The few adventurous settlers who succeeded in making Jamestown the first permanent English settlement in North America were the ancestors of a huge master class numbering nearly 400,000 persons in 1860.

Different patterns of economic development influenced the colonial slaveholding class. In the Chesapeake region, tobacco became the chief crop, and its fortunes shaped the destinies of numerous Virginia "aristocrats" as well as thousands of small slaveholding farmers. In the backcountry, the slaveholders grew prosperous, albeit more modestly, on the diversified products of slave labor. And in the lowcountry of the Carolinas and Georgia, the cultivation of rice provided the basis for a third pattern of slaveholding in the colonial South.

The American Revolution stimulated further economic changes. It virtually destroyed the once flourishing indigo trade, crippled the economic influence of the Scottish tobacco merchants, and provoked the closing of the African slave trade, thereby eliminating a major source of profit among colonial planters. But the growth of the cotton market, beginning in the 1790's, revitalized the slave economy, prolonged its life, and guaranteed the significance of slavery to southern culture and American economic development.

By the revolutionary era the typical slaveholder might be French, German, or Scottish as well as English. Overwhelmingly Christian, slaveholders were nonetheless divided among Catholics, Episcopalians, and increasingly Baptists, Methodists, and other Protestant sects. Evangelicalism thrived on the diversity of the slaveholding class. Beginning just prior to the Revolution and accelerating immediately thereafter, the evangelization and conversion of the slaveholders continued into the earliest decades of the nineteenth century. As its influence spread, evangelical Protestantism became one of the outstanding features of antebellum slaveholding culture.

Economic and cultural changes were paralleled by the political development of the slaveholders. Born to an age that rewarded wealth with political power, the master class eventually thrust itself into the struggle for democracy. Slaveholders took the lead in the American Revolution, authored its most cherished documents, and carried the struggle into the nineteenth century. Taking its name from one of America's wealthiest planters, the "age of Jackson" saw the principles of democratic egalitarianism implemented by slaveholding politicians who made the white man's freedom the black man's burden. As late as the last decade of the antebellum era, the oldest slaveholding states were still reforming their constitutions, bringing them closer to the democratic ideal that previous generations of slaveholders had inspired.

More or less continuous economic growth and sustained physical and demographic expansion within the context of political democratization and religious evangelization—these were the bases of the dominant slaveholding ideology. Beginning with the assumption that their prosperity was divinely inspired, slaveholders went on to view black slaves and western lands as core elements in the construction of a physically and economically mobile culture. In their singular unwillingness to settle down, in their relentless pursuit of personal prosperity, hundreds of thousands of individual masters gave living testimony to the immediacy of their world view.

In these fundamental ways, the slaveholding experience coincided with the American experience at large. Except for its defense of bondage, the slaveholders' ideology was strikingly similar to the Republican party ideology of the 1850's. Indeed it was this closeness that so frightened the master class. In articulating the antislavery principles of the Republicans, William H. Seward must have appeared to slaveholders as the devil quoting scripture. Free soil and free labor were for most slaveholders the inalienable rights of free white men. Furthermore, they were rights that the institution of slavery sustained.

But where Northerners increasingly viewed slavery as an anachronistic institution antithetical to freedom, slaveholders continued to insist that "freedom is not possible without slavery." With good reason, they viewed human bondage as the basis of their entire civilization. The president of the Florida secession convention declared that "at the south, and with our people of course, slavery is the element of all value, and a destruction of that destroys all that is property." Mississippi secessionists publicly announced that their position was "thoroughly identified with the institution of slavery—the greatest material interest of the world." Alexander Stephens called slavery "the cornerstone of the Confederacy." By placing slavery at the heart of their society, the master class came into conflict with a northern tradition that claimed the same ideological heritage. In its famous capacity for pragmatic accommodation of conflicting positions, the American liberal tradition had managed to embrace two views of slavery so fundamentally incompatible as to bring a nation to civil war.[1]

FOR MORE THAN TWO CENTURIES history seemed to side with the slaveholders. The master class met and absorbed each new development with a resiliency that confounded the most confident predictions of slavery's inevitable demise. But in the late antebellum period, the slaveholders became increasingly frightened that their peculiar institution could no longer withstand the pace and direction of historical change. While the slave economy was being transformed from within, its importance outside the South was waning. Corresponding declines in the South's demographic predominance and political authority were brought into sharp relief by the increasing volume of northern antislavery rhetoric. It was through the lens of their liberal ideology that slaveholders viewed the frightening crises of the 1850's, and upon that vision they justified their withdrawal from the Union.

The slaveholders were understandably proud of their contribution to American economic growth. Indeed, slavery had played a pivotal role in precipitating the commercial development of the Western world. "Cotton is King," the *Southern Cultivator* declared in 1859, "and wields an astonishing influence over the world's commerce." From 1815 to 1839 the cotton trade provided much of the export capital to finance northeastern economic growth. But, after 1840, slavery's importance to the northern economy declined even as the southern slave economy continued to prosper. Indeed, so successfully had the American economy developed outside the South that the rest of the nation was increasingly able to prosper independently of the cotton trade. Northern urbanization—prompted in no small measure by the cotton export trade—disrupted the population balance between the North and South, giving the former an increasing demographic advantage.[2]

In still other ways the profits of the cotton economy came to work against the long-range interests of the slaveholders. Having sustained an increasingly independent industrial economy in the North, slaveholders watched as that section became more closely tied to the food-producing regions of the West. This was the beginning of the great era of nationwide railroad construction, and the discovery of gold in California only enhanced the strengthening bonds between West and East. Thus, just when the South's predominance was declining, western lands became increasingly important to northern economic growth. That the traditionally expansive slave economy should come into conflict with the North over the issue of western lands was hardly surprising. For both the North and the South, territorial expansion spoke directly to the great questions of slavery and freedom.

Equally frightening were the internal changes within the southern economy, changes readily understood by the slaveholders and sufficiently serious to provoke their leaders. In the democratic polity of the Old South, the basis of the slaveholders' authority had always been the capacity of the slave economy to distribute its wealth, however unequally, to a significant fraction of the southern white population. But, beginning around 1830, that population began to expand so quickly as to create demands that the slave economy could no longer meet. The percentage of slaveholding families in the South was shrinking, and with increasing velocity in the 1850's. Thirty-six percent of southern white families held slaves in 1830, thirty-one percent in 1850, and twenty-six percent in 1860. A drop in the growth rate of the slave population compounded the problem.[3] But whatever its ultimate cause, the declining proportion of slaveholders threatened to undermine their authority by closing off popular avenues of material advancement, thus jeopardizing the masters' ability to sustain the loyalty of the nonslaveholding whites. Whether they were justified or not, slaveholders approached the secession crisis fearful of an uncertain consensus among free Southerners.

The shrinking proportion of slaveholders did not mean that slave wealth became more concentrated among the planters. Nor was the distribution of slaves within the master class substantially altered. In the 1850's there was a tendency for slaves to accumulate among middle-class masters at the expense of large and small slaveholders. But it was a mild tendency at best.[4] In fact, the absolute number of slaveholders continued to grow by tens of thousands every decade, and in the 1850's the population of the slaveholding class grew by fourteen percent. Thus the increasingly substantial hostility on the part of nonslaveholding whites may have been muted by the fact that despite the declining proportion of slaveholders within southern society as a whole, the opportunities for advancement in the slave economy were not completely closed off.

But those opportunities were shrinking, and in the market culture of the slaveholders this was a threat. The increase in the relative scarcity of slaves drove their prices beyond the reach of aspiring non-slaveholders. Far from indicating the masters' faith in the future of slavery, high prices were seen by slaveholders as a threat to the legitimacy of the entire system. "Let things go on as they are now tending, and the days of the peculiar institution of the South are necessarily few," a Louisiana editor warned in 1858. "The present tendency of supply and demand is to concentrate all the slaves in the hands of the few, and thus excite the envy rather than cultivate the sympathy of the people." A Texas editor similarly warned that "exorbitant monopoly prices" for slaves made it difficult for "many thousands among us to be slaveowners."[5]

It was the promise as much as the reality of upward mobility that traditionally sustained the dreams of many non-slaveholding whites. One Tennessee farmer in an area with few slaves explained in the 1850's that "the people here all wanted it [Nebraska] to be Slave States, because they might want to move out there, and a fellow might get a nigger and have to sell him" if slavery was prohibited there. The slaveholders feared that such loyalty would soon diminish. "The minute you put it out of the power of common farmers to purchase a negro man or woman to help him in his farm, or his wife in the house, you make him an abolitionist at once."[6]

Southern leaders therefore sought to ensure the diffusion of slave property. "Ours is a pro-slavery form of Government, and the pro-slavery element should be increased," a Georgia newspaper editor concluded. "For our part we would like to see every white man at the South the owner of a family of negroes." As self-serving as this proposition was, it nevertheless appealed to the slaveholders' traditional devotion to white democracy and equality as well as to the conservative slaveholders' concern with the organic unity of interests among whites. "Increase the supply of labor, and thus cheapen the cost of slaves and the South will escape this *internal peril*," the Charleston *Mercury* declared. "The number of slaveholders would multiply, the direct interest in its preservation would be more universally diffused, and the great necessity of the South—union in defense of slavery, more readily accomplished."[7]

But slaveholders disagreed over the steps necessary to effect the diffusion of slave property. Some advocated the reopening of the African slave trade. Having insisted for decades that slavery was humane and uplifting for the blacks, conservatives like Edmund Ruffin came to see the reopening of the slave trade as an opportunity to spread their benevolence even as they advanced their own material interests. "Under such operation of self interest and legal regulation," Ruffin explained, "there is no reason why the African slaves, even in the 'Middle Passage' should not be even more comfortable, (physically,) than their lives were before under their barbarous & inhuman African masters and rulers."[8]

In the end, advocates of the slave trade found that they had hurled themselves into an unpopular cause that flew in the face of long-standing southern traditions. It was their constant complaint that most slaveholders remained committed to the fallacious moral objections to the slave trade that had led the South to withdraw from the commerce a half-century earlier. Slave-trade advocates explicitly disavowed the legitimacy of the moral question involved. "We have had enough of that," one Georgian explained. It is revealing testimony to their impotence that in raising the issue of the African slave trade advocates succeeded only in intensifying the hostility of the North. In the South their proposals were all but dismissed out of hand. The Alabama and Georgia secession conventions openly declared their opposition. "Suppose we re-open the African slave trade, what would be the result?" a Georgia secessionist asked the Virginia convention. "Why, we would soon be drowned in a black pool; we would be literally overwhelmed with a black population."[9]

As they groped for solutions to the internal crisis of the 1850's, southern leaders most often proposed laws that would encourage whites to maintain at least some slave property. In 1858 the governor of Florida told the state legislature that "the passage of a law securing every person in the possession of at least one slave . . . would inspire every man with an ambition . . . [and] make hundreds of our citizens actual slave owners who, without some such encouragement, would probably never own a slave." The governor of South Carolina recommended "the passage of a law exempting from sale . . . at least one slave. Such an immunity would stimulate every one to exert himself to possess his family of at least a property in some degree above the casualties of debt. As you multiply the number who acquire the property, so you will widen and deepen the determination to sustain the institution."[10]

Governor John A. Winston of Alabama tied the diffusion of slave property to the slaveholders' ideology of individual achievement. He proposed a law exempting at least one slave from taxation in order to ensure that "the investment of money in that kind of property will be preferred to all others." He argued that "the continued prosperity of the South will be greatly advanced by the more diffuse distribution of slave property. . . . The ownership of slaves will become more general; the benefits of the institution more generally felt, acknowledged, and defended." Furthermore, Winston explained, "experience teaches us that when a family, before [in] indigent circumstances, once become possessors of this kind of property, the regular progression to wealth is uninterrupted—acting as a wholesome incentive to further industry and economy."[11] Slaveholders clearly understood that the legitimacy of the slave system among whites depended on a good deal more than periodic barbecues and free ginning for the local non-slaveholders.

Not surprisingly, the 1850's witnessed an enhanced determination among slaveholders to press their territorial claims in the face of rising northern hostility. To have done otherwise would have been to abandon the premises on which masters had always justified slavery. As early as 1820, the Richmond *Enquirer* declared that the proposal to exclude slavery from Missouri "strikes at the very root of our Union, and prosperity." If they believed that the diffusion of slave property was essential to the legitimacy of the slave system, so too did slaveholders see westward migration as a principle that could never be abandoned if slavery was to survive. They made their case in the language of constitutional rights. To Isaac Johnson it was patently discriminatory for Congress to pass legislation "which permits and invites a Rhode Islander to emigrate with his property of every description, whilst it refuses and prohibits to the Louisianan the same privilege." The territorial question remained active in the slaveholders' minds well into the secession crisis. "We want land, and have a right to it," a Georgia secessionist declared. "How are we to get our share of it? Can we get it in the Union? Never." One delegate to the Texas secession convention proposed a resolution expressing the conviction that "the 'Monroe Doctrine' is of the most vital importance to the State of Texas."[12]

Already fearful that the legitimacy of their institution was being undermined by a shrinking base of popular support for slavery, and concerned that both political and natural limits to slavery expansion had been reached by the 1850's, slaveholders were ill prepared to meet the challenge of rising antislavery sentiment in the North. Here was an external threat that could not be met by innovative reforms to ensure that the fruits of slavery would be widely distributed. On the contrary, the same proposals devised to meet the internal crisis of the slaveholding South—reopening the African slave trade, greater expansion of the slave economy—further antagonized the most hostile elements in the North. If the slaveholders felt compelled to advocate measures that would ensure the survival of slavery, abolitionists opposed those measures precisely because they hoped to see slavery die. In so doing, they brought to the surface the gravest fear of the slaveholding class: that emancipation of the slaves would so threaten the "purity" of whites as to raise the specter of a bloody race war across the South.

All about them slaveholders saw evidence of the hideous intentions of the abolitionists. They were "determined to make the South a wilderness," a Florida master wrote, "and give the 'nigger' more privileges than the white man." In its thirty-year-old war against slavery, one South Carolinian declared, the North had, in effect, "suggested to the subject race—rising and murdering their masters."[13]

Nothing seemed to confirm these fears more than John Brown's failed effort to incite a slave insurrection at Harpers Ferry, Virginia, in 1859. To Sereno Taylor, a Louisiana master, slave insurrection was indistinguishable from race war, and the success of John Brown's plot therefore would have resulted in the deaths of "thousands of poor deluded servants." For this reason alone life imprisonment was not enough punishment for Brown. "It seems to me far preferable that the sentence of death be executed on him than that one misled servant should have been killed in Brown's enterprise of blood and insurrection." Yet Taylor's was a relatively calm response among slaveholders. Brown's execution was grimly noted in diaries throughout the South. His "murderous designs" were "the work of Abolitionists," a Mississippi mistress declared. "It is dreadful to think of a set of white scoundrels rising and killing persons with the plea to liberate the slaves. They ought to be hung," Susan Sillers Darden wrote. "Burning would be nothing but right." On the day after the execution, a Tennessee slaveholder noted that Brown's was "the first scheme of this kind which has ever been openly attempted in this country and it has promptly met with just retribution." Nevertheless, William Lawrence feared that Harpers Ferry was "but the beginning of a chain of events which will ultimately end in the dissolution of our glorious Union."[14]

Each new development brought forth fears of racial degeneration. In the summer of 1860 the Richmond *Enquirer* declared that Abraham Lincoln's "bosom friends and advocates seem willing to sink the proud Anglo-Saxon and other European races into one common level with the lowest races of mankind."[15] The slaveholders could not conceive of a society in which blacks and whites lived in equality and harmony. This powerful conviction informed their actions throughout the sectional crisis.

E. S. Dargan told Alabama's secession convention that "if pecuniary loss alone were involved in the abolition of slavery, I should hesitate long before" voting for secession. But "there are now in the slaveholding States over four millions of slaves," he noted. "To remove them from amongst us is impossible. . . . If the relation of master and slave be dissolved, and our slaves turned loose amongst us without restraint, they would either be destroyed by our own hands—the hands to which they look, and look with confidence, for protection—or we ourselves would become demoralized and degraded. The former result would take place, and we ourselves would become the executioners of our own slaves."[16]

The apocalyptic horror of emancipation left slaveholders with no alternative but to separate from the Union, a Georgia commissioner told the Virginia secession convention. "If things go on as they are it is certain that slavery is to be abolished," he warned. "By the time the North shall have attained the power, the black race will be in a large majority, and then we will have black governors, black legislatures, black juries, black everything. . . . We will be completely exterminated, and the land will be left in the possession of the blacks, and then it will go back into a wilderness and become another Africa or St. Domingo." Such would be the legacy of centuries of benevolent affection. A hundred abolitionist tracts could not have exposed

the cynicism and self-deception of the slaveholders' ideology more
effectively than the horrible visions projected by the advocates of
immediate secession.[17]

MOST SLAVEHOLDERS viewed their decision to secede not as a rejection of the principles upon which the Union was founded but as a
reaffirmation of those principles. Eccentrics like Edmund Ruffin
and fire-eaters like William Lowndes Yancey notwithstanding,
most slaveholders resisted the calls for secession throughout the
1850's. In 1854, the slaveholding governor of Tennessee announced
that "the storm of sectional passion and agitation which swept over
the country, and for a time created some alarm for the safety of our
institutions has happily subsided." But the sense of relief in the
governor's remarks was tempered by his overriding concern for the
safety of the South's "institution." In the 1850's slaveholding politicians repeatedly affirmed their devotion to the Constitution but
warned that abolitionism in the North was undermining their unionist impulses. In a lengthy address to the Mississippi legislature in
1854, Governor H. S. Foote spent over ten printed pages attacking
John C. Calhoun, South Carolina, and opponents of the Compromise of 1850, but for another ten pages he attacked abolitionists for
not supporting the compromise and for denying Southerners their
rights, thus advancing the cause of disunion. The reluctance to ex-
press secessionist principles openly waned as the decade progressed,
but concern for the Union was not uncommon among slaveholders
as late as 1860. On July 4 of that year, at the New Hope plantation
in Louisiana, Leonidas Pendleton Spyker noted "the 84th Anniversary of American Independence. How many shall we see a united
people? The prospect looks gloomy." A month after Lincoln's election, a Mississippi planter, G. W. Sargent, explained that as the
"son of one who shed his blood and gave a lifetime to obtain and
secure this Union, I regret to see such a blessing lost to us, yet as
a Southern Man I cannot see how we can longer bear the wrongs
heaped upon us by the North."[18] Allowing for differences of timing, emphasis, and enthusiasm, Sargent's thinking was in line with
that of most slaveholders.

Yet, in the frenetic months between Lincoln's election and the firing on Fort Sumter, such differences of timing, emphasis, and enthusiasm were points of major distinction among white Southerners. The position of the secessionists had always been clear, but their opponents were not so easily classified: a vote for a "cooperationist" in late 1860 did not necessarily indicate opposition to secession the following spring. Indeed, within a month of Lincoln's inauguration, the white South was remarkably unified in its readiness to secede.

At the beginning of the crisis, Southerners were divided in several ways over the question of secession: conservative vs. mainstream slaveholders, Upper South vs. Deep South, slaveholders vs. non-slaveholders. The divisions within the slaveholding class were fairly clear. In the Upper South, particularly the border states, the slaveholders were reluctant to secede merely because a Republican president had been elected. With the 1860 voting returns still incomplete, a Tennessee planter cautioned that if Lincoln was elected "all ought to acquiesce till he does some overt act for which if contrary to the Constitution he ought to suffer & not till then."[19] Slavery was less important to the Upper South's economy, and slaveholding was not as widespread in states like Virginia, Kentucky, North Carolina, and Tennessee as in the Deep South. Ties to the North were stronger, and in the back of their minds, many Upper South masters feared that when the war came their states would suffer the most violence.

But what most frightened Upper South slaveholders was the prospect of losing everything secession was supposed to defend. "The political troubles hang like a portentous cloud," a Kentucky slaveholder wrote in late 1860. "May God preserve us from blood." William Lawrence feared "civil war and servile insurrection." The Tennessee master voted against secession, hoping to save a Union which for him "was once the home of plenty and happiness." A Virginia mistress agreed. "There is too much to lose to lightly break up the Union of the States," Eliza Ann Willson wrote in late 1860. Appalled by the arrogance of South Carolina's secessionist leaders, she declared that "the idea of a great Southern Republic is but a chimera."[20]

Throughout the Upper South, particularly in Virginia, slaveholders expressed alarm over the pressure from the Deep South to secede. In the Virginia secession convention, Samuel Moore declared that he would not be "bound hand and foot, to the Cotton States, which have disregarded us in their proceedings." There was, he believed, "a conflict of interest between Virginia and the cotton States." His state's convention was thus the most divided in the South. But even staunch unionist slaveholders in the Upper South did not rule out secession altogether. "I shall recede only when I must," a Virginia planter explained, "and when at length it becomes necessary, if it ever should." For Virginia, secession became necessary in mid-April, 1861. Having been in session for two months, the convention had adopted most of the provisions of a cooperationist resolution, along with a series of proposed amendments to the United States Constitution designed to protect slavery. But on April 13 news of the firing on Fort Sumter reached the delegates. The following Tuesday they went into secret session, and on the next day Virginia seceded.[21]

In different states and within each convention the cooperationist position could imply several different strategies. The cooperationists themselves were divided between those who favored a unified, or "cooperative," secession of all the southern states, those who would secede only if the federal government did not "cooperate" by acquiescing in a series of proslavery demands, and unionists who would justify secession only in the face of overt federal provocation. Southerners who were firmly opposed to secession in principle were virtually nonexistent in the Deep South conventions of late 1860 and early 1861.[22] In practical terms, therefore, the chief difference between cooperationist and secessionist masters was whether slavery was better protected in or out of the Union.

Tying secession from the federal Union to a union of confederate states was in logical contradiction to the states' rights position of most slaveholders. The point of secession was that the individual state was sovereign before all else, and as a sovereign state it could decide for itself the kind of relationship it wanted to have with a confederation of states. Thus, for most delegates, secession had to come first, and it had to be independent of the move to join the confederacy, even though most assumed that the southern states would unite, and even though that unity was to be based on principles identical to those of the United States Constitution. So when S. W. Dorsey introduced a resolution for Louisiana's withdrawal from the "Federal Union, with a view to the establishment of a new confederacy, to be composed of the seceding states," his resolution was quickly amended to remove everything "after the word 'Union.' "[23]

Despite the fact that the cooperationist position was explicitly proslavery, it attracted only a small minority of slaveholders in the Deep South. For what motivated these masters was a conservative fear of anarchy and revolution and an antipathy to democracy that rendered their arguments meaningless to the slaveholding majority. Conservatives evoked images of bloodshed no less startling than those projected by the advocates of secession. But by cooperationist reasoning, secession itself would bring on the cataclysm disunionists were hoping to avert. "It will be the downfall of slavery," a South Carolina planter wrote when his state left the Union. "Peaceable secession" is "impossible," an Alabama master declared. "No liquid but blood has ever filled the baptismal fount of nations." James S. Clark opposed secession, fearing it would destroy Alabama's economic base, causing the whites to do what they had always done—emigrate. "The dismal proportion of negroes which we have already, would then become absolutely alarming," Clark wrote. "Our lovely State, with its few Caucasian inhabitants, would be converted into a kind of American Congo."[24]

Thus, cooperationist masters in the Deep South used many of the same arguments as the secessionists, but came to the opposite conclusion about the propriety of secession. "It is important to the State that you of the majority should be right and that I should be wrong," an Alabama cooperationist warned his fellow delegates. He voted for secession—against his own principles—because it seemed to be the will of the people. That they were overwhelmed by popular sentiment was hardly a strange predicament, for their distrust of democracy was the basis of their position to begin with. They recoiled from secession not because they opposed slavery or saw the Union as a bulwark of democracy, but because they feared its revolutionary implications. Nevertheless, few cooperationists were willing to leave the impression that in voting against secession they were somehow less than faithful to the southern cause. "I was elected to this Convention as a Cooperationist," a Mississippi delegate declared. But "the proposition has now narrowed down to *submission* or *secession,* and as between the two, I am for secession." Cooperationists often felt compelled to explain their positions publicly. Some justified their change of heart by declaring that they had done all they could to resist secession until they realized popular opinion was against them. Others insisted that in voting against secession they were simply carrying out the wishes of their constituents. Whatever their explanations, by the spring of 1861, cooperationists were clearly overwhelmed.[25]

If they are to be taken at their word, the slaveholders left the Union in order to preserve liberty, democracy, and prosperity, to uphold black slavery so that whites might continue to enjoy freedom. "We are for the Union as Gen. Jackson understood it," a Georgia newspaper explained. "A Union of equal rights to every citizen of this Confederacy; a Union which secured to the slave-holder the same privileges as a non-slaveholder; a Union which afforded protection to slave property throughout the length and breadth of our vast domain; a Union which guarantees the right of property of *every kind* in the common territories of the Union."[26]

Secessionist slaveholders consistently invoked the wisdom of their ancestors. Freedom was "the richest jewel in our heritage as Americans," a Florida secessionist declared. If we remain in the Union, a Virginia slaveholder added, "we will be deprived of that right for which our fathers fought the battles of the revolution. . . . I would rather see the standard of revolution roll through the land." The actions of the Founding Fathers served as a model to the slaveholders. "We must either submit to degradation, and the loss of property worth four billions of money, or we must secede," the Mississippi convention declared. "For far less cause than this, our fathers separated from the Crown of England." The situation facing the South "closely resembles that which existed prior to the American Revolution," a Texas secessionist explained. If the federal government did not act to protect southern rights, the governor of Tennessee observed, "to follow the example of our fathers of 1776, will be the only alternative left to us."[27]

In the debates between cooperationist and secessionist slaveholders, "the nomenclature of the Revolution of 1776 will have to be revived," William Lowndes Yancey proclaimed. "The friends of the country were then called Whigs, and the enemies of the colonies were then called Tories." An Alabama newspaper explained: "Were the Whigs of the Revolution, the men of 1776, who withdrew their allegiance from George III and set up for themselves and posterity the mighty Republic of ours Secessionists? and were not those who opposed them Tories?"[28]

Throughout the South the analogy between the Revolution and secession was accepted uncritically. The first state to leave the Union, South Carolina, cited the Declaration of Independence as a model for the South's "free and independent states" to follow. In North Carolina, one of the last states to withdraw, secessionists formally disavowed their subservience to the President. "George the Third was the rightful occupant of the British throne," John Ellis wrote, "yet our fathers submitted not to his authority." In many states Southerners formed local groups of "minute men" to defend their new nation. When the fighting began, the revolutionary precedent continued to inspire slaveholders. "On the 19th of April 1775 the first blood of the revolution was shed in Lexington," one Virginian wrote in the spring of 1861. "Nearly a century after this, in the town of Lexington, Va., a band of noble youths, the pride of the surrounding country, bidding farewell to weeping friends, started to the defense of their country."[29]

Like most nineteenth-century Americans, slaveholders did not usually distinguish between the dual legacies of the Revolution and the Constitution. But when they did, they were as likely to invoke the right of revolution as their constitutional liberties in justifying secession. During the war a Confederate officer, the son of a prosperous slaveholder, declared that he "never believed the Constitution recognized the right of secession. I took up arms, sir, upon a broader ground—the right of revolution. We were wronged. Our properties and liberties were about to be taken from us. It was a sacred duty to rebel." Thus, the conservatives' fear of revolution was sparked as much by the behavior of their fellow Southerners as by their own fantasies of anarchy and dissolution. A. P. Calhoun called secession "an up-heaving of the people. No leaders could have resisted it, or stemmed its impetuosity." If secession is revolution, a Georgia judge declared, "then I am for it." In Texas a "spontaneous and voluntary concert of the people of this State" forced the governor to recognize the authority of a secession convention that he had refused to call into session.[30]

No one doubted for a minute that this was a revolution whose aim was to protect slavery, and the legacy of the Founding Fathers was not seen as a hindrance. "The prospect before us, in regard to our Slave Property, if we continue in the Union, is nothing less than utter ruin," a South Carolina master wrote in his diary. "In the struggle for maintaining the ascendancy of our race in the South," an Alabama editor declared, "we see no chance for victory but in withdrawing from the Union. To remain in the Union is to lose all that white men hold dear in government. We vote to go out."[31]

Colonial slaveholders had enthusiastically joined the Revolution against Britain; most saw no conflict between its libertarian principles and the perpetuation of slavery. All that had passed from 1776 to 1860 had served only to reinforce the slaveholders' convictions. For when they cited the legacy of their revolutionary forebears, slaveholding secessionists openly proclaimed what they had always believed. "In the formation of the Government of our Fathers, the Constitution of 1787, the institution of domestic slavery is recognized, and the right of property in slaves is expressly guaranteed." The "revolutionary forefathers of '76" had established that "all political power is inherent in the people," O. M. Roberts observed. "The crisis upon us not only involves the right of self government, but the maintenance of a great principle in the law of nations—the immemorial recognition of the institution of slavery." Would the dissolution of the Union "prove the failure of our federative and representative government?" *DeBow's Review* asked in 1858. "By no means, any more than the occasional divorce or separation of man and wife proves the failure of the institution of marriage."[32]

The slaveholders did not leave the Union in the name of southern nationalism. They made no effort to construct a patriarchal republic, for no such effort was necessary. "There is no defect in our fundamental law; therefore it needs no alteration," an Alabama fire-eater explained. "The great defect in the Union is the public conscience and education of the northern masses upon the slavery question." Far from repudiating their ancestors, secessionists called up their powerful revolutionary heritage and acted in the name of prosperity, white supremacy, and democracy—the essential components of the only America they had ever known. So the slaveholders built their fated Confederacy, to be governed, they insisted, "upon the principles of the Constitution of the United States."[33]

William Wells Brown understood as much. He recalled his feelings during an unsuccessful effort to escape to Canada from his master in Missouri. "As we travelled towards a land of liberty, my heart would at times leap for joy. At other times, being, as I was, almost constantly on my feet, I felt as though I could travel no further. But when I thought of slavery with its Democratic whips—its Republican chains—its evangelical blood-hounds, and its religious slave-holders—when I thought of all this paraphernalia of American Democracy and Religion behind me, and the prospect of liberty before me, I was encouraged to press forward, my heart was strengthened, and I forgot that I was tired and hungry."[34]

APPENDIX,
NOTES,
AND
BIBLIOGRAPHY

Appendix

~

Sample of Slaveholders from the 1850 Census

T HE RANDOM SAMPLE has achieved the exalted status of tradition among historians of the nineteenth-century South. Conclusions based on the careful selection of representative counties have enhanced some of the most important works in southern history, among them Lewis Cecil Gray's classic *History of Agriculture in the Southern United States,* the Parker-Gallman sample of the cotton South in 1860, and the recent sample of 11,000 southern farms in 1880 taken for the Southern Economic History Project. The most widely used source for these samples is the manuscript returns of the United States Census.

The sample used in this study is modest compared to those mentioned above, but the needs were more limited and the goals more specific. Using the manuscript census returns for 1850, the following ten counties were selected for their diversity and representativeness:

Covington, Alabama   Georgetown, South Carolina
Dallas, Alabama   Sullivan, Tennessee
Coweta, Georgia   Weakley, Tennessee
Natchitoches, Louisiana   Red River, Texas
Attala, Mississippi   Halifax, Virginia

This selection includes counties from the upper and lower South, from the oldest regions of the eastern seaboard and the Texas frontier.

The cash crops of the counties selected were cotton, sugar, rice, and tobacco, and they produced various amounts of grain and livestock as well. Dallas is the only county that had anything like a city— Selma—in 1850, though most counties had at least a small town. The ratio of blacks to whites varied between counties. Georgetown had 18,109 slaves and only 3,013 whites; Weakley had 13,985 whites and 4,213 slaves. In Coweta, the slave population of just over 7,000 was nearly equal to the white population. Some counties were extraordinarily wealthy, while others were well below the southern average.

The number of slaveholders in each county was determined and a sample of names was taken from the slave schedules. I tried to select as close to fifty slaveholders as possible from each county. If there were 200 masters listed, a random number determined the first slaveholder selected and approximately every fourth name thereafter was used. If there were 300 masters in the county, every sixth name was used, and so on. Variations in the readability of the microfilm, the number of absentees, the diligence or penmanship of the enumerator, resulted in variations in the actual number of masters taken from each county.

From the slave schedules a total of 530 slaveholders was selected, twenty-five of whom could not be located in the population schedules. Conclusions are based on the remaining 505 masters and their households. In addition to the number of slaves, the 1850 census included information on the age, sex, race, occupation, real-estate value, birthplace, education, and literacy of the free white population, all of which was recorded for all 505 masters.

Similar information was collected for all free persons living in the same household as the master for all but Weakley and Sullivan counties, a total of 408 households. The age, sex, and race (black or mulatto) of 4,632 slaves were collected from seven of the ten counties —excluding Weakley, Sullivan, and Halifax.

The validity of the samples is confirmed by comparisons of collected data with the results published by the Bureau of the Census for the South as a whole. Thus the distribution of slaves among masters falls into roughly the same pattern in both the sample and the South in 1850. However, there is a bias toward large slaveholders that puts the average holding at 10.9 slaves for the sampled masters, whereas the average holding across the South was closer to eight slaves in 1850. This upward bias was largely caused by the inclusion in the sample of rice- and sugar-producing counties (Georgetown and Natchitoches), which, by their nature, were inordinately wealthy. To have eliminated these counties, however, would have detracted from the diversity of the sample. Since the statistics for average slaveholdings are well known, and since the conclusions are not heavily dependent on the accuracy of the mean slaveholding, the bias does not detract from the validity of the sample.

The following tables summarize the conclusions of the sample, most of which have been incorporated into the text.

A. Slaveholders

TABLE A.1.   UPWARD MOBILITY
(AS MEASURED IN DISTRIBUTION OF SLAVES BY AGE OF THE MASTER)*

Master's Age	Mean Slaveholding	Median Slaveholding
15–29 years	6.1	—
30–39	10.7	7.6
40–49	11.1	14.6
50–59	12.3	14.8
60 or over	13.9	16.0

*N = 505

TABLE A.2. DISTRIBUTION OF OCCUPATIONS AMONG SLAVEHOLDERS

Occupation	N*	%	Projected estimate †
Agriculture		(79)	
"Farmer"	325	71	240,743
"Planter"	26	6	26,851
Overseer	10	2	6,950
Professional	37	8	27,802
Businessman	26	6	26,851
Artisan or Craftsman	27	6	26,851
Miscellaneous	5	1	3,475

*N = 456. 49 masters listed no occupation; 44 of these were women.
†Percentage multiplied by the number of slaveholders in 1850.

B. Variations by Sex

TABLE B.I.   AGE DISTRIBUTION OF MALE AND FEMALE MASTERS

Age	Men (N=455)	Women (N=50)	Total
15–30 years	15%	8%	14%
31–40	27	10	25
41–50	26	32	27
51–60	21	28	22
61–99	11	22	12
Median Age	42.7 years	50.0 years	43.4 years
Mean Age	43.2	49.0	43.8

TABLE B.2. LAND DISTRIBUTION OF MALE AND FEMALE MASTERS*

Land Value	Men	Women	Total
$0.	18%	18%	18%
1–99.	1	2	1
100–499.	11	18	12
500–999.	15	16	15
1,000–4,999.	38	38	38
5,000–9,999.	9	2	8
10,000 and over	8	6	8

*N=505.

TABLE B.3.   SLAVE DISTRIBUTION
AMONG MALE AND FEMALE MASTERS*

Number of Slaves	Men	Women	Total
1	16%	20%	16%
2	10	20	10
3	7	4	7
4	11	4	11
5–9	23	22	23
10–19	19	28	20
20–29	6	10	7
30–49	4	0	4
50 or more	3	2	3
Mean	—	8.3	10.9

*N=505.

TABLE B.4.   MISCELLANEOUS VARIATIONS AMONG
SLAVEHOLDERS BY SEX*

	Men	Women	Total
1. Born outside the South	7%	5%	7%
2. Illiterate	5	22	7
3. No "occupation" in census	1	88	10
4. Free black masters	1	2	1

*N = 505.

C. Regional Variations

County	Mean Slaves	Median Slaves	Mean Land	Median Land	Mean Age	Employed outside Agriculture
Attala	7	6	$1471.	$2616.	42	11%
Covington	5	3	268.	200.	48	9
Coweta	10	6	3076.	1750.	42	13
Dallas	21	12	8740.	5875.	44	17
Georgetown	23	11	8049.	3307.	40	37
Halifax	13	10	2826.	2989.	48	13
Natchitoches	12	7	—	—	40	20
Red River	10	7	1717.	688.	43	33
Sullivan	5	4	3185.	2356.	47	25
Weakley	6	5	1252.	833.	—	14

D. Ages of Masters and Slaves

Age	Masters (N = 505)	Slaves*
Under 5 years	0.0%	16.9%
5–9	0.0	15.0
10–14	0.0	13.6
15–19	0.4	11.2
20–29	13.9	17.9
30–39	25.4	11.0
40–49	26.7	6.9
50–59	21.6	4.0
60–69	8.3	2.1

D. Ages of Masters and Slaves (cont'd)

Age	Masters (N = 505)	Slaves*
70–79	2.8	0.8
80 and over	1.0	0.4
Median Age	43 years	18 years
Mean Age	44	20

*Source: J. D. B. DeBow, *Statistical View of the United States* (Washington, D.C., 1854), 88–89.

E. Education in Slaveholding Families
(preliminary statistics)

While five percent of male slaveholders were listed as illiterate in the census returns, fifteen percent of their wives (N = 297) could not read or write. To some extent, this was a function of age: illiteracy was twice as common as literacy among wives sixty years of age or older. But among wives thirty years old or younger, literacy was four times as common as illiteracy.

All of the children of slaveholders in the sample who had attended school within the previous year fell between the ages of four and twenty-two. But only 396 out of 933 children (42 percent) between the ages of four and twenty-two had attended school within a year of the time the 1850 census data were collected. Education was not strictly reserved for male children in slaveholding families—46 percent of the schoolchildren were female, although of these none was over twenty years old. In addition, the average age of the male schoolchild was higher than the female's, probably a reflection of the fact that young men were more likely to go to college than young women.

Abbreviations Used in Notes and Bibliography

Agric. Hist.	*Agricultural History*
Ala. Hist. Quar.	*Alabama Historical Quarterly*
Ala. Rev.	*Alabama Review*
AHR	*American Historical Review*
Ark. Hist. Quar.	*Arkansas Historical Quarterly*
Fla. Hist. Quar.	*Florida Historical Quarterly*
Ga. Hist. Quar.	*Georgia Historical Quarterly*
Ga. Hist. Soc., *Coll.*	Georgia Historical Society, *Collections*
JAH	*Journal of American History*
Jour. Econ. Hist.	*Journal of Economic History*
Jour. Miss. Hist.	*Journal of Mississippi History*
Jour. Negro Hist.	*Journal of Negro History*
JSH	*Journal of Southern History*
La. Hist.	*Louisiana History*
La. Hist. Quar.	*Louisiana Historical Quarterly*
Md. Hist. Mag.	*Maryland Historical Magazine*
Miss. Hist. Soc., *Publ.*	Mississippi Historical Society, *Publications*
N.Y. Hist. Soc., *Coll.*	New York Historical Society, *Collections*
So. Car. Hist. Geneal. Mag.	
	South Carolina Historical and Genealogical Magazine
So. Car. Hist. Mag.	*South Carolina Historical Magazine*
So. West. Hist. Quar.	*Southwestern Historical Quarterly*
Tyler's	*Tyler's Quarterly Historical and Genealogical Review*
Va. Mag. Hist. Biog.	*Virginia Magazine of History and Biography*
WMQ	*William and Mary Quarterly*

Notes

Chapter 1: Revolutionary Slaveholders

1. Abner Cheney Goodell, "John Saffin and His Slave Adam," Colonial Society of Massachusetts, *Publications,* I (Boston, 1895), 85–112; Lawrence W. Towner, "The Sewall-Saffin Dialogue on Slavery," *William and Mary Quarterly,* 3rd Ser., XXI (1964), 40–52. The court did not actually free Saffin's slave, it simply refused to deny Adam's petition for freedom. The case dragged on for eight years before the slave was freed, twelve months before his death; Samuel Sewall, *The Selling of Joseph* (Boston, 1700); John Saffin, *A Brief and Candid Answer to a late Printed Sheet, Entituled, The Selling of Joseph . . .* (Boston, 1701), partially reprinted in George H. Moore, *Notes on the History of Slavery in Massachusetts* (New York, 1866), 251–256.

2. On the influence of this literature in colonial Virginia, see Louis B. Wright, *The First Gentlemen of Virginia* (Charlottesville, Va., 1940), 1–37. Peacham's book was published in 1622; Defoe's was written around 1729 but was not published until 1890.

3. Richard Brathwait, *The English Gentleman: Containing Sundry excellent Rules, or exquisite Observations, tending to Direction of every Gentleman, of selecter ranke and Qualitie,* 2d ed. (London, 1633), 58, 65–68, 154–164.

4. *Ibid.,* 123. For a fuller definition of "paternalism" as the term is used here, see above, Chap. 7.

5. George Alsop, *A Character of the Province of Maryland* (London, 1666), 53; Hugh Jones, *The Present State of Virginia* (London, 1724), 38; John Brickell, *The Natural History of North Carolina* (Dublin, 1737), 272.

6. Reverend Thomas Bacon, *Sermons addressed to Masters and Servants . . .* (Winchester, Va., 1742), 1–3.

7. Brathwait, *English Gentleman,* 58–61; Edmund S. Morgan, "The First American Boom: Virginia 1618 to 1630," *WMQ,* 3rd Ser., XXVII (1971), 169–198, suggests that speculative fever was part of the southern tradition almost from the beginning; Alsop, *Character of Maryland,* 64.

8. William Bullock, *Virginia Impartially Examined . . .* (London, 1649), introduction. Promotional pamphlets were frequently distributed among prospective European immigrants. See the examples cited in Herrmann Shuricht, *History of the German Element in Virginia* (Baltimore, Md., 1898, reprinted 1977), I, 62.

9. Brickell, *Natural History of North Carolina,* 256, 12, 269; [?], *A New and Accurate Account of the Provinces of South Carolina and Georgia* (London, 1733), Georgia Historical Society, *Collections* (Savannah, Ga., 1840), I, 49.

10. Lawrence Stone, *The Crisis of the Aristocracy, 1558–1641* (Oxford, 1965), 41; J. H. Plumb, "The Growth of the Electorate in England from 1600 to 1715," *Past & Present,* 45 (1969), 90–166, estimates that as late as 1842, after two centuries of expansion, the English electorate included only 15% of the adult male population; Robert E. and B. Katherine Brown, *Virginia, 1705–1786: Democracy or Aristocracy?* (East Lansing, Mich., 1964), 125–150; Alice Hanson Jones, *Wealth of a Nation to Be: The American Colonies on the Eve of the Revolution* (New York, 1980), 164 and throughout, demonstrates that whether slaves are counted as wealth or not, there was no significantly greater inequality in wealth distribution in the southern colonies than in the middle or New England colonies.

11. Even in New England the list of wealthy slaveholders reads like a roster of prominent colonial citizens. See Lorenzo Johnston Greene, *The Negro in Colonial New England* (New York, 1942; reprinted 1974), 350–359; Charles S. Sydnor, *Gentlemen Freeholders: Political Practices in Washington's Virginia* (Chapel Hill, N.C., 1952); Bernard Bailyn, "Politics and Social Structure in Virginia," in James Morton Smith, ed., *Seventeenth-Century America* (Chapel Hill, N.C., 1959), 90–115.

12. Aubrey C. Land, "Economic Base and Social Structure: The Northern Chesapeake in the Eighteenth Century," *Journal of Economic History,* 25 (1965), 639–654; Thomas Jefferson Wertenbaker, *The Planters of Colonial Virginia* (Princeton, N. J., 1922), 153; Peter Wood, *Black Majority: Negroes in South Carolina from 1670 Through the Stono Rebellion* (New York, 1974), 160–161; Philip D. Curtin, *The Atlantic Slave Trade: A Census* (Madison, Wisc., 1969), 140, estimates that slave imports to North America rose steadily through the eighteenth century and peaked in the years 1741–1760, the same years in which European emigration to the colonies became heavy.

13. Jackson T. Main, "The One Hundred," *WMQ,* 3rd Ser., XI (1954), 355–356, 362; David Curtiss Skaggs, *Roots of Maryland Democracy 1753–1776* (Westport, Conn., 1973), 43; George B. Tatum, "Architecture," in Louis B. Wright, *et al., The Arts in America: The Colonial Period* (New York, 1966; reprinted 1975), 41–145, esp. 116–125.

14. Louis B. Wright, ed., *Letters of Robert Carter, 1720–1727* (San Marino, Calif., 1940), vii–viii, 37, 40, 50–52; Main, "One Hundred," 364.

15. Aubrey Land, "Genesis of a Colonial Fortune," *WMQ*, 3rd Ser., VII (1950), 255–269; Devereux Jarratt, *The Life of the Reverend Devereux Jarratt* (Baltimore, Md., 1806); "Personal Property List of Dinwiddie County, 1782," *WMQ*, 1st Ser., XXVI (1917), 101.

16. [Lyon G. Tyler], "The Medical Men of Virginia," *WMQ*, 1st Ser., XIX (1911), 152; Clement Eaton, "A Mirror of the Southern Colonial Lawyer," *WMQ*, 3rd Ser., VII (1951), 520–534.

17. William Dunbar Letterbook; Mrs. Dunbar Rowland, comp., *Life, Letters and Papers of William Dunbar* (Jackson, Miss., 1930).

18. Klaus Wust, *The Virginia Germans* (Charlottesville, Va., 1969), 19–26; Land, "Genesis of a Colonial Fortune."

19. Robert Carter to George Eskridge, Sept. 21, 1727, Robert Carter Letterbook; Rowland, comp., *Letters of William Dunbar*, 23; William Dunbar to [?], Oct. 20, 1776, Dunbar Letterbook.

20. Mississippi River Expeditions, Miscellaneous Manuscripts Collection; see also Robert R. Rea, "Planters and Plantations in British West Florida," *Alabama Review*, XXIX (1976), 220–235; William Dunbar to [?], Aug. 15, 1783, Dunbar Letterbook. See Ulrich Bonnell Phillips, ed., *Plantation and Frontier, 1649–1873*, in *A Documentary History of American Industrial Society* (Cleveland, Ohio, 1910), I, 78, 84, on the cultural divisions within the slaveholding class caused by the creation of a demographic belt of immigrants whose mere presence "segregated" the low-country planters.

21. Edmund S. Morgan, *American Slavery American Freedom: The Ordeal of Colonial Virginia* (New York, 1975), 83–84; Bailyn, "Politics and Social Structure." David W. Jordan, "Maryland's Privy Council, 1637–1715," in Aubrey Land, *et al.*, eds., *Law, Society and Politics in Early Maryland* (Baltimore and London, 1977), 65–87, points out that high mortality rates in colonial Maryland hampered the development of an entrenched ruling elite until after 1700.

If indentured servants who died, returned to Europe, or left their county of settlement are not counted in the calculations, a much higher rate of upward mobility can be deduced. See, for example, Russell R. Menard, "From Servant to Freeholder: Status, Mobility and Property Accumulation in Seventeenth-century Maryland," *WMQ*, 3rd Ser., XXX (1973), 37–64; see also Lorena S. Walsh, "Servitude and Opportunity in Charles County, Maryland, 1658–1705," in Land, *et. al*, eds., *Law, Society and Politics in Early Maryland*, 111–133; Lois Green Carr and Lorena S. Walsh, "The Planter's Wife: The Experience of White Women in Seventeenth-Century Maryland," *WMQ*, 3rd Ser., XXXIV (1977), 542–571, conclude that perhaps 85% of the white immigrants in 17th-Century Maryland arrived as indentured servants; Mildred Campbell, "English Emigration on the Eve of the American Revolution," *American Historical Review*, LXI (1955), 1–20; E. P. Thompson, "Eighteenth-century English Society: Class Struggle without Class?" *Social History*, 3 (1978), 133–165; George Rude, *Wilkes and Liberty; A Social Study of 1763 to 1764* (Oxford, 1962).

22. R. J. Dickson, *Ulster Emigration to Colonial America 1718–1775* (London, 1966), 69–97, 221–227.

23. E. Estyn Evans, "The Scotch Irish: Their Cultural Adaptation and Heritage in the American Old West," in E. R. R. Green, ed., *Essays in Scotch-Irish History* (New York, 1969), 69–86.

24. Albert Bernhard Faust, *The German Element in the United States,* I (New York, 1927), 53–72, 177–247; Wust, *Virginia Germans,* 121–128; Richard H. Shryock, "British Versus German Traditions in Colonial Agriculture," *Mississippi Valley Historical Review*, XXVI (1939–1940), 39–54.

25. Hester Walton Newton, "The Industrial and Social Influences of the Salzburgers in Colonial Georgia," *Georgia Historical Quarterly,* XVIII (1934), 335–353; Klaus G. Loewald et al., eds. and trans., "Johann Martin Bolzius Answers a questionnaire on Carolina and Georgia," *WMQ,* 3rd Ser., XIV (1957), 226.

26. Harold E. Davis, *The Fledgling Province: Social and Cultural Life in Colonial Georgia, 1733–1776* (Chapel Hill, N.C., 1976), 131; Hester Walton Newton, "The Agricultural Activities of the Salzburgers in Colonial Georgia," *Ga. Hist. Quar.,* XVIII (1934), 259–260; Loewald et al., eds. and trans., "Bolzius Answers a questionnaire," 226.

27. J. M. Hofer, "The Georgia Salzburgers," *Ga. Hist. Quar.,* XVIII (1934), 113–117. See also Clarence L. Ver Steeg, *Origins of a Southern Mosaic: Studies of Early Carolina and Georgia,* Mercer University Lamas Memorial Lectures, 17 (Athens, Ga., 1975), 86–88.

28. Ian C. C. Graham, *Colonists from Scotland: Emigration to North America, 1707–1783* (Ithaca, N. Y., 1956), 43–63, 89, 107–108; Viola Root Cameron, comp., *Emigrants from Scotland to America 1774–1775* (Baltimore, Md., 1965), 14–15.

29. Graham, *Colonists from Scotland,* 114–115; Duane Meyer, *The Highland Scots in North Carolina* (Chapel Hill, N.C., 1957; reprinted 1961), 108–109.

30. Jacob Price details how the French, in the late 1600's, decided to take monopoly control of the world's tobacco market. They centralized domestic production, encouraged tobacco cultivation in Louisiana, and eventually moved into the British market in an effort to buy up a controlling share of the tobacco from the Chesapeake. It was largely as a result of these efforts that Scottish merchant houses in Glasgow, buying for the French, surpassed the London merchants and had a profound effect on the economic development of the Chesapeake. See Jacob Price, *France and the Chesapeake, A History of the French Tobacco Monopoly, 1674–1791, and Its Relationship to the British and American Tobacco Trades* (Ann Arbor, Mich., 1973), esp. v. I, 592–593, 608–613, 616–617, 662–671, and throughout.

31. Graham, *Colonists from Scotland,* 121–122; Jacob M. Price, "The Rise of Glasgow in the Chesapeake Trade, 1707–1775," *WMQ,* 3rd Ser., XI (1954), 179–199.

32. George Fraser Black, *Scotland's Mark on America* (New York, 1921), 33–35; Alexander R. MacDonell, "The Settlement of Scotch Highlanders at Darien," *Ga. Hist. Quar.,* XX (1936), 250–262; Charles G. Sellers, Jr., "Private Profits and British

Colonial Policy: The Speculations of Henry McCulloh," *WMQ*, 3rd Ser., VIII (1951), 535–551; Graham, *Colonists from Scotland*, 139.

33. Graham, *Colonists from Scotland*, 157; Price, "Rise of Glasgow."

34. John M. Graham, "The Exclusion of the Scotch from Georgia," *Ga. Hist. Quar.*, XVII (1933), 37–39.

35. *Extract of the Journals of Mr. Commissary Von Reck and of the Rev. Mr. Bolzius* (London, 1734), in Peter Force, ed., *Tracts and Other Papers, relating principally to the origin, settlement, and progress of the colonies in North America* . . . (Washington, D.C., 1846), IV, 9; *An Impartial Inquiry into the State and Utility of the Province of Georgia* (London, 1741), Ga. Hist. Soc., *Coll.* (Savannah, Ga., 1840), I, 167; Wood, *Black Majority*, 224.

36. Ralph B. Flanders, *Plantation Slavery in Georgia* (Cos Cob, Conn., 1967), 122.

37. The following paragraphs are based on Gerald W. Mullin, *Flight and Rebellion: Slave Resistance in Eighteenth-century Virginia* (New York, 1972), and Wood, *Black Majority*.

38. Dixon and Hunter's *Virginia Gazette*, Nov. 18, 1775; Purdie's *Virginia Gazette*, April 21, 1775.

39. Rowland, comp., *Letters of William Dunbar*, 55, 30.

40. Louis B. Wright and Marion Tinling, eds., *The Secret Diary of William Byrd of Westover, 1709–1712* (Richmond, Va., 1941), 53, 75, 112–113, 119, 205, 199, 117.

41. Jones, *Present State of Virginia*, 37; Brickell, *Natural History of North Carolina*, 276; *The Letters of Honorable James Habersham, 1756–1775*, Ga. Hist. Soc., *Coll.*, VI (Savannah, Ga., 1904), 15–17, 21; Hunter Dickinson Farish, ed., *Journal & Letters of Philip Vickers Fithian, 1773–1774: A Plantation Tutor in the Old Dominion*, new ed. (Williamsburg, Va., 1957), 38.

42. Brickell, *Natural History of North Carolina*, 275.

43. *Virginia Gazette*, Oct. 12, 1739; Purdie and Dixon's *Virginia Gazette*, Sept. 27, 1770; Frances Christien to Edmund Wilcox, March, 1760, Hubard Family Papers; J. Bryan Grimes, ed., *North Carolina Wills and Inventories* (Raleigh, N. C., 1912), 73; Rind's *Virginia Gazette*, Feb. 18, 1768; *Virginia Gazette*, April 7, 1738.

44. Edward Porter Alexander, ed., *The Journal of John Fontaine: An Irish-Huguenot Son in Spain and Virginia, 1710–1719* (Williamsburg, Va., 1972), 28.

45. Brickell, *Natural History of North Carolina*, 273; A. Leon Higginbotham, Jr., *In the Matter of Color: Race and the American Legal Process; The Colonial Period* (New York, 1978), 52, 78, 204, 252.

46. Grimes, *North Carolina Wills*, 20–22.

47. See Pauline Maier, "Early Revolutionary Leaders and the Problem of Southern Distinctiveness," in Jeffrey J. Crow and Larry E. Tise, eds., *The Southern Experience in the American Revolution* (Chapel Hill, N.C., 1978), 3–24; Elias Ball to [?], Nov. 22, 1784, Elias Ball Papers; *A Sermon Preached at the Anniversary Meeting of the Planter's Society . . . August 7, 1769* (Charleston, S.C., 1769), 12; John Clopton to William Clopton, Dec. 25, 1775, John Clopton Papers.

48. *Tyler's,* II (1920), 323–324; Evangeline Walker Andrews and Charles McLean Andrews, eds., *Journal of a Lady of Quality* (New Haven, Conn., 1939), 199; Purdie's *Virginia Gazette,* Dec. 29, 1775, supplement 2, and March 29, 1776.

49. Josiah Quincy, *Memoir of the Life of Josiah Quincy, Jun., of Massachusetts* (Boston, 1825), 115, 116, 127; *A Sermon Preached . . .* , I, 8–19.

50. Jack P. Greene, ed., *The Diary of Colonel Landon Carter of Sabine Hall, 1752–1778* (Charlottesville, Va., 1965), II, 1056, 1009, 1015.

51. Winthrop D. Jordan, *White over Black: American Attitudes Toward the Negro, 1550–1812* (Chapel Hill, N.C., 1968), esp. 3–98, 429–481. For more on Jefferson and slavery, see David Brion Davis, *The Problem of Slavery in the Age of Revolution, 1770–1823* (Ithaca, N.Y., 1975), 164–184.

52. Purdie and Dixon's *Virginia Gazette,* July 18, 1771; François Jean de Chastellux, *Travels in North America in the Years 1780, 1781, and 1782* (New York, 1827), I, 193.

53. Richard Randolph's Will, Feb. 18, 1796.

54. Duncan J. McLeod, *Slavery, Race and the American Revolution* (London, 1974), 138–139, 143; *The Lee Papers,* New York Historical Society, *Collections,* V (New York, 1873), 218.

55. Richard Cogdell to [?], April 25, 1770, Richard Cogdell Papers; "Official Letters of Governor John Martin, 1782–1783," *Ga. Hist. Quar.,* I (1917), 284.

56. Fredrika Teute Schmidt and Barbara Ripel Wilhelm, eds., "Early Proslavery Petitions in Virginia," *WMQ,* 3rd Ser., XXX (1973), 139.

57. McLeod, *Slavery, Race and the American Revolution,* 34–35; *Lee Papers,* V, 219.

58. Robert McColley, *Slavery in Jeffersonian Virginia,* 2d ed. (Urbana, Ill., 1964: 1973), 163–170; McLeod, *Slavery, Race and the American Revolution,* 31–47, 101–102; Rind's *Virginia Gazette,* July 28, 1774; Purdie and Dixon's *Virginia Gazette,* June 30, 1774.

59. John Mills to Gilbert Jackson, May 19, 1807, John Mills Letters; Manuscript of a public address by A. L. C. Magruder, April 19, 1828, James Trueman Magruder Papers.

60. Curtin, *Atlantic Slave Trade,* 73, 92; Russell R. Menard, "The Maryland Slave Population, 1658–1730," *WMQ,* 3rd Ser., XXXII (1975), 29–54.

61. *Letters of James Habersham,* 71–72.

Chapter 2: Master-class Pluralism

1. Daniel R. Hundley, *Social Relations in our Southern States* (New York, 1860), 68–69.

2. The modern argument for a slaveholders' aristocracy is most forcefully presented in several works by Eugene D. Genovese, all of which stress ideology

and culture over statistical demonstrations of wealth concentration or maldistribution. See especially his first two monographs, *The Political Economy of Slavery* (New
York, 1965), and *The World the Slaveholders Made* (New York, 1969). *Roll, Jordan,
Roll: The World the Slaves Made* (New York, 1974) incorporates Genovese's interpretation into a discussion of slave life and culture.

Various historians have emphasized the egalitarian aspects of the Old South,
most often by reference to its democratic politics. See especially Fletcher Melvin
Green, "Democracy in the Old South," *Journal of Southern History*, XII (1946);
Charles S. Sydnor, *The Development of Southern Sectionalism* (Baton Rouge, La.,
1948), 275–293. A recent variation is J. Mills Thornton III, *Politics and Power in
a Slave Society* (Baton Rouge, La., 1978).

But the statistical argument for wide distribution of wealth has not advanced
much beyond Frank L. Owsley, *Plain Folk of the Old South* (Baton Rouge, La.,
1949), primarily because subsequent historians have concentrated on finding out
how much wealth the wealthy had rather than on how much land the "typical"
Southerner had. Owsley's interpretation is highly romantic, but his figures demonstrating that landholding was widespread even though wealth was concentrated
have never been successfully refuted. Curiously, an article by Fabian Linden,
"Economic Democracy in the Slave South: An Appraisal of Some Recent Views,"
Journal of Negro History, XXXI (1946), 140–189, is frequently cited as a "brilliant"
refutation of Owsley's thesis, even though it was published three years before
Owsley's book. Linden's analysis explicitly exempted much of the work that
Owsley had published in article form up to that time, and even a cursory comparison of the critique and the book reveals that most of Linden's attack was quite
irrelevant. Even when it was published, Linden's article was only half logical and
was based on sources far more disreputable than those he was criticizing. See the
brief but trenchant remarks of Joseph G. Tregle, Jr., "Another Look at Shugg's
Louisiana," *Louisiana History*, XVII (1976), 245–279, esp. 256–259.

3. Gavin Wright, " 'Economic Democracy' and the Concentration of Agricultural Wealth in the Cotton South, 1850–1860," *Agricultural History*, XLIV
(1970), 63–85, demonstrates the concentration of improved acreage among the
wealthiest slaveholders; see also the evidence in Lewis Cecil Gray, *History of
Agriculture in the Southern United States to 1860* (Washington, D.C., 1933), I, 480,
and in general chapters 21 and 23; Lee Soltow, *Men and Wealth in the United States,
1850–1870* (New Haven, Conn., 1975), 24; James C. Bonner, "Profile of a Late
Ante-bellum Community," *AHR*, XLIX (1944), 672; see Appendix, Table B.2.

4. Ralph B. Flanders, "Two Plantations and a County of Ante-bellum
Georgia," *Ga. Hist. Quar.*, XII (1928), 24–32; Randolph B. Campbell, "Planters
and Plain Folk: Harrison County, Texas, as a Test Case, 1850–1860," *JSH*, XL
(1974), 379.

5. Gavin Wright, *The Political Economy of the Cotton South* (New York, 1978),
29–33; Warren I. Smith, "Land Patterns in Ante-bellum Montgomery County,

Alabama," *Ala. Rev.,* VIII (1955), 197–198; Donnie D. Bellamy, "Slavery in Microcosm: Onslow County, North Carolina," *Jour. Negro Hist.,* LXII (1977), 341.

6. Lee Soltow, "Economic Inequality in the United States in the Period from 1790 to 1860," *Jour. Econ. Hist.,* XXXI (1971), 825, 833; Joseph Karl Menn, *The Large Slaveholders of Louisiana—1860* (New Orleans, 1964), 75–76. The 1860 U.S. Census mistakenly dropped 10,332 slaveholders from its compilations by an incorrect transcription of the statistics from Arkansas to the nationwide totals. The commonly cited figure of 384,884 slaveholders in 1860 is therefore wrong. Assuming no other errors, the correct figure should be 395,216. The percentage of slaveholding families in 1860 is adjusted upward in a brief discussion of the changes in these slaveholding statistics in the Epilogue of the present work; see Joseph G. Kennedy, *Agriculture of the United States in 1860* (Washington, D.C., 1864), 244, 247.

7. Soltow, *Men and Wealth,* 25, 66, 101, 166–167. It is this southern domination of American wealthholders that explains the higher statistical inequality of the South more than the presence of a larger number of poor whites.

8. James D. B. DeBow, *Statistical View of the United States* (Washington, D. C., 1854), 95; see Appendix, C.

9. Soltow, *Men and Wealth,* 57; Otto H. Olsen, "Historians and the Extent of Slave Ownership in the Southern United States," *Civil War History,* 18 (1972), 111.

10. Eugene D. Genovese, "Yeomen Farmers in a Slaveholders' Democracy," *Agric. Hist.,* XLIX (1975), 331–342. For a different view see Robert R. Russell, "The Effects of Slavery upon Nonslaveholders of the Ante Bellum South," *Agric. Hist.,* XV (1941), 112–126.

11. Timothy Flint, *Recollections of the Last Ten Years* (Boston, 1826), 228–229.

12. Ralph D. Gray, ed., "A Tour of Virginia in 1827, Letters of Henry D. Gilpin to his Father," *Virginia Magazine of History and Biography,* 76 (1968), 450; John Fredrick Nau, *The German People of New Orleans, 1850–1890* (Leiden, 1958), 35; Frederick Law Olmsted, *A Journey in the Back Country* (New York, 1860), 42.

13. Frederick Law Olmsted, *A Journey in the Seaboard Slave States* (New York, 1856), 356; Earl F. Niehous, *The Irish in New Orleans* (Baton Rouge, La., 1965), 54–55. For the circumstances surrounding Olmsted's unusually extensive tour of the South, see *The Papers of Frederick Law Olmsted,* ed., Charles Capen McLaughlin, II: *Slavery and the South, 1852–1857,* ed., Charles E. Beveridge *et al.* (Baltimore, Md., 1981), 1–35. These papers reaffirm Olmsted's well-deserved reputation as the most careful, thorough, and reliable observer of life in the Old South.

14. See for example, John D. Barnhart, "Frontiersmen and Planters in the formation of Kentucky," *JSH,* VII (1941), 19–36; Herbert Weaver, "Foreigners in Ante-bellum Towns of the Lower South," *JSH,* XIII (1947), 70–71; Harris Gaylord Warren, "Population Elements in Claiborne County, 1820–1860," *Journal of Mississippi History,* IX (1947), 82; Barnes F. Lathrop, "Migration into East Texas,"

Southwestern Historical Quarterly, LII (1948–1949), 198; Ralph A. Wooster, "Foreigners in the Principal Towns of Ante-bellum Texas," *So. West. Hist. Quar.,* LXVI (1962), 217–218.

15. Brief descriptions of the origins of slavery in Louisiana can be found in W. J. Eccles, *France in America* (New York, 1972), 158–166; Joe Gray Taylor, *Negro Slavery in Louisiana* (Baton Rouge, La., 1962), chap. I. Much more intriguing is the discussion of France's attempt to build a tobacco empire in Louisiana, in Price, *France and the Chesapeake.*

16. V. Alton Moody, "Slavery on Louisiana Sugar Plantations," *Louisiana Historical Quarterly,* 7 (1924), 201; Olmsted, *Seaboard States,* 649. See also, Joseph G. Tregle, Jr., "Early New Orleans Society: A Reappraisal," *JSH,* XVIII (1952), 20–30.

17. Charles Lyell, *A Second Visit to the United States* (New York, 1849), II, 157–158; *DeBow's Review,* XI (1851), 606; Menn, *Large Slaveholders,* 83–84.

18. Theda Perdue, *Slavery and the Evolution of Cherokee Society* (Knoxville, Tenn., 1979), 3–49. I have relied heavily on this excellent analysis of the disruptive effects of black slavery on Cherokee culture and society.

19. Annie Heloise Abel, *The American Indian as Slaveholder and Secessionist,* vol. I of *The Slaveholding Indians* (Cleveland, Ohio, 1915), 19–21, 41–46; Kenneth W. Porter, *The Negro on the American Frontier* (New York, 1971), 42–43; Perdue, *Slavery and Cherokee Society,* 61, 70–71.

20. Abel, *Indian as Slaveholder,* 46, 77, 86n.; Porter, *Negro on Frontier,* 42; Charles S. Sydnor, *Slavery in Mississippi* (New York, 1933), 131–133.

21. Porter, *Negro on Frontier,* 46, 44; Perdue, *Slavery and Cherokee Society,* 56–58.

22. Abel, *Indian as Slaveholder,* 122n.

23. John H. Russell, "Colored Freedmen as Slave Owners in Virginia," *Jour. Negro Hist.,* I (1916), 239–241; R. Halliburton, Jr., "Free Black Owners of Slaves: A Reappraisal of the Woodson Thesis," *South Carolina Historical Magazine,* LXXVI (1975), 135, 142.

24. Carter G. Woodson, "Free Negro Owners of Slaves in the United States in 1830," *Jour. Negro Hist.,* IX (1924), 42; Henry S. Robinson, "Some Aspects of the Free Negro Population of Washington, D.C., 1800–1862," *Maryland Historical Magazine,* 64 (1969), 50–51.

25. Quoted in Ira Berlin, *Slaves Without Masters: The Free Negro in the Antebellum South* (New York, 1974), 276; William Ransom Hogan and Edwin Adams Davis, eds., *William Johnson's Natchez: The Ante-bellum Diary of a Free Negro* (Baton Rouge, La., 1951), 514n.

26. Hogan and Davis, eds., *William Johnson's Natchez, passim.* See also Berlin, *Slaves Without Masters,* 276.

27. David O. Whitten, "Slave Buying in 1835 Virginia as Revealed in the Letters of a Louisiana Negro Sugar Planter," *La. Hist.,* XI (1970), 231–234; Ulrich

Bonnell Phillips, *American Negro Slavery* (New York, 1918; reprinted Baton Rouge, La., 1966), 434–436.

28. Russell, "Colored Freedmen," 242; Frederick Law Olmsted, *A Journey Through Texas* (London, 1859), 399.

29. For a descriptive analysis, see Richard C. Wade, *Slavery in the Cities, The South 1820–1860* (New York, 1964); Claudia Dale Goldin, *Urban Slavery in the American South, 1820–1860: A Quantitative History* (Chicago, 1976), 16–26.

30. See Appendix, Tables B.1–B.4. For a representative example of a woman who had considerable experience managing slaves in her husband's absence, see the Mary Ann Colvin Mayfield Biography.

31. See Appendix.

32. Kenneth M. Stampp, *The Peculiar Institution: Slavery in the Antebellum South* (New York, 1956), 30–31, 36, 38, defines a planter as an owner of at least 20 slaves, but he divides slaveholders into three groups: those with fewer than ten bondsmen, substantial farmers and small planters with between 10 and 30 bondsmen, and those with 30 slaves or more, who achieved maximum efficiency.

33. Genovese, *Roll, Jordan, Roll,* 7–9, argues that "plantations defined by contemporaries" included "units of twenty slaves or more." But Roger L. Ransom and Richard Sutch, *One Kind of Freedom: The Economic Consequences of Emancipation* (Cambridge, 1977), 73, assert that "fifty slaves was usually taken by contemporaries as a minimum size for a farm to deserve the title 'plantation.'" Where Stampp argues that 30 slaves were necessary for plantation efficiency, Winthrop Jordan implies that "plantations" could have fewer than twenty bondsmen, *New York Review of Books,* April 17, 1980.

34. Beulah M. D'Olive Price, ed., "Excerpts from the Diary of Walter Alexander Overton, 1860–1862," *Jour. Miss. Hist.,* XVII (1955), 194–197.

35. Thomas W. Chadwick, ed., "The Diary of Samuel Edward Burges, 1860–1862," *South Carolina Historical and Genealogical Magazine,* XLVIII (1947), 63–75, 141–163, but esp. 151, 75, 148.

36. James K. Greer, ed., "The Diary of James Buckner Barry, 1860–1862," *So. West. Hist. Quar.,* XXXVI (1932), 146, 149–150.

37. W. J. Simpson Diary, entries for Sept. 19, 1855, Jan., 1856, and Jan., 1861.

38. "Autobiography of Gideon Lincecum," Mississippi Historical Society, *Publications,* VIII (1904), 451–452, 457.

39. *Ibid.,* 464, 468–478.

40. *Ibid.,* 486, 491.

41. *Ibid.,* 516–519.

42. Olmsted, *Back Country,* 226.

43. *Ibid.,* 159; Grady McWhiney, "The Similar Class Status of Alabama's Party Leaders," reprinted in Edward Pessen, ed., *New Perspectives in Jacksonian Parties and Politics* (Boston, 1969), 134–135.

44. See Appendix, Table A.2; Samuel Lewis Moore Autobiography.

45. Weymouth T. Jordan, ed., *Herbs, Hoecakes and Husbandry* (Tallahassee, Fla., 1960), introduction.

46. See Appendix, Table A.2; Robert Partin, ed., "A Connecticut Yankee's Letters from Conecuh County, Alabama, 1847–1866," *Ala. Rev.*, IV (1951), 68–69.

47. Newton Haskin James, "Josiah Hinds: Versatile Pioneer of the Old Southwest," *Jour. Miss. Hist.*, II (1940), 22–33.

48. See Appendix, Table A.2.

49. Henry Watson, Jr., to Julia Watson, May 18, 1834, Henry Watson, Jr., Papers.

50. Benjamin Fitzpatrick Papers, Folders I and II; Moses Bledsoe Papers.

51. Robert Remini, *Andrew Jackson and the Course of American Empire, 1767–1821* (New York, 1977), 133.

52. Thomas Gale to Benjamin Johns, Oct. 25, 1817, Gale and Polk Family Papers; William P. Graham Papers, see esp. folder 6.

53. Everard Green Baker Diary, entry for March 19, 1854.

54. Alex Allen to George Allen, Dec. 24, 1849 and Dec. 29, 1849, George Washington Allen Papers.

55. "James M. Torbert's Plantation Journal for 1856," *Alabama Historical Quarterly*, 18 (1956), 279; "James M. Torbert's Journal for 1857–1874," *Ala. Hist. Quar.*, 22 (1960), 46–48; James Monette Plantation Diary; Pinckney Cotesworth Harrington Papers.

56. Dugal McCall Plantation Journal and Diary.

57. Thus, the correlation between age and slaveholding is stronger than for age and landholding. The slaveholding middle class was in large part responsible for this dichotomy, since masters with non-agricultural careers were fifty percent more likely to own no land than those employed chiefly in farming. This information has been derived from the slaveholding sample described in the Appendix.

58. Kollock Plantation Books; John Houston Bills Diary.

59. Archibald Hunter Arrington Papers, folders 1, 1-C, 7.

60. Soltow, "Economic Inequality," 825, 829, 834.

61. Wright, " 'Economic Democracy,' " 63–85; Albert W. Niemi, Jr., "Inequality in the Distribution of Slave Wealth: The Cotton South and Other Southern Agricultural Regions," *Jour. Econ. Hist.*, XXXVII (1977), 747–753; Nancy C. Roberson, "Social Mobility in Ante-bellum Alabama," *Ala. Rev.*, XIII (1960), 135–145.

Chapter 3: The Slaveholder's Pilgrimage

1. Moore Autobiography, 13; Franklin L. Riley, "Diary of a Mississippi Planter, January 1, 1840, to April, 1863," Miss. Hist. Soc., *Publ.*, X (1909), 464.

2. Wm. Byrd to Wm. Byrd, April 8, 1859, William Byrd Papers; Isaac Guion to John Guion, May 2, 1820, Guion Family Papers.

3. Reverend Charles Pettigrew, 1797, Pettigrew Papers.

4. Isaac Guion to John and Frederick Guion, Sept. 15, 1816, Guion Papers; R. Hinton to Laurens Hinton, Dec. 16, 1836, Jan. 10, 1837, and Feb. 4, 1837, Laurens Hinton Papers.

5. Thomas Harrison to James T. Harrison, March 11, 1834 and May 24, 1835, James Thomas Harrison Papers.

6. Henry Watson, Jr., to Julius Reed, Jan. 8, 1831, Watson Papers; James Silk Buckingham, *The Slave States of America* (London, 1842), II, 295.

7. John Houston Bills Diary, entry for Dec. 25, 1853; Olmsted, *Seaboard States,* 561; Joseph Holt Ingraham, *The Southwest. By a Yankee* (New York, 1835), II, 91; Olmsted, *Texas,* 359.

8. Oscar Hamilton to G. W. House, July 9, 1859, George W. House Papers.

9. Henry Watson, Jr., to Henry Watson, Esq., Feb. 10, 1834, Watson Papers; Leslie Howard Owens, *This Species of Property: Slave Life and Culture in the Old South* (New York, 1976), 16.

10. Alva Fitzpatrick to Phillips Fitzpatrick, Aug. 20, 1849, Fitzpatrick Papers.

11. James Winchester to J. R. Eaton, Sept. 3, 1806, John Rust Eaton Papers; Margaret Burr Des Champs, ed., "Some Mississippi Letters to Robert Fraser, 1841–1844," *Jour. Miss. Hist.,* XV (1953), 184; Rufus Amis to Bettie Amis, Feb. 28, 1857, Rufus Amis Papers; Thomas [?] to W. P. Graham, Oct. 26, 1835, Graham Papers; Thomas Maitland Marshall, ed., *The Life and Papers of Frederick Bates* (St. Louis, Mo., 1926), II, 156.

12. Marshall, ed., *Papers of Frederick Bates,* II, 156; G. W. Carter to Ebenesor Carter, Dec. 13, 1853, McDonald and Irving Family Papers; Thomas [?] to W. P. Graham, June 23, 1835, Graham Papers; Rufus Amis to Bettie Amis, Feb. 28, 1857, Amis Papers.

13. Bayrd Still, ed., "The Westward Migration of a Planter Pioneer in 1796," *WMQ,* 2d Ser., XXI (1941), 340; Marshall, ed., *Papers of Frederick Bates,* II, 155; Henry Watson, Jr., to Henry Watson, Esq., Jan. 30, 1839, Watson Papers; Champs, ed., "Some Mississippi Letters," 184.

14. G. W. Carter to Ebenesor Carter, Dec. 13, 1853, McDonald & Irving Papers; Champs, ed., "Some Mississippi Letters," 184; [?] to W. P. Graham, July 4, 1831, Graham Papers; Rufus Amis to Bettie Amis, Feb. 28, 1857, Amis Papers; Albert Fitzpatrick to Phillips Fitzpatrick, Aug. 20, 1849, Fitzpatrick Papers.

15. Ariella Hawkins to Sarah M. Alston, April 11, 1847, Archibald Davis Alston Papers; William A. Chaney, ed., "A Louisiana Planter in the Gold Rush," *La. Hist.,* III (1962), 133–144.

16. "Recollections" of 1836, Chap. II, James Rowe Coombs Papers; Bills Diary, entry for June 9, 1857; Clement Eaton, *The Growth of Southern Civilization* (New York, 1961), 31–32; Edward Strutt Abdy, *Journal of a Residence and Tour in the United States 1833–1834* (London, 1835), II, 183.

17. Jonathan M. Wiener, *Social Origins of the New South: Alabama, 1860–1885* (Baton Rouge, La., 1978), 9. Wiener's evidence shows that between 1850 and 1870 the persistence rate of much of Alabama's "planter elite" was only 21%. The statistics for Dallas County, Alabama, were generously provided by William Barney of the University of North Carolina at Chapel Hill and are from his forthcoming study of Alabama during the Civil War. I derived the Jasper County, Ga., statistics from the manuscript slaveholding schedules of the United States Census for 1850 and 1860.

Persistence rates of this kind must be used carefully. They are subject to all the difficulties associated with the U.S. census returns, plus the added problem of interpreting why individuals left and how far they actually went. Thus many slaveholders may not have been located because their names were unrecognizable, because they were missed by enumerators, or because they died. Many who moved may have gone no farther than a few miles, into the next county. Nevertheless, the extraordinary rates of change have been corroborated by at least three separate studies of the manuscript census returns, and they are confirmed by overwhelming literary evidence as well.

18. Peter R. Knight, "Population Turnover, Persistence, and Residential Mobility in Boston, 1830–1860," in Stephen Thernstrom and Richard Sennett, eds., *Nineteenth-century Cities: Essays in the New Urban History* (New Haven, Conn., 1969), 262–265; Stephen Thernstrom, *Poverty and Progress: Social Mobility in a Nineteenth Century City* (Cambridge, Mass., 1964), 96, 102.

19. Mrs. E. A. Carter to Mary N. Bailey, Nov. 27, 1853, James B. Bailey Papers; Fletcher M. Green, ed., *The Lides Go South . . . And West, The Record of a Planter Migration* (Columbia, S.C., 1952), 12–14.

20. Lyell, *Second Visit*, II, 61–63, 109–110; Orville W. Taylor, *Negro Slavery in Arkansas* (Durham, N.C., 1958), 51. Internal migration was a national phenomenon which did not escape the attention of the U.S. government. See Joseph C. G. Kennedy, *Preliminary Report on the Eighth Census* (Washington, D.C., 1862), 120–121, and his *Population of the United States in 1860* (Washington, D.C., 1864), xxxiii–xxxiv.

21. Douglass C. North, *The Economic Growth of the United States, 1790–1860* (Englewood Cliffs, N.J., 1961), argues that slaveholders moved in rhythm with cotton price fluctuations. Analyzing population shifts in South Carolina, he writes: "Emigration and plantation consolidation were the old South's answer to the low cotton prices of the 1820's," p. 191. But in a footnote on the same page North says that emigration from South Carolina doubled in the 1830's. "With rising cotton prices, the lure of rich western lands attracted the large planters and their slaves." North seems to be arguing that slaveholders moved because cotton prices were high *and* because they were low. In a chart on p. 124 North uses public land sales as a measure of southern expansionism, again relating them to cotton price fluctuations. But the use of federal land sales excludes state sales of Indian lands and private land speculation as well, two important omissions. Still more damaging to North's

argument, as Peter Temin points out, is the assumption that price fluctuations were entirely a response to changes in the *supply* of cotton—fluctuations that could thus be met by opening new lands to cotton cultivation. In fact, 41% of the southern cotton in the 1830's was sold abroad, and price fluctuations clearly resulted from shifts in international *demand* as well as supply. Thus migration could follow a demand-induced price rise rather than an exhausted capacity. Contrary to North, Temin concludes that there is "no evidence" of a "periodic exhaustion" of cotton lands which was presumably responsible for "long swings" in cotton price fluctuation. Peter Temin, "The Causes of Cotton-price Fluctuations in the 1830's," *Review of Economics and Statistics,* XLIX (1967), 463–470. See also Paul Gates, "Charts of Public Land Sales and Entries," *Jour. Econ. Hist.,* XXIV (1964).

22. Henry Watson, Jr., to Julia Watson, Sept. 27, 1836, Watson Papers.

23. Herbert A. Kellar, ed., "A Journey Through the South in 1836: Diary of James D. Davidson," *JSH,* I (1935), 355, 356.

24. Charles Lyell, *Travels in North America* (New York, 1845), I, 156; Harrod C. Anderson Diary, entry for Feb. 21, 1854.

25. Lyell, *Second Visit,* II, 72.

26. Julian Dwight Martin, ed., "The Letters of Charles Caleb Cotton, 1798–1802," *So. Car. Hist. Geneal. Mag.,* LI (1950), 138; George Allen to William Williams, Sept. 12, 1850, Allen Papers; Lyell, *Second Visit,* II, 13.

27. Green, ed., *Lides Go South, passim;* Thomas Harrison to James Harrison, March 11, 1834, July 27, 1834, Harrison Papers.

28. Flint, *Recollections,* 234; Nath Winfield, ed., "A Letter from Texas," *So. West. Hist. Quar.,* LXXI (1968), 426.

29. [Mr. or Mrs. Smith Lipscomb ?] to his or her mother, July 11, 1846, Lipscomb Family Papers; Joseph B. Thompson to Rebecca Thompson, March 3, 1839, Thompson Family Papers; Green, ed., *Lides Go South,* 13, 18–19.

30. Ingraham, *Southwest,* II, 51; Olmsted, *Seaboard States,* 386.

31. Philip Henry Gosse, *Letters from Alabama* (London, 1859), 153–156; Olmsted, *Back Country,* 20; Olmsted, *Seaboard States,* 575; Olmsted, *Texas,* 115–117.

32. Buckingham, *Slave States,* II, 305; Henry Watson, Jr., to Julius Reed, Jan. 8, 1831, Watson Papers; Daniel Lord, Journal of a trip from Baltimore to Savannah and return, 1824; Olmsted, *Back Country,* 269; Olmsted, *Seaboard States,* 330, 350.

33. Sam Bowers Hilliard, *Hog Meat and Hoecake: Food Supply in the Old South, 1840–1860* (Carbondale, Ill., 1972), 40–55, and *passim;* Olmsted, *Texas,* 116.

34. Buckingham, *Slave States,* I, 234–235, II, 198–199; Lyell, *Second Visit,* I, 244; Dr. Francis J. Kron Diary, entry for 1835, W. K. Littleton Collection.

35. Eaton, *Growth of Southern Civilization,* 34; Lucy Clanton to Mary Arrington, May 14, 1848, Arrington Papers; Ingraham, *Southwest,* II, 101.

36. Olmsted, *Texas,* 47–51; Henry Watson, Jr., to Theodore Watson, March 11, 1831, Watson Papers.

37. Flint, *Recollections,* 198; Buckingham, *Slave States,* I, 258.

38. Mayfield Biography; Olmsted, *Seaboard States*, 576.

39. Pauline [?] to Elizabeth Goode, April 8, 1851, Mrs. William Buchanan Papers; Green, ed., *Lides Go South*, 1, 8; Mary Drake to Gray Sills, June 14, 1839, Louisa M. (Jelks) Sills Papers.

40. Green, ed., *Lides Go South*, 35–36; Alex Allen to George Allen, Sept. 26, 1850, Allen Papers.

41. *Farmers' Register*, IV (1836), 10–11.

42. *Southern Cultivator*, II (1844), 121; *Farmers' Register*, III (1835), 138; *Southern Cultivator*, II (1844), 121.

43. *American Farmer*, XIV (1858), 92; *Farmers' Register*, I (1833), 124.

44. *Southern Agriculturist*, VIII (1835), 243; *Southern Cultivator*, II (1844), 121.

45. *Southern Agriculturist*, VIII (1835), 128; *American Farmer*, XIV (1858), 92; *Farmers' Register*, IV (1837), 577.

46. *Farmers' Register*, VII (1839), 436–437; *Southern Cultivator*, II (1844), 95.

47. *Southern Cultivator*, XV (1857), 114.

48. Eaton, *Growth of Southern Civilization*, 34.

49. Ingraham, *Southwest*, II, 205–206.

50. Champs, ed., "Some Mississippi Letters," 188; Abdy, *Journal of Residence*, II, 193–198; Ingraham, *Southwest*, II, 159ff. The town was also a gathering place for slaveholders of various occupations. Port Gibson, Miss., had 62 slaveholders in 1860. They included three women—two teachers and a "planter" with five slaves —a free black barber with two slaves, five agriculturists, four clerks, fourteen merchants including a druggist, four physicians, a dentist, seven lawyers, four teachers, a preacher, and eleven craftsmen, including tinsmiths, gunsmiths, and a brickmason. The remaining eleven masters included a sailor, government workers, a gardener, and a liveryman. Harris Gaylord Warren, "People and Occupations in Port Gibson, 1860," *Jour. Miss. Hist.*, X (1948), 104–115. See also U. B. Phillips, "Historical Notes of Milledgeville, Ga.," *Gulf States Historical Magazine*, II (1903), 162–163.

51. Green, ed., *Lides Go South*, 18.

52. Flint, *Recollections*, 65–66; Ingraham, *Southwest*, II, 170–172; the factorage system is described in detail in Harold D. Woodman, *King Cotton and His Retainers* (Lexington, Ky., 1968); Kron Diary, entry for 1835; Olmsted, *Seaboard States*, 330.

53. William D. Moseley Diary, entries for Dec. 1850.

54. Woodman, *King Cotton*, 74; Harold D. Woodman, "Itinerant Cotton Merchants in the Antebellum South," *Agric. Hist.*, XL (1966), 79–90.

55. Lewis E. Atherton, *The Southern Country Store, 1800–1860* (Baton Rouge, La., 1949), 21 and *passim*.

56. Raleigh A. Suarez, "Bargains, Bills, and Bankruptcies: Business Activity in Rural Antebellum Alabama," *La. Hist.*, VII (1966), 189–206.

57. Green, ed., *Lides Go South*, 42; see above, p. 158.

Chapter 4: The Convenient Sin

1. See Edwin Scott Gaustad, *Historical Atlas of Religion in America* (New York, 1962, rev. ed. 1976), 69, 105, for the locations of Episcopal and Roman Catholic churches in the Old South.

2. Wesley M. Gewehr, *The Great Awakening in Virginia* (Gloucester, Mass., 1930; reprinted 1965), 68–105, 34, and *passim*.

3. David T. Morgan, Jr., "The Great Awakening in North Carolina, 1740–1775: The Baptist Phase," *North Carolina Historical Review,* XLV (1968), 264–283. See also David T. Morgan, Jr., "The Consequences of George Whitefield's Ministry in the Carolinas and Georgia, 1739–1740," *Ga. Hist. Quar.,* LV (1971), 62–82.

4. See John B. Boles, *The Great Revival: The Origins of the Southern Evangelical Mind, 1787–1805* (Lexington, Ky., 1972).

5. Ingraham, *Southwest,* II, 72; George C. Osborn, ed., "A Religious Revival in Tallahassee in 1843," *Florida Historical Quarterly,* XXXIII (1954), 293; Olmsted, *Seaboard States,* 453.

6. Rosa Kleburg, "Some of My Early Experiences in Texas," Texas State Historical Association, *Quarterly,* I (1898), 300; William Ethelbert Ervin Books, entries for Oct. 17–21, 1841; John W. Jones Diary, entry for Dec. 31, 1859. There were revivals at the Univ. of Alabama at Tuscaloosa in 1833, the Univ. of Georgia at Athens in 1839, and the Univ. of Virginia at Charlottesville in 1859.

7. James, "Josiah Hinds," 22–23, 26, 27; Sarah Guion to John Guion, July 30, 1818, Guion Papers.

8. M. A. R. Kirkland to Octavia Wyche, April 16, 1843, Wyche and Otey Family Papers; "Last Advice . . ." of the Reverend Charles Pettigrew, 1797, Pettigrew Papers; Octavia Wyche-Otey to [?], Nov. 19, 1851, Wyche-Otey Papers; Alexander Allen to George Allen, March 31, 1852, Allen Papers.

9. Faye Acton Axford, ed., *The Journals of Thomas Hubbard Hobbs* (University, Ala., 1976), 26; Eliza Burruss to John Burruss, June 15, 1825; John C. Burruss and Family Papers; William Byrd to William Byrd, April 8, 1859, Byrd Papers; Mary (Jeffreys) Bethell Diary, entry for Oct. 16, 1856.

10. Donald Mathews, *Religion in the Old South* (Chicago, 1978), is a useful introduction to southern evangelicalism. See also Boles, *Great Revival,* 25–35, 131.

11. Journal of a Voyage up the Mississippi and Red Rivers from New Orleans, entry for Jan. 15, 1806; Flint, *Recollections,* 75.

12. Lyder L. Unstad, ed., "Norwegian Migration to Texas," *So. West. Hist. Quar.,* XLIII (1939), 188.

13. Jeremiah Clemens to Clement C. Clay, Jan. 14, 1834, Clement C. Clay Papers; John N. Evans to John William Burruss, Jan. 1, 1836, Burruss Papers.

14. Buckingham, *Slave States,* II, 274–275; Boles, *Great Revival,* 168.

15. Dr. Thomas Gale to Benjamin Johns, July 3, 1816, Gale and Polk Papers; Baker Diary, entry for March 23, 1860; Bills Diary, entry for Dec. 1858.

16. William Byrd to William Byrd, Aug. 21, 1851, Byrd Papers.

17. Anderson Diary, entry for Dec. 23, 1859; James, "Josiah Hinds," 27; C. P. Pettit to Joshua Lipscomb, Oct. 10, 1858, Lipscomb Papers; David Thomas Bailey, "Slavery and the Churches: The Old Southwest" (Ph.D. dissertation, University of California at Berkeley, 1979), 72.

18. Sarah McCulloh Lemmon, ed., *The Pettigrew Papers* (Raleigh, N.C., 1971), I, 285; Olmsted, *Back Country,* 67.

19. Larry E. Tise, "Proslavery Ideology: A Social and Intellectual History of the Defense of Slavery in America, 1790–1840" (Ph.D. dissertation, University of North Carolina at Chapel Hill, 1974).

20. Higginbotham, *In the Matter of Color,* 37; Albert J. Raboteau, *Slave Religion: The "Invisible Institution" in the Antebellum South* (New York, 1978), 102–103, 119.

21. Kenneth L. Carroll, "Religious Influences on the Manumission of Slaves in Caroline, Dorchester, and Talbot Counties," *Md. Hist. Mag.,* LVI (1961), 188.

22. Charles Woodmason, *The Carolina Backcountry on the Eve of the Revolution,* ed. Richard J. Hooker (Chapel Hill, N.C., 1953), 240–241; see also Rhys Isaac, "Evangelical Revolt: The Nature of the Baptists' Challenge to the Traditional Order in Virginia, 1765 to 1775," *WMQ,* 3rd. Ser., XXIV (1974), 345–368; Orville W. Taylor, "Baptists and Slavery in Arkansas: Relationships and Attitudes," *Arkansas Historical Quarterly,* XXXVIII (1979), 212.

23. Charles C. Jones, *The Religious Instruction of the Negroes in the United States* (Savannah, Ga., 1842), 193.

24. South Carolina, *Journal of the General Assembly* (1835), 6; see also Mathews, *Religion in the Old South,* 136–184.

25. Jacob Stroyer, *My Life in the South* (Salem, Mass., 1898), 64; Axford, ed., *Journal of Thomas H. Hobbs,* 74; Mary Burruss McGehee to John W. Burruss, March 17, 1836, Burruss Papers.

26. "Last Advice . . ." of the Reverend Charles Pettigrew, 1797, Pettigrew Papers; Ronald T. Takaki, *A Pro-Slavery Crusade: The Agitation to Reopen the African Slave Trade* (New York, 1971), 77.

27. Taylor, "Baptists and Slavery in Arkansas," 222; Hepzibah Church Records, I, entries for Nov. 20, 1819, Dec. 14, 1822, March 15, 1823, May 17, 1823. Eventually "Br. Edds. Confessed his fault to the Church and was restored"; Lemmon, ed., *Pettigrew Papers,* I, 286.

28. William Allen Smith, *Lectures on the Philosophy and Practice of Slavery* (Nashville, Tenn., 1856), 23; Gosse, *Letters from Alabama,* 253; John Witherspoon to Susan McDowall, Feb. 18, 1836, Witherspoon and McDowall Family Papers.

29. Jo Ann Carrigan, "Impact of Epidemic Yellow Fever on Life in Louisiana," *La. Hist.,* IV (1963), 30; Kenneth F. and Virginia H. Kiple, "Black Tongue and Black Men: Pellagra and Slavery in the Antebellum South," *JSH,* XLIII (1977), 411–428. See the discussions of black mortality and morbidity in Wood, *Black Majority,* 63–91; and in Paul A. David, *et al., Reckoning with Slavery: A Critical Study in the Quantitative History of American Negro Slavery* (New York, 1976), 282–292.

30. Isaac Guion to Frederick Guion, April 25, 1819, Guion Papers; Philip Pitts Diary, v. 1.

31. Lemmon, ed., *Pettigrew Papers,* I, 586; Henry Watson, Jr., to Julius Reed, June 22, 1833, Watson Papers.

32. Baker Diary, entry for Aug. 22, 1850; Andrew Buchanan to William Buchanan, Nov. 26, 1836, Buchanan and McClellan Family Papers; Lucy Horton to her husband, Sept. 24, 1826, Wyche-Otey Papers.

33. Florida, *Journal of the Legislative Council* (Tallahassee, Fla., 1840), 9; Carrigan, "Impact of Epidemic Yellow Fever," 22; Susan Sillers Darden Diary, entry for Sept. 23, 1855; Mrs. Eliza Eve Carmichael Diary, entry for May 26, 1844.

34. William Luther Bigelow Lawrence Diary, entry for Sept. 8, 1854; Boles, *Great Revival,* 101.

35. Louis M. DeSaussure Plantation Record, entry for Nov. 11, 1857; Samuel Arrington to [Archibald Arrington?], Jan. 26, 1857, Arrington Papers; Green, ed., *Lides Go South,* 43.

36. Frank L. Owsley, "The Clays of Early Alabama History," *Ala. Rev.,* II (1949), 267–268.

37. "Torbert's Journal for 1857–1874," 46; Owens, *This Species of Property,* 116–117; Baker Diary, entry for June 30, 1854; Rodah Horton to Lucy Ann Horton, Nov. 23, 1836, Wyche-Otey Papers; "Recollections," p. 5, Coombs Papers; Owsley, "Clays of Alabama," 266.

38. Edwin Adams Davis, ed., *Plantation Life in the Florida Parishes of Louisiana, 1836–1846, As Reflected in the Diary of Bennet H. Barrow* (New York, 1943, reprinted 1967), 374; Robert Raymond Reid Diary, entry for Feb. 1, 1833; Barrow Family Paper, misc. entries for 1819–1824.

39. Olmsted, *Back Country,* 133; Clarissa E. Leavitt Town Diary, entry for March 15, 1853; Bethell Diary, entry for Jan. 13, 1853.

40. Taylor, "Baptists and Slavery in Arkansas," 202; Sydnor, *Slavery in Mississippi,* 58; M. A. R. Kirkland to Octavia Wyche, April 16, 1843, Wyche-Otey Papers; Mrs. Cain to Minerva Cain, [1850's?], Tod Robinson Caldwell Papers.

41. Bailey, "Slavery and the Churches," 86; John W. Blassingame, *The Slave Community,* 2d rev. ed. (New York, 1979), 79–90.

42. Lewis O. Saum, "Death in the Popular Mind of Pre-Civil War America," 30–48, and Ann Douglass, "Heaven Our Home: Consolation Literature in the Northern United States, 1830–1880," 49–68, both in David E. Stannard, ed., *Death in America* (Philadelphia, 1975). Saum does not argue for a sectional division in attitudes toward death, but a close reading of his evidence reveals that with few exceptions such a division existed.

43. Frederick Douglass, *My Bondage and My Freedom* (New York, 1855), 68; Louis Hughes, *Thirty Years a Slave* (Milwaukee, Wisc., 1897), 90–91; Lawrence W. Levine, *Black Culture and Black Consciousness: Afro-American Folk Thought from Slavery to Freedom* (New York, 1977), 34–35. See also Raboteau, *Slave Religion,* 290–293.

44. Moses Grandy, *Narrative of the Life of Moses Grandy* (Boston, 1844), 19; Solomon Northup, *Twelve Years a Slave*, edited by Sue Eakin and Joseph Logsdon (Auburn, N.Y., 1953, reprinted Baton Rouge, La., 1968), 32, 120.

45. Reid Diary, entry for Jan. 31, 1833; "Last Advice . . ." of the Reverend Charles Pettigrew, 1797, Pettigrew Papers.

46. *Lee Papers,* V, 218–219; John Witherspoon to Susan McDowall, Jan. 14, 1836, Witherspoon and McDowall Papers; Martha von Briesen, ed., *The Letters of Elijah Fletcher* (Charlottesville, Va., 1965), 122; Charles B. Dew, "David Ross and the Oxford Iron Works: A Study of Industrial Slavery in the Early Nineteenth-century South," *WMQ,* 3rd Ser., XXXI (1974), 202; Olmsted, *Seaboard States,* 94.

47. William Kaufman Scarborough, ed., *The Diary of Edmund Ruffin* (Baton Rouge, La., 1972), I, 238; Marshall, ed., *Papers of Frederick Bates,* II, 228.

48. Anne C. Loveland, *Southern Evangelicals and the Social Order, 1800–1860* (Baton Rouge, La., 1980), 186–189.

49. Henry Clay Bruce, *The New Man* (York, Pa., 1895), 85; John Witherspoon to Susan McDowall, May 23, 1837, Witherspoon and McDowall Papers.

50. John Mills to Gilbert Jackson, May 19, 1807, Mills Letters; Phillips, ed., *Plantation and Frontier,* I, 56.

51. Olmsted, *Texas,* 386; James, "Josiah Hinds," 27; Lemmon, ed., *Pettigrew Papers,* I, 286; Takaki, *Pro-Slavery Crusade,* 78.

52. James L. Roark, *Masters Without Slaves: Southern Planters in the Civil War and Reconstruction* (New York, 1977), 10; [?] to J. H. Whitten, Feb. 18, 1855, J. H. Whitten Letter.

53. Mary Burruss McGehee to John W. Burruss, May 29, 1836, Burruss Papers; Olmsted, *Back Country,* 133; Henry Watson, Jr., to Sophia Watson, May 11, 1848, Watson Papers.

Chapter 5: Freedom and Bondage

1. John Mills to Gilbert Jackson, May 19, 1807, Mills Letters.

2. Henry Marston Diary, entry for Jan. 1, 1827; A. R. Boteler Diary, entry for May 16, 1845.

3. "Recollections of John Mitchell Davidson," Theodore Davidson Morrison Papers.

4. Edward W. Phifer, "Slavery in Microcosm: Burke County, North Carolina," *JSH,* XXVIII (1962), 147.

5. Olmsted, *Back Country,* 23; John C. Jenkins Dairy, entries for Jan. 1, 1844 and Jan., 1850.

6. See in general, Woodman, *King Cotton;* Henry Watson, Jr., to Henry Watson, Esq., June 11, 1837, Watson Papers; James, "Josiah Hinds," 24; Olmsted, *Back Country,* 328.

7. Alex Dortch to William Baskerville, Oct. 8, 1850, William Baskerville Papers; Henry Watson, Jr., to Julius Reed, Jan. 8, 1831, Watson Papers.

8. J. E. Pirie, ed., "A Letter from Lamar County in 1844," *So. West. Hist. Quar.,* LIII (1949), 67; *Southern Planter,* I (1941), 4; "Torbert's Journal for 1856," 246.

9. Smith Lipscomb to Joshuah Lipscomb, March, 1853, Lipscomb Papers; Joseph B. Thompson to Aunt Rebecca, Dec. 18, 1852, Thompson Papers; *Farmers' Register,* IV (1837), 733.

10. Still, ed., "Westward Migration of a Planter Pioneer," 340–341; Alex Dortch to William Baskerville, Oct. 8, 1850, Baskerville Papers.

11. South Carolina, *Journal of the Senate* (Columbia, S.C., 1854), 12–13.

12. *Farmers' Register,* I (1833), 124; *Southern Agriculturist,* II (1829), 4–6.

13. Mississippi, *Journal of the Senate* (Jackson, Miss., 1842), 13; Georgia, *Journal of the Senate* (Milledgeville, Ga., 1828), 18; *ibid.* (1848), Nov. 2, 1847.

14. Eliza Burruss to John C. Burruss, June 15, 1825, Burruss Papers; Edward Harden Diary, entry for Feb. 9, 1839; Baker Diary, entry for June 16, 1850.

15. North Carolina, *Journal of the House of Commons* (Raleigh, N.C., 1837), Nov. 22, 1836; Green, ed., *Lides Go South,* 17; Texas, *Journal of the House of Representatives* (Austin, Tex., 1853), II, 31; Georgia, *Journal of the Senate* (Milledgeville, Ga., 1818), 5–6.

16. Arkansas, *Journal of the House of Representatives* (Little Rock, Ark., 1859), 32–33.

17. Georgia, *Journal of the Senate* (Columbus, Ga., 1858), Nov. 3, 1858; Tennessee, *Journal of the House of Representatives* (Nashville, Tenn., 1854), 37.

18. Richmond *Enquirer,* Oct. 2, 1860.

19. Green, ed., *Lides Go South,* 23; Baker Diary, entry for Sept. 27, 1849; Esther Wright Boyd Memoirs, p. 2.

20. Olmsted, *Texas,* 126, 245; Henry Watson, Jr., to Rosanna Reed, April 9, 1834, Watson Papers; Flint, *Recollections,* 133.

21. For a discussion of how southern intellectuals fretted over the origins of alleged black inferiority, see George M. Fredrickson, *The Black Image in the White Mind: The Debate on Afro-American Character and Destiny, 1817–1914* (New York, 1971), chapters 1–3.

22. Jordan, *White Over Black,* 436; John Mills to Gilbert Jackson, May 19, 1807, Mills Letters; *Appendix to Congressional Globe,* April 10, 1848, 526.

23. Olmsted, *Back Country,* 239; Buckingham, *Slave States,* I, 272; Richmond *Enquirer,* Aug. 30, 1831; John Campbell, *Negro Mania: Being an Examination of the Falsely Assumed Equality of the Various Races of Men* (Philadelphia, 1851), 10.

24. George H. Reese, ed., *Proceedings of the Virginia State Convention of 1861* (Richmond, Va., 1965), IV, 385–386.

25. Northup, *Twelve Years a Slave,* 205–206; Buckingham, *Slave States,* I, 66.

26. *Farmers' Register,* II (1834), 253.

27. Buckingham, *Slave States,* I, 66.

28. *American Farmer*, 10 (1828), 273; Olmsted, *Texas*, 32.

29. Olmsted, *Seaboard States*, 623; John Mills to Gilbert Jackson, May 19, 1807, Mills Letters; *American Cotton Planter*, I (1853), 283–285; *DeBow's Review*, XXII (1857), 76.

30. William Dunbar to David Ross, Nov. 21, 1800, Dunbar Letterbook; Louis-Phillipe, *Diary of My Travels in America* (1797, reprinted New York, 1977), 19.

31. *Farmers' Register*, III (1836), 180; *DeBow's Review*, VII (1849), 220. For evidence of the increased legal oppression of slaves in the 1850's, see Michael S. Hindus, "Black Justice Under White Law: Criminal Prosecutions of Blacks in Antebellum South Carolina," *Journal of American History*, LXII (1976), 590.

32. Thomas Glover, *An Account of Virginia, Its Scituation, Temperature, Productions, Inhabitants and Their Manner of Planting and Ordering Tobacco & c.* (1676, reprinted at Oxford, 1904), 12; Alexander, ed., *Journal of John Fontaine*, 28; J. R. Eaton to Charles R. Eaton, May 31, 1794, Eaton Papers.

33. *DeBow's Review*, XI (1951), 350; Buckingham, *Slave States*, II, 8.

34. Lyell, *Second Visit*, I, 225, 241; Richmond *Enquirer*, April 15, 1856; Abdy, *Journal*, II, 196.

35. Buckingham, *Slave States*, I, 215; Olmsted, *Seaboard States*, 44–45. So averse were some Southerners to attacking the North that in two reviews of Harriet Beecher Stowe's antislavery novel, *Uncle Tom's Cabin*, the normally aggressive *DeBow's Review* concentrated on criticizing gullible English readers for believing the book. In one case the critic offered the usual comparison of free labor in England and slave labor in the South. See XIV (1853), 258–280 and XV (1853), 95–105.

36. Lyell, *Second Visit*, II, 69–70; Henry Watson, Jr., to Henry Watson, Esq., Aug. 7, 1834, Watson Papers.

37. Lyell, *Second Visit*, II, 210, 211.

38. Alabama, *Journal of the Senate* (Montgomery, Ala., 1854), 37.

39. John Clopton to James Apperson, April 4, 1796, Clopton Papers; Harden Diary, misc. entries for 1826–1828; William Luther Bigelow Lawrence Diary, entry for Sept. 20, 1842.

40. John Clopton to [?], Jan. 16, 1796, Clopton Papers; Virginia, *Journal of the House of Delegates* (Richmond, Va., 1842), 7.

41. Louisiana, *Journal of the House of Representatives* (Baton Rouge, La., 1820), 30; Kentucky, *Journal of the House of Representatives* (Lexington, Ky., 1827), 14.

42. Richmond *Enquirer*, April 15, 1856.

43. Buckingham, *Slave States*, I, 138–139, 375. See Epilogue of the present work for the slaveholders' historical justification of secession in defense of slavery.

44. Monette Dairy; Bills Diary, entries for Dec. 16, 1843 and May 29, 1845; Marston Diary, entry for June 17, 1822; John Nevitt Diary, entry for July 4, 1827; John Fletcher Comer Book, entry for July 4, 1846.

45. Mary E. Bateman Dairy, entries for July 4–6, 1856; Monette Diary; Edgar

A. Stewart, ed., "The Journal of James Mallory," *Ala. Rev.,* XIV (1961), 222–223.

46. Northup, *Twelve Years a Slave,* 206; *Appendix to Congressional Globe,* April 10, 1848, 524, 526; Reese, ed., *Proceedings,* IV, 385–387.

47. Robert M. Ireland, *The County Courts of Antebellum Kentucky* (Lexington, Ky., 1972), 3–4, 13–14; Ralph A. Wooster, *The People in Power: Courthouse and Statehouse in the Lower South, 1850–1860* (Knoxville, Tenn., 1969), 54–55; Ralph A. Wooster, *Politicians, Planters and Plain Folk: Courthouse and Statehouse in the Upper South, 1850–1860* (Knoxville, Tenn., 1975), 63.

48. Wooster, *People in Power,* 41; Wooster, *Politicians,* 40.

49. Thornton, *Politics and Power,* 65–66.

50. Fitzpatrick Papers. Receipts for purchases of land and slaves are found especially in folders 3–5. Manuscript inaugural address is in folder 4.

51. Lyell, *Second Visit,* II, 226; Leonard L. Richards, "The Jacksonians and Slavery," in Lewis Perry and Michael Fellman, eds., *Antislavery Reconsidered: New Perspectives on the Abolitionists* (Baton Rouge, La., 1979), 99–118.

52. For Jackson's influence on southern politics, see William J. Cooper, *The South and the Politics of Slavery* (Baton Rouge, La., 1978), 5–22; Reid Diary, entry for Oct. 10, 1833; Henry Watson, Jr., to Julius Reed, June 22, 1833, Watson Papers; Bills Dairy, entries for June 13, 1845, Jan. 8, 1859.

53. Charles G. Sellers, Jr., "Who Were the Southern Whigs?" in Pessen, ed., *New Perspectives,* 109–123, Sellers's notes are a useful guide to the literature on southern Whigs.

54. Buckingham, *Slave States,* II, 76, 80–81.

55. Mississippi, *Journal of the Senate* (Jackson, Miss., 1848), 30; Bills Diary, entry for May 6, 1844; Davis, ed., *Plantation Life in Louisiana,* 340; see also, Robert E. May, *The Southern Dream of a Caribbean Empire, 1854–1861* (Baton Rouge, La., 1973).

56. Richmond *Enquirer,* Dec. 21, 1819.

57. Letter of Rep. John Clopton to his constituents, Feb. 24, 1804, Clopton Papers; Baker Diary, entry for Aug. 29, 1849.

58. *DeBow's Review,* IV (1847), 31; Hundley, *Social Relations,* 50.

59. Alabama, *Journal of the Senate* (Montgomery, Ala., 1857), 25; *DeBow's Review,* X (1851), 132.

60. Adam McChesney to George Houston, Jan. 31, 1852, Willson, Whitehead and Houston Papers.

Chapter 6: Factories in the Fields

1. *Southern Cultivator,* IV (1846), 114. See also R. Keith Aufhauser, "Slavery and Scientific Management," *Jour. Econ. Hist.,* XXXIII (1973), 811–824.

2. *Cotton Planter and Soil of the South,* I (1857), 233; *Southern Agriculturist,* II (1842), 534; *DeBow's Review,* III (1847), 419, and XXV (1858), 55.

3. *Farmers' Register,* VI (1837), 32; *Southern Agriculturist,* VI (1833), 281–282.

4. *Southern Agriculturist,* I (1828), 524, and X (1837), 505; *Farmers' Register,* I (1834), 565.

5. *Farmers' Register,* III (1836), 115; *Southern Cultivator,* VII (1849), 103; *American Farmer,* VII (1852), 397; *Farmers' Register,* VIII (1840), 426.

6. *DeBow's Review,* XXI (1856), 618; *Farmers' Register,* I (1834), 565; *Southern Cultivator,* VII (1849), 103, and XVIII (1860), 131.

7. *Southern Agriculturist,* VI (1833), 571.

8. *American Cotton Planter,* II (1854), 353, 356. For examples of proposed rules governing overseers, see *Southern Agriculturist,* XI (1838), 344–345; *Farmers' Register,* VIII (1840), 230–231; *Southern Cultivator,* VI (1848), 134; *American Cotton Planter,* II (1854), 353–356, reprinted the following year in *DeBow's Review,* XVIII (1855), 339–345; *Southern Planter,* XVI (1856), 48–51, 147–148.

9. *Southern Agriculturist,* VI (1833), 571. See also, for example, *DeBow's Review,* XIV (1853), 177–178.

10. *Southern Agriculturist,* VI (1833), 572.

11. Davis, ed., *Plantation Life in Louisiana,* 408; *DeBow's Review,* XIV (1853), 177–178.

12. *Cotton Planter and Soil of the South,* I (1857), 374; *Southern Agriculturist,* IX (1836), 627, 626.

13. *Southern Agriculturist,* I (1828), 525.

14. *Southern Cultivator,* IV (1846), 114; *Southern Agriculturist,* IV (1831), 352, 350.

15. *American Farmer,* VII (1852), 350; *DeBow's Review,* XI (1851), 371.

16. *Southern Cultivator,* VII (1849), 103; *Southern Planter,* XII (1852), 107; *Farmers' Register,* I (1834), 564; *DeBow's Review,* XXII (1857), 376.

17. *Southern Cultivator,* XVIII (1860), 131; *DeBow's Review,* XXII (1857), 43; *Southern Agriculturist,* II (1842), 533; *Southern Cultivator,* VII (1849), 103, and V (1847), 62, and VII (1849), 103.

18. *Southern Agriculturist,* V (1832), 231; *Farmers' Register,* III (1836), 68; *Southern Agriculturist,* XI (1838), 512.

19. *Farmers' Register,* II (1834), 248–249, and VI (1837), 32, and VII (1840), 426–427; *Southern Cultivator,* XIV (1856), 17.

20. *Southern Cultivator,* IV (1846), 113; *Southern Agriculturist,* I (1828), 524, 525; *Southern Cultivator,* VII (1849), 105, and II (1844), 107; *American Farmer,* XII (1856), 131.

21. *Cotton Planter and Soil of the South,* II (1858), 20; *Southern Cultivator,* X (1852), 88.

22. See, for example, *Farmers' Register,* III (1836), 69, for indirect evidence that the sectional controversy inhibited discussion of plantation management. On the

shift in emphasis, see for example, *Cotton Planter and Soil of the South*, I (1857), 374–375.

23. *Southern Agriculturist*, XI (1838), 513, and III (1830), 238, 239; *Southern Planter*, XII (1852), 107; *Southern Cultivator*, XIV (1856), 192, and XVII (1860), 130–131.

24. *DeBow's Review*, XVII (1854), 425, 424; *Cotton Planter and Soil of the South*, II (1858), 21; *Southern Cultivator*, VII (1850), 163; *DeBow's Review*, XVIII (1855), 53. One writer spoke with uncharacteristic tenderness of his slaves as "rational beings," part of "the great brotherhood of man." But he was also unusually blunt about the important "profits" from "the little negroes he succeeds in raising," by treating "the breeding women, when lusty," with special care, *Cotton Planter and Soil of the South*, I (1857), 374–375.

25. "Inventory of books belonging to Roslin estate," 1829, Robert Leslie Account Book; Baker Diary, entry for April 9, 1850; "Plantation Rules" for Green Valley Plantation, 1840, Andrew Flinn Plantation Book.

26. "Rules to be observed on my place from & after the *First* of *January 1847,*" Ervin Books; "General Rules to govern time of an overseer," Haller Nutt Journal.

27. Jerdone Family Slave Record Book, 1762–1865; John Brown of North Carolina, Journal and Accounts; John Peter Broun Papers, 1843; John Francis Page Commonplace Book; Henry L. Pinckney Plantation Book, entry for May, 1850; "Inventory of Property at Cedar Bluff," Turner Reavis Account Book.

28. Lewis Plantation Records, late 1850's and early 1860's; Robert Jemison Proclamation to his slaves.

29. *DeBow's Review*, XI (1851), 371; Olmsted, *Seaboard States*, 145.

30. *American Farmer*, II (1821), 402.

31. Olmsted, *Seaboard States*, 618, 206; *Southern Planter*, I (1841), 138; Moseley Diary, entry for July 7, 1851; "Torbert's Journal for 1856," 241.

32. Austin Steward, *Twenty-two Years a Slave and Forty Years a Freeman* (Rochester, N.Y., 1857), 28; Douglass, *Bondage and Freedom*, 150; Davis, ed., *Plantation Life in Louisiana*, 148.

33. Phillips, ed., *Plantation and Frontier*, II, 31–32; Thomas Maskell [?] to Dr. Samuel Plaisted, Aug. 8, 1838, Samuel Plaisted Correspondence; Olmsted, *Seaboard States*, 207; David Gavin Diary, entry for Jan. 2, 1856.

34. Riley, ed., "Diary of a Mississippi Planter," 323, 327, 339.

35. Joseph B. Thompson to Uncle Lawrence, Sept 14, 1849, Thompson Papers; William Ogbourne, July 22, 1856, Bailey Papers; Thomas Gale to Josiah Gale, Aug. 22, 1833, Gale and Polk Papers; Anderson Diary, entry for Aug. 16, 1860.

36. Davis, ed., *Plantation Life in Louisiana*, 182.

37. [?] to William Berkeley, June 1, 1810, William Berkeley Papers.

38. Peter Carr Minor and Hugh Minor Notebooks, entries for winter 1830–1831; A. M. Reed Diary, 1861; *Farmers' Register*, II (1834), 95; Pitts Diary, entry for May 28, 1852. See also, Robert Gallman and Ralph V. Anderson, "Slaves as Fixed Capital," *JAH*, LXIV (1977), 24–46.

39. Olmsted, *Back Country,* 226; Ervin Books, entries for Jan. 11–12, 1848; James F. Jordan Paper, March 21, 1851; Lawrence Diary, entry for June 27, 1858; Bills Diary, entry for Jan. 4, 1846; Riley, ed., "Diary of a Mississippi Planter," 334; Olmsted, *Seaboard States,* 570.

40. John Brown Journal, entry for June 16, 1787; William Dinwiddie to his brother, Feb. 25, 1854, Roulstone and Dinwiddie Family Papers; J. L. Watkins to Samuel Bryarly, Feb. 23, 1829, Samuel Bryarly Papers; Davis, ed., *Plantation Life in Louisiana,* 259; Steward, *22 Years a Slave,* 23.

41. Olmsted, *Back Country,* 284.

42. *Farmers' Register,* II (1834), 253–254; *Southern Agriculturist,* XI (1838), 77; Sterling Gee to Nevill Gee, March 10, 1826, Sterling, Nevill, and Charles Gee Papers.

43. Thomas Houston to J. H. Dalton, May 11, 1857, Placebo Houston Papers; A. H. Arrington to Kate Arrington, Jan. 13, 1857, Arrington Papers; Buckingham, *Slave States,* I, 60; Douglass, *Bondage and Freedom,* 78; Ulrich B. Phillips and James David Glunt, eds., *Florida Plantation Records from the Papers of George Noble Jones* (St. Louis, Mo., 1927), 124; Phillips, ed., *Plantation and Frontier,* I, 179.

44. Alabama, *Journal of the House of Representatives* (Tuscaloosa, 1843), 28.

45. Olmsted, *Seaboard States,* 91; Kollock Books, entry for April 28, 1838 made by Kollock's overseer, William Hoffman; Olmsted, *Back Country,* 207; Phillips and Glunt, eds., *Florida Plantation Records,* 150.

46. Baker Diary, entry for July 1, 1858; Davis, ed., *Plantation Life in Louisiana,* 154; Lemmon, ed., *Pettigrew Papers,* I, 167, 285. See also, for example, John Couturier to John Ewing Colhoun, Aug. 10, 1792, and Archibald McKewn to J. E. Colhoun, Sept. 14, 1792, John Ewing Colhoun Papers; A. H. Arrington to Kate Arrington, Feb. 17, 1857, Arrington Papers.

47. Sydnor, *Slavery in Mississippi,* 69; Riley, ed., "Diary of a Mississippi Planter," 452–453; "Torbert's Journal for 1857–1874," 4, 38. See in general, William K. Scarborough, *The Overseer: Plantation Management in the Old South* (Baton Rouge, La., 1966).

48. Stroyer, *My Life in the South,* 30–33; William Wells Brown, *Narrative of William W. Brown, a Fugitive Slave* (Boston, 1847), 22; Douglass, *Bondage and Freedom,* 230–231.

49. Von Briesen, ed., *Letters of Elijah Fletcher,* 24; Douglass, *Bondage and Freedom,* 132; *Southern Agriculturist,* II (1842), 536; Phillips and Glunt, eds., *Florida Plantation Records,* 58–59, 63.

50. William Macon Waller to his mother, Feb. 17, 1848, William Macon Waller Letters; Taylor, *Slavery in Louisiana,* 25; Nevitt Diary, entry for Nov. 18, 1830; Thomas Sparks to Thomas Blewed, July 21, 1819, Harrison Papers; Elizabeth Keckley, *Behind the Scenes* (New York, 1868), 28.

51. Douglass, *Bondage and Freedom,* 174–175; "A Copy of Mary Houston's Will," April 27, 1833, Houston Papers; see, for example, Mark Grady's will, Aug. 1, 1845, Rosalie Ferrell Collection; John Brownrigg to Thomas Brownrigg, Sept.

18, 1789, and John Brownrigg to John Hunter, Sept. 18, 1789, Brownrigg Family Papers.

52. Hughes, *Thirty Years a Slave,* 5–12, 59; Bruce, *New Man;* Douglass, *Bondage and Freedom.*

53. Keckley, *Behind the Scenes,* 23, 43–44; Olmsted, *Texas,* 230.

54. Stampp, *Peculiar Institution,* esp. chapters 2 and 3, sees slave resistance as following logically from the exploitation of the slaves' labor. Recent interpretations which more or less follow this reasoning are Wood, *Black Majority,* and Mullin, *Flight and Rebellion.*

55. Genovese, *Roll, Jordan, Roll.* I frame these points as questions because, while I disagree with Genovese's interpretation of the slaveholders, I remain impressed —if not entirely convinced—by the subtlety of his compelling analysis of slave life. I also believe that his evocation of the dialectical interrelationship of accommodation and resistance can retain its validity whether or not the slaveholders were a paternalistic class.

Most of the work published since Stampp, *Peculiar Institution,* reinforces his emphasis on the importance of slave resistance: Blassingame, *Slave Community,* 147, argues that slaves created a sense of communalism that "called for support for those slaves who broke plantation rules"; Owens, *This Species of Property,* 104, asserts that "again and again bondsmen attacked slavery . . . at its core"; George P. Rawick, *From Sunup to Sundown: The Making of the Black Community* (Westport, Conn., 1972), 95, suggests that the fear of dehumanization was a motivation for slave resistance. Thus, "while blacks were oppressed and exploited, they fought back in a constant struggle by all available means"; Mullin, *Flight and Rebellion,* and Wood, *Black Majority,* both see rebellion as the logical conclusion of endemic slave resistance; Raboteau, *Slave Religion,* 305, argues that "religion itself, in a very real sense, could be an act of rebelliousness—an assertion of slave independence, which sometimes required outright defiance of the master's command"; Herbert G. Gutman, *The Black Family in Slavery and Freedom, 1750–1925* (New York, 1976), sees the development of adaptive family structures in the slave community which enhanced its cultural independence from white society; Levine, *Black Culture and Black Consciousness,* 133, argues that slave culture "intensified feelings of distance from the world of the slaveholders." All of these works are concerned with questions that go well beyond slave resistance. For present purposes, however, it is important to note that it was through pervasive resistance that the slaves made their greatest impact on the master class.

56. Davis, ed., *Plantation Life in Louisiana,* 406–410.

57. *Ibid.,* 213, 214, and *passim.*

58. *Ibid.,* 214, 85, 154, 373, 370, 239.

59. Nevitt Diary, entries for Oct. 2, 1827, May 21, 1828, Dec. 26, 1828, Jan. 27, 1828, Feb. 18, 1828, April 4, 1830, Aug. 27, 1830, Dec. 11, 1830, April 26, 1831.

60. Lemmon, ed., *Pettigrew Papers,* I, 612; Davis, ed., *Plantation Life in Louisiana,*

311; Douglass, *Bondage and Freedom,* 145–146; Olmsted, *Seaboard States,* 91; Buckingham, *Slave States,* I, 135. Rebecca S. C. Pilsbury Diary, entry for Dec. 20, 1848; [?] to James Bailey, March 24, 1856, Bailey Papers.

61. Olmsted, *Seaboard,* 684; Northup, *Twelve Years a Slave,* 157; James W. C. Pennington, *The Fugitive Blacksmith* (London, 1849), vii; Norman Yetman, ed., *Life Under the 'Peculiar Institution': Selections from the Slave Narrative Collection* (New York, 1970), 15–18; Abdy, *Journal,* II, 211.

62. Nathaniel Macon Papers.

63. Phillips, ed., *Plantation and Frontier,* I, 127–128; Pennington, *Fugitive Blacksmith,* 4; Lemmon, ed., *Pettigrew Papers,* I, 427; Dew, "David Ross and the Oxford Iron Works," 197.

64. Lyell, *Second Visit,* I, 267; Isaac Mason, *Life of Isaac Mason as a Slave* (Worcester, Mass., 1893), 22.

65. Lemmon, ed., *Pettigrew Papers,* I, 307; Robert S. Starobin, ed., *Blacks in Bondage: Letters of American Slaves* (New York, 1974), 13–35; Olmsted, *Back Country,* 143, 151, 155, 156.

66. May Brown to [?], April 30, 1839, Alexander and Hillhouse Family Papers; Thomas Purdie to Benajah Nicholls, April 4, 1824, Benajah Nicholls Papers; Nutt Journal, entry for Christmas, 1843.

67. Olmsted, *Seaboard States,* 5; Phillips and Glunt, eds., *Florida Plantation Records,* 130; Grandy, *Narrative of Moses Grandy,* 19.

68. Axford, ed., *Journals of Thomas H. Hobbs,* 139; Phillips and Glunt, eds., *Florida Plantation Records,* 96; Town Diary, entries for Feb. 8, 1853 and Feb. 24, 1853; Olmsted, *Seaboard States,* 196.

69. Texas, *Journal of the House of Representatives* (Austin, 1860), 35–36; Davis, ed., *Plantation Life in Louisiana,* 323–324; Douglass, *Bondage and Freedom,* 168; Phillips and Glunt, eds., *Florida Plantation Records,* 156–157.

70. Olmsted, *Seaboard States,* 11, 210, 198; Town Diary, entry for Jan. 25, 1853.

71. Rowland, comp., *Letters of William Dunbar,* 46–47; John A. Hamilton to William S. Hamilton, July 29, 1851, William S. Hamilton Papers; Richmond *Enquirer,* April 8, 1856.

72. Mason, *Life of Isaac Mason,* 33; Davis, ed., *Plantation Life in Louisiana,* 133, 135, 329.

73. Northup, *Twelve Years a Slave,* 191; Mason, *Life of Isaac Mason,* 27; Phillips and Glunt, eds., *Florida Plantation Records,* 116, 98, 107, 123–124; Grandy, *Narrative of Moses Grandy,* 8.

74. Buckingham, *Slave States,* I, 208; Olmsted, *Texas,* 104–105; *Seaboard States,* 189.

75. Lyell, *Travels,* I, 135.

Chapter 7: Masters of Tradition

1. The following paragraphs draw heavily on David Roberts, *Paternalism in Early Victorian England* (New Brunswick, N.J., 1979).

2. Gavin Diary, entry for May 31, 1856; Alfred Huger Papers, *passim.*

3. Bruce E. Steiner, "A Planter's Troubled Conscience," *JSH,* XXXVIII (1962), 346. For evidence of the pervasiveness of familial rhetoric throughout antebellum America, along with a provocative interpretation, see George B. Forgie, *Patricide in the House Divided: A Psychological Interpretation of Lincoln and His Age* (New York, 1979).

4. See Appendix, Table D.

5. Buckingham, *Slave States,* I, 166, 284–308. For the historical origins of this perimeter, see text, chap. 1.

6. Isaac Guion to Frederick Guion, April 22, 1816 and June 21, 1819, Guion Papers; G. W. Sargent to George Sargent, Dec. 28, 1851, George Washington Sargent Papers.

7. LeRoy P. Graf and Ralph W. Haskins, eds., "The Letters of a Georgia Unionist: John G. Winter and Secession," *Ga. Hist. Quar.,* XLV (1961), 385–391; von Briesen, ed., *Letters of Elijah Fletcher, passim;* Tise, "Proslavery Ideology," shows that a substantial percentage of proslavery ideologues were born or educated in the North and were influenced by northeastern federalism.

8. Henry Watson, Jr., to Henry Watson, Esq., Jan. 30, 1839, Watson Papers.

9. Henry Watson, Jr., to Julia Watson, April 29, 1842; Henry Watson, Jr., to Henry Watson, Esq., Aug. 23, 1835; Henry Watson, Jr., to William Watson, April 30, 1834; Henry Watson, Jr., to Henry Watson, Esq., Feb. 6, 1837, Watson Papers.

10. Henry Watson, Jr., to Henry Watson, Esq., Feb. 10, 1834 and Dec. 15, 1836; Henry Watson, Jr., to Julius Reed, July 23, 1834, Watson Papers.

11. Henry Watson, Jr., to Rev. Philip B. Wiley, Nov. 28, 1835; Henry Watson, Jr., to Julia Watson, July 15, 1834; Henry Watson, Jr., to Henry Watson, Esq., Feb. 10, 1834, Watson Papers.

12. Henry Watson, Jr., to Sarah Carrington, Jan. 28, 1861, Watson Papers.

13. Samuel Walker Diary, entry for Feb. 22, 1856. See also Michael P. Johnson, "Planters and Patriarchy: Charleston, 1800–1860," *JSH,* XLVI (1980), 45–72.

14. Clement Comer Clay to Clement C. Clay, John W. Clay, and Hugh L. Clay, July 7, 1827; William Clay to Clement Comer Clay, March 22, 1829, Clay Papers.

15. G. W. Sargent to G. W. Sargent, Dec. 28, 1851, Sargent Papers.

16. Henry Watson, Jr., to Julia Watson, April 25, 1841, Watson Papers; William Withers to Clement Claiborne Clay, Aug. 3, 1834, Clay Papers.

17. Henry L. Duffel Book.

18. Walker Diary, entry for Feb. 17, 1856.

19. DeSaussure Plantation Record; "Last Will and Testament," July 20, 1843, Zephaniah Kingsley Papers; J. M. C. Breaker to W. E. Ellis, Nov. 30, 1852, Ellis Family Papers; David B. Witherspoon to Susan McDowall, July 2, 1840, Witherspoon and McDowall Papers.

20. Henry Watson, Jr., to Julia Watson, May 26, 1844, Watson Papers; Juliana Margaret Conner Diary, entries for 1827; *American Farmer,* III (1841), 229.

21. Gaustad, *Historical Atlas of Religion in America,* 69, 105; Baker Diary, entry for Sept. 25, 1855.

22. Duffel Book; Sarah Guion to John Isaac Guion, July 30, 1818, Guion Papers.

23. Avery Craven, *Edmund Ruffin, Southerner: A Study in Secession* (New York, 1932; reprinted Baton Rouge, La., 1972), 39–40.

24. For a brief discussion of southern Whigs within the context of slaveholding politics, see text, chap. 5; Duffel Book; Walker Diary, entry for Feb. 22, 1856.

25. Von Briesen, ed., *Letters of Elijah Fletcher,* 105; Gavin Diary, entry for Feb. 9, 1856.

26. Ulrich B. Phillips, "The Course of the South to Secession: An Answer of Race," *Ga. Hist. Quar.,* XXI (1937), 313; Herbert J. Doherty, Jr., "Union Nationalism in Florida," *Fla. Hist. Quar.,* XXIX (1950), 90; Gavin Diary, entry for Feb. 9, 1856.

27. Scarborough, ed., *Diary of Edmund Ruffin,* I, 237; Alfred Huger to Judge King, Oct. 12, 1853, Huger Papers; Gavin Diary, entry for July 4, 1856.

28. Gavin Diary, entry for Nov. 9, 1855; Henry Watson, Jr., to William Watson, April 30, 1834; Henry Watson, Jr., to Edward Watson, March 21, 1850. See also Henry Watson's hostile reaction to New York City's expanding immigrant population in a letter to his wife, June 18, 1848, Watson Papers.

29. Henry Watson, Jr., to Saul Judson, June 6, 1833; Henry Watson, Jr., to Sophia Watson, June 12, 1848, Watson Papers.

30. "A Treatise on the Patriarchal or Cooperative System of Society . . . Under the Name of Slavery," Kingsley Papers.

31. *Ibid.;* see also Kingsley's "Last Will . . ."; Scarborough, ed., *Diary of Edmund Ruffin,* I, 277, 102.

32. George Fitzhugh, *Sociology for the South, or the Failure of Free Society* (Richmond, Va., 1854), 221; *DeBow's Review,* VIII (1850), 235, and XXVI (1859), 554.

33. George Fitzhugh, *Cannibals All! or, Slaves Without Masters,* ed. and introd., C. Vann Woodward (Cambridge, Mass., 1960), 57–64; Scarborough, ed., *Diary of Edmund Ruffin,* I, 240–241. As Ruffin put it: Fitzhugh's "opposition to interest or capital, which is in fact opposition to the accumulation of capital (as what inducement would there be to accumulate, if it could yield no profit?) is foolish." *DeBow's Review,* VIII (1850), 235–236; *American Cotton Planter,* II (1854), 66–67; *Cotton Planter and Soil of the South,* IV (1860), 57–64.

34. *Cotton Planter and Soil of the South,* III (1859), 12.

35. Fitzhugh, *Sociology,* 70–71; *DeBow's Review,* XVIII (1855), 475; *ibid.,* VIII

(1850), 339–347; *ibid.*, VII (1849), 379; Scarborough, ed., *Diary of Edmund Ruffin*, I, 200, and see also 202, 248, 304, 315.

36. Alfred Huger to Dr. Benjamin Huger, Sept. 4, 1853, Huger Papers; Scarborough, ed., *Diary of Edmund Ruffin*, I, 220; *DeBow's Review*, XXVII (1859), 522–523. See also Fitzhugh, *Cannibals All!*, 11, 40, 58, 81, 199, 258–259, for Fitzhugh's repeated insistence that the North was an exception.

37. Fitzhugh, *Sociology*, 23, 45, 84, 113–114; Baker Diary, entry for Feb. 13, 1849. Baker resolved to avoid companions who were "lax of morals or dissolute of habits"; Gavin Diary, entry for Sept. 29, 1855. Ill health convinced Gavin to end his self-imposed chastity. "If a man lives single until he is forty years old, he should have intercourse, even unlawfully, or his health will be impaired." See also *American Cotton Planter*, I (1857), 7, for a typical assault on northern "Universalism, Mormonism, Fourierism, Freelovism, Higherlawism, and the like."

38. Alfred Huger to Henrietta Huger, Dec. 3, 1853, Huger Papers; *American Cotton Planter*, II (1854), 76. Despite intertwined racial destinies, the writer warned whites to "take care that *contact do not assimilate* us too much to him [the black man]."

39. Fitzhugh, *Cannibals All!*, 134.

40. *American Cotton Planter*, II (1854), 76; *DeBow's Review*, XI (1851), 185–188. The best discussion of Cartwright's place in the racist defense of bondage is in Fredrickson, *Black Image in the White Mind* (New York, 1971), esp. chap. 2.

41. Fitzhugh's "abhorrence" was for the theory that blacks and whites were not descended from a "common parentage." He still believed, however, that blacks—for whatever reasons—were inferior to whites. See *Sociology*, 95, and the chapters on "Negro Slavery" in both *Sociology*, 82–95, and *Cannibals All!*, 199–203. Part of the problem stems from Fitzhugh's well-known inability to make himself clearly understood. Partly it was Fitzhugh's 1861 announcement that he had become convinced of what he previously denied, that "the negro is of a different species," not simply inferior to the white man.

42. Fitzhugh, *Cannibals All!*, 201, and Fitzhugh, *Sociology*, 147.

43. Fitzhugh, *Cannibals All!*, 199.

44. *DeBow's Review*, XXIV (1858), 314; J. Minor to L. M. Blackford, March 4, 1860, Blackford Letters; Walker Diary, entry for Feb. 15, 1856; *DeBow's Review*, XXIV (1858), 508–509.

45. Drew Gilpin Faust, *A Sacred Circle: The Dilemma of the Intellectual in the Old South, 1840–1860* (Baltimore, Md., 1977), 2, 18, and *passim*.

46. "Treatise . . . ," Kingsley Papers; Fitzhugh, *Sociology*, 106.

47. *Cotton Planter and Soil of the South*, IV (1860), 261.

48. Alfred Huger to Henrietta Huger, Dec. 5, 1853, Huger Papers; Scarborough, ed., *Diary of Edmund Ruffin*, I, 18–20, 355–356, 456, 464, 470.

49. Scarborough, ed., *Diary of Edmund Ruffin*, I, 288, 81–82; Henry Watson, Jr., to Julia Watson, Nov. 27, 1851, Watson Papers; G. W. Sargent to George Sargent, April 29, 1852, Sargent Papers.

50. Clement Claiborne Clay to Clement Comer Clay, May 28, 1832, Clay Papers.

51. Conservatives were not the Whig party's only constituency by any means. See, for example, Sellers, "Who Were the Southern Whigs?" in Pessen, ed., *New Perspectives,* 109–123; Carl N. Degler, *The Other South: Southern Dissenters in the Nineteenth Century* (New York, 1974), 160–163, demonstrates the continuity of Whiggery and Unionism. For a different view, see Michael P. Johnson, *Toward a Patriarchal Republic* (Baton Rouge, La., 1977).

52. Reid Diary, entry for Aug. 12, 1835; Doherty, Jr., "Union Nationalism in Florida," 88.

53. G. W. Sargent to Winthrop Sargent, Dec. 15, 1859, Sargent Papers; Henry Watson, Jr., to [?], Dec. 12, 1859, Watson Papers.

54. J. Minor to [?], Oct. 13, 1860, Blackford Letters; Doherty, Jr., "Union Nationalism in Florida," 90; William M. E. Rachal, ed., " 'Secession Is Nothing but Revolution': A Letter of R. E. Lee to his son Rooney," *Va. Mag. Hist. Biog.,* 69 (1961), 6.

55. Graf and Haskins, eds., "Letters of a Georgia Unionist," 390; Johnson, *Toward a Patriarchal Republic,* 54.

56. Anderson Diary, entries for June, 1862; Edward Taylor to J. Minor, 1861, Blackford Letters; Graf and Haskins, eds., "Letters of a Georgia Unionist," 390.

57. Anderson Diary, entry for Oct. 24, 1860; G. W. Sargent to Winthrop Sargent, Dec. 5, 1860, Sargent Papers.

58. Henry Watson, Jr., to Messrs. Thayer and Peck, Dec. 14, 1860; Henry Watson, Jr., to Julia Watson, Dec. 28, 1860; Henry Watson, Jr., to [?], Dec. 12, 1859, Watson Papers; Johnson, *Toward a Patriarchal Republic,* 28–31; J. Minor to [?], 1861, Blackford Letters; Rachal, ed., " 'Secession Is Revolution,' " 6; J. Carlysle Sitterson, "The William J. Minor Plantations: A Study in Ante-bellum Absentee Ownership," *JSH,* IX (1943), 61; G. W. Sargent to Winthrop Sargent, Oct. 30, 1860, Sargent Papers; Anderson Diary, entries for June, 1862.

59. Henry Watson, Jr., to Messrs. Thayer and Peck, Dec. 14, 1860, Watson Papers. Cooperationists were not all conservative, but most conservatives were cooperationist. For a brief discussion of the divisions among white Southerners at secession, see the Epilogue of the present work.

60. G. W. Sargent to Winthrop Sargent, Oct. 30, 1860, Sargent Papers; Rachal, ed., " 'Secession Is Revolution,' " 6.

Epilogue: The Slaveholders' Revolution

1. Florida, *Journal of the Proceedings of the Convention of the People of Florida* (Tallahassee, Fla., 1861), 8; Mississippi, *Proceedings of the Mississippi State Convention* (Jackson, Miss., 1861), 47; "Alexander H. Stephens and Judge Henry Baldwin. "Slavery, the Corner Stone," *Tyler's,* XI (1930), 11.

2. Eric Williams, *Capitalism and Slavery* (New York, 1944), argues that slavery built and was in turn destroyed by capitalism. See also D. A. Farnie, *The English Cotton Industry and the World Market, 1815–1896* (Oxford, 1979), 3–44, 81–134. *Southern Cultivator,* XVII (1859), 125. This and the following paragraph draw heavily on North, *Economic Growth of the United States,* 69–74, 205–206, and *passim.*

3. Soltow, *Men and Wealth,* 57. The figures are analyzed effectively in Wright, *Political Economy of the Cotton South,* 29–37, but see below, Chapter 2, n. 6. The slave population never grew as quickly as the white population in the Old South, but after 1830 the difference in the growth rates widened, despite erratic rises and falls from decade to decade. From 1800 to 1830 the slave population grew by 125%; from 1830 to 1860 it grew by 97%. Kennedy, *Preliminary Report on the Eighth Census,* 133.

4. Wright, *Political Economy of the Cotton South,* 29–32.

5. Takaki, *Pro-Slavery Crusade,* 63.

6. Olmsted, *Back Country,* 240; Takaki, *Pro-Slavery Crusade,* 66.

7. Johnson, *Toward a Patriarchal Republic,* 127; Takaki, *Pro-Slavery Crusade,* 64–65.

8. Scarborough, ed., *Diary of Edmund Ruffin,* I, 67–68.

9. *Southern Cultivator,* XVI (1858), 137.

10. Florida, *Journal of the Proceedings of the House of Representatives* (Tallahassee, Fla., 1858), 29–30; *DeBow's Review,* XXIII (1857), 211.

11. Alabama, *Journal of the Senate* (Montgomery, Ala., 1858), 23.

12. Richmond *Enquirer,* Jan. 1, 1820; Louisiana, *Journal of the House of Representatives* (New Orleans, La., 1850), 11; Reese, ed., *Proceedings,* I, 71; Texas, *Journal of the Secession Convention of Texas* (Austin, Tex., 1861; reprinted 1912), 46.

13. Christian Boye to his son, Sept. 23, 1862, Christian Boye Letter; Reese, ed., *Proceedings,* I, 80.

14. Sereno Taylor to Calvin Taylor, Nov. 7, 1859, Calvin Taylor and Family Papers; Darden Diary, entry for Nov. 3, 1859; Lawrence Diary, entry for Dec. 3, 1859.

15. Richmond *Enquirer,* Aug. 17, 1860.

16. William R. Smith, *The History and Debates of the Convention of the People of Alabama* (Atlanta, Ga., 1861), 94.

17. Reese, ed., *Proceedings,* I, 66.

18. Tennessee, *Journal of the House of Representatives* (Nashville, Tenn., 1854), 43; Mississippi, *Journal of the Senate of the State of Mississippi* (Jackson, Miss., 1854); Leonidas Pendleton Spyker Diary, entry for July 4, 1860; G. W. Sargent to Mary Duncan, Dec. 21, 1861, Sargent Papers. I have not attempted to analyze in detail the secessionist movement in the South, but have tried to show that the way slaveholders viewed the crisis followed logically from their traditional assumptions. For a thorough review of the literature on secession, see David M. Potter, *The Impending Crisis, 1848–1861,* completed and edited by Don E. Fehrenbacher (New York, 1976), 485–554.

19. Bills Diary, entry for Nov. 7, 1860. Stephen Howard Hahn, "The Roots of Southern Populism: Yeomen Farmers and the Transformation of Georgia's Upper Piedmont" (Ph.D. dissertation, Yale University, 1979), is the best study to date. Hahn presents evidence of increasing class conflicts between slaveholders and non-slaveholders in the 1850's, climaxing in widespread opposition to secession in low-slaveholding areas. He is careful not to suggest that this tension represented yeoman repudiation of racism, or hostility to slavery per se. Instead, Hahn argues that the roots of this tension grew from intrinsic contradictions between the subsistence culture of the yeomen and the culture of the slaveholders.

20. Jones Diary, entry for Jan. 10, 1861; Lawrence Diary, entry for Dec. 25, 1860; Eliza Ann Willson to Willson, Dec. 29, 1860, Willson, Whitehead, and Houston Papers.

21. Reese, ed., *Proceedings,* I, 43, 47; J. Minor to M. B. Blackford, [?] 1861, Blackford Letters. The "Majority Report of the Committee on Federal Relations" included a clearly cooperationist resolution, number six, and a series of proposed amendments to protect slavery. For the text of the report see Reese, ed., *Proceedings,* I, 523–528. The sixth resolution was adopted on April 5, but eight days later news of Fort Sumter reached the convention, see *ibid.,* III, 189. Lincoln's Secretary of War asked Virginia to supply troops to the Union Army, provoking renewed debate which ended in secession, *ibid.,* IV, 74.

22. Clarence Phillips Denman, *The Secession Movement in Alabama* (Montgomery, Ala., 1933), 93–95.

23. Louisiana, *Official Journal of the Proceedings of the Convention of the State of Louisiana* (New Orleans, La., 1861), 5.

24. Greenwood Plantation Journal, entry for Dec. 20, 1860; see also above, chap. 7, 283–288; Smith, *Alabama Debates,* 29, 82–83.

25. Smith, *Alabama Debates,* 97–98; Mississippi, *Proceedings,* 15, and in general 13–15, 68–69.

26. Johnson, *Toward a Patriarchal Republic,* 14.

27. Florida, *Journal of the Proceedings of the House of Representatives* (Tallahassee, Fla., 1848), 17; Reese, ed., *Proceedings,* II, 533; see the remarkable "Declaration of the immediate causes which induce and justify the secession of the State of Mississippi from the Federal Union," in Mississippi, *Proceedings,* 47–48; Texas, *Journal of the House of Representatives* (Austin, Tex., 1860), 49; Tennessee, *Journal of the House of Representatives* (Nashville, Tenn., 1854), 832.

28. The cooperationist response to Yancey's speech was typically conservative. "What a commentary on the charity of party majorities!" Robert Jemison declared. "The history of the reign of terror furnishes not a parallel to the bloody picture shadowed forth in the remarks of the gentleman." Also: "Is this in the spirit of Southern chivalry?" Smith, *Alabama Debates,* 69, 72; William L. Barney, *The Secessionist Impulse, Alabama and Mississippi in 1860* (Princeton, N.J., 1974), 110.

29. *Declaration of the immediate causes which induce and justify the Secession of South Carolina* (Charleston, S.C., 1860), 40; North Carolina, *Journal of the House*

of Commons (Raleigh, N.C., 1861), 40; "Extracts from the Circular of the Minute Men of South Carolina," Grace Elmore Diary, entry for Oct. 7, 1860; Frank [?] to Eliza Willson, April 26, 1861, Willson, Whitehead, and Houston Papers.

30. George Ward Nichols, *The Story of the Great March* (New York, 1865), 302; Smith, *Alabama Debates,* 32; Johnson, *Toward a Patriarchal Republic,* 28–29; Texas, *Convention Journal,* 16–17.

31. "Diary of John Berkley Grimball, 1858–1865," *So. Car. Hist. Mag.,* LVI (1955), 101; Denman, *Secession Movement in Alabama,* 88n.

32. Florida, *Convention Proceedings,* 8; Texas, *Convention Journal,* 16–17; *DeBow's Review,* XXIV (1858), 314–315.

33. See the important analysis in Potter, *Impending Crisis,* 448–484; Denman, *Secession in Alabama,* 96; Alabama, *Ordinances and Constitution of the State of Alabama* (Montgomery, Ala., 1861), 32.

34. Gilbert Osofsky, ed., *Puttin' on Ole Massa* (New York, 1969), 205.

Bibliography

Manuscripts Consulted

Duke University Library, Durham, North Carolina

William Baskerville Papers
William Berkeley Papers
A. R. Boteler Diary
Branch Family Papers
Samuel Bryarly Papers
Clement C. Clay Papers
John Clopton Papers
James Rowe Coombs Papers
Bolling R. Chinn Account and Plantation Records
James Dove Papers
Sterling, Nevill, and Charles Gee Papers
Edward Harden Papers and Diary

Benjamin Harper Letters
David Hicks Ledgers and Day Books
Placebo Houston Papers
Alfred Huger Papers
Dugal McCall Plantation Journal and Diary
Peter Carr Minor and Hugh Minor Notebooks
Haller Nutt Journal
Henry L. Pinckney Plantation Book
A. M. Reed Diary
Louisa M. (Jelks) Sills Papers
Henry Watson, Jr., Papers

University of Florida Library, Gainesville, Florida

Henry Bond Accounts
Christian Boye Letter
William Cason Papers

James Gonzalez Papers
Zephaniah Kingsley Papers
J. H. Whitten Letter

Florida State Library, Tallahassee, Florida (WPA typescripts)

Blackford Letters
Grace Elmore Diary

Samuel Lewis Moore Autobiography
William Morton Travel Diary

William D. Moseley Diary
Sallie Camp Norfleet Autobiography
Robert Raymond Reid Diary
W. J. Simpson Diary

David L. White Diary
Judge William B. Young Autobio-
    graphy

University of Kentucky Library, Lexington, Kentucky

J. Winston Coleman Papers on Slavery
    in Kentucky

John W. Jones Diary

Library of Congress, Washington, D.C.

Anonymous Journal, Trip to New
    Orleans, 1811
John Brown of North Carolina, Jour-
    nal and Accounts
Charlotte Browne, Voyage from Lon-
    don to Virginia, 1754
George S. Denison Papers
Gideon Denison [Dennison] Letter-
    books
Stephen D. Doar Plantation Accounts
William Dunbar Letterbook
Edmund Pendleton Gaines Papers
Greenwood Plantation Journal
Habersham Family Papers
Journal of a Voyage up the Mississippi
and Red Rivers from New Orleans

Duncan Farrar Kenner Papers
Daniel Lord, Journal of a Trip from
    Baltimore to Savannah and
    return
William Lowndes Letterbook and
    Plantation Diary
Mississippi River Expeditions, Mis-
    cellaneous Manuscripts Collec-
    tions
James Monette Plantation Diary
William B. Randolph Plantation
    Accounts and Letters
Turner Reavis Account Book
Shirley Farm Journal
Stone Family of Maryland Papers
Moses Waddel Diary and Letters

Louisiana State University Library, Baton Rouge, Louisiana

Harrod C. Anderson Diary
James P. Bowman Papers
John C. Burruss and Family Papers, in
    the George M. Lester Collection
Martin Gordon, Jr., Letters, in the
    Benjamin Tureaud Papers
William S. Hamilton Papers
Hepzibah Church Records, 1813–1861
John C. Jenkins Diary
Eliza L. Magruder Diary
Henry Marston Diary

Mary Ann Colvin Mayfield Biography
John Mills Letters
Samuel Plaisted Correspondence
Alexander F. Pugh Diary
Joseph Toole Robinson Plantation
    Diary
H. M. Seale Diary
Leonidas Pendleton Spyker Diary
Calvin Taylor and Family Papers
Clarissa E. Leavitt Town Diary

Mississippi State Archives, Jackson, Mississippi

James Allen Plantation Book
Aventine Plantation Diary
Jefferson J. Birdsong Plantation Journal
Brookdale Farm Journal
Susan Sillers Darden Diary

Alden Spooner Forbes Diary
Killona Plantation Journals
James Trueman Magruder Papers
Walter Wade Plantation Diary

University of North Carolina, Chapel Hill, North Carolina
(Southern Historical Collection)

Samuel Agnew Diary
Alexander and Hillhouse Family Papers
George Washington Allen Papers
Archibald Davis Alston Papers
Rufus Amis Papers
Archibald Hunter Arrington Papers
James B. Bailey Papers
Everard Green Baker Diary
Barrow Family Paper
Mary E. Bateman Diary
Mary (Jeffreys) Bethell Diary
John Houston Bills Diary
Branch Family Papers
John Peter Broun Papers
Brownrigg Family Papers
Mrs. William Buchanan Papers
Buchanan and McClellan Family Papers
William Byrd Papers
Tod Robinson Caldwell Papers
Mrs. Eliza Eve Carmichael Diary, in Carmichael Family Books
John Fletcher Comer Book
Louis M. DeSaussure Plantation Record
Henry L. Duffel Book
John Rust Eaton Papers
William Ethelbert Ervin Books
Benjamin Fitzpatrick Papers
Gale and Polk Family Papers
David Gavin Diary
William Proctor Gould Diary
William P. Graham Papers

Guion Family Papers
Pinckney Cotesworth Harrington Papers
James Thomas Harrison Papers
Laurens Hinton Papers
George W. House Papers
Hubard Family Papers
Robert Jemison Proclamation to his slaves
Johnston and McFaddin Family Papers
David and Mary Ker Papers
Kollock Plantation Books
Edward McCrady L'Engle Papers
Francis Terry Leak Books
Lewis Plantation Records
Lipscomb Family Papers
William Lytle Papers
McDonald and Irving Family Papers
John Morel Paper
Theodore Davidson Morrison Papers
Myers Family Papers
John Nevitt Diary
Rebecca S. C. Pilsbury Diary
Philip H. Pitts Diary
William Polk Papers
Douglas Watson Porter Papers
Randolph and Yates Family Papers
Roulstone and Dinwiddie Family Papers
George Washington Sargent Papers
James Shackelford Paper
Thompson Family Papers
Whitaker and Snipes Family Papers

Robert W. Withers Papers
Witherspoon and McDowall Family
   Papers

Wooley Family Papers
Wyche and Otey Family Papers

North Carolina State Archives, Raleigh, North Carolina

Moses Bledsoe Papers
Richard Cogdell Papers
Juliana Margaret Conner Diary, in
   Alexander Brevard Papers
Rosalie Ferrell Collection
James F. Jordan Paper

Dr. Francis J. Kron Diary, in W. K.
   Littleton Collection
Nathaniel Macon Papers
Benajah Nicholls Papers
Pettigrew Papers
William S. Pettigrew Papers

University of South Carolina, Columbia, South Carolina
(South Caroliniana Library)

Elias Ball Papers
John Ewing Colhoun Letters
Margaret Colleton Papers
Ellis Family Papers
Andrew Flinn Plantation Book
Samuel Porcher Gaillard Plantation
   Journals

Michael Gramling Plantation Journal
Alexander Keith Commonplace Book
Thomas Lowndes Letter
William Gilmore Simms Plantation
   Book
Samuel Thomas Letters, in Thomas
   Family Papers

South Carolina Department of Archives and History, Columbia, S.C.

Charleston County Record of Wills
General Assembly Slave Manumission

Petitions, 1815–1830

Tennessee State Library and Archives, Nashville, Tennessee

Esther Wright Boyd Memoirs
Joseph Brown Papers

William Luther Bigelow Lawrence
   Diary, in Lawrence Family Papers

Tulane University Library, New Orleans, Louisiana

Dr. McGuire Diary
David Washington Pipes Diary

Samuel Walker "Diary of a Louisiana
   Planter"

University of Virginia, Charlottesville, Virginia
(Alderman Library)

Richard Randolph's Will

Willson, Whitehead, and Houston
   Papers

Virginia Historical Society, Richmond, Virginia

William Cabell Commonplace Book   B. C. Rousseau "Negro Book"
Robert Carter Letterbook   William Macon Waller Letters
Robert Leslie Account Book   Henry Alexander Wise Papers
John Francis Page Commonplace Book   John George Woolfolk Account Book

Virginia State Library, Richmond, Virginia

Jerdone Family Slave Record Book   William Massie Farm Journal

Selected Bibliography

(This list includes only those works cited more than once in the notes.)

Abdy, Edward S. *Journal of a Residence and Tour in the United States of North America, 1833–1834.* 3 vols. London, 1835.

Abel, Annie Heloise. *The Slaveholding Indians.* 3 vols. Cleveland, Ohio, 1915.

Alexander, Edward Porter, ed. *The Journal of John Fontaine: An Irish-Huguenot Son in Spain and Virginia, 1710–1719.* Williamsburg, Va., 1972.

Alsop, George. *A Character of the Province of Maryland.* London, 1666.

Axford, Faye Acton, ed. *The Journals of Thomas Hubbard Hobbs.* University, Ala., 1976.

Bailey, David Thomas. "Slavery and the Churches: The Old Southwest." Ph.D. dissertation, University of California, Berkeley, 1979.

Barney, William L. *The Secessionist Impulse: Alabama and Mississippi in 1860.* Princeton, N.J., 1974.

Berlin, Ira. *Slaves Without Masters: The Free Negro in the Antebellum South.* New York, 1974.

Blassingame, John W. *The Slave Community: Plantation Life in the Antebellum South.* Rev. ed. New York, 1979.

Boles, John B. *The Great Revival: The Origins of the Southern Evangelical Mind, 1787–1805.* Lexington, Ky., 1972.

Brathwait, Richard. *The English Gentleman: Containing Sundry excellent Rules, or exquisite Observations, tending to Direction of every Gentleman, of selecter ranke and Qualitie.* 2d ed. London, 1633.

Brickell, John. *The Natural History of North Carolina.* Dublin, 1737.

Bruce, Henry Clay. *The New Man: Twenty-nine Years a Slave, Twenty-nine Years a Freeman.* York, Penn., 1895.

Buckingham, James Silk. *The Slave States of America.* 2 vols. London, 1842.

Bullock, William. *Virginia Impartially Examined . . .* London, 1649.

Carrigan, Jo Ann. "Impact of Epidemic Yellow Fever on Life in Louisiana." *La. Hist.,* IV (1963), 5–34.

Curtin, Philip D. *The Atlantic Slave Trade: A Census.* Madison, Wisc., 1969.

Davis, Edwin Adams, ed. *Plantation Life in the Florida Parishes of Louisiana, 1836–1846, As Reflected in the Diary of Bennet H. Barrow.* New York, 1943, reprinted 1967.

Denman, Clarence Phillips. *The Secession Movement in Alabama.* Montgomery, Ala., 1933.

Des Champs, Margaret Burr, ed. "Some Mississippi Letters to Robert Fraser, 1841–1844." *Jour. Miss. Hist.,* XV (1953), 181–189.

Dew, Charles B. "David Ross and the Oxford Iron Works: A Study of Industrial Slavery in the Early Nineteenth-century South." *WMQ,* 3rd Ser., XXXI (1974), 189–224.

Doherty, Herbert J., Jr. "Union Nationalism in Florida." *Fla. Hist. Quar.,* XXIX (1950), 83–95.

Douglass, Frederick. *My Bondage and My Freedom.* New York, 1855.

Eaton, Clement. *The Growth of Southern Civilization.* New York, 1961.

Fitzhugh, George. *Cannibals All! or, Slaves Without Masters.* Ed. C. Vann Woodward. Cambridge, Mass., 1960.

Fitzhugh, George. *Sociology for the South, or the Failure of Free Society.* Richmond, Va., 1854.

Flint, Timothy. *Recollections of the Last Ten Years.* Boston, 1826.

Florida. *Journal of the Proceedings of the Convention of the People of Florida.* Tallahassee, Fla., 1861.

Fredrickson, George M. *The Black Image in the White Mind: The Debate on Afro-American Character and Destiny, 1817–1914.* New York, 1971.

Gaustad, Edwin Scott. *Historical Atlas of Religion in America.* Rev. ed. New York, 1976.

Genovese, Eugene D. *Roll, Jordan, Roll: The World the Slaves Made.* New York, 1974.

Gosse, Philip Henry. *Letters from Alabama.* London, 1859.

Graff, Leroy P. and Ralph W. Haskins, eds. "The Letters of a Georgia Unionist: John G. Winter and Secession." *Ga. Hist. Quar.,* XLV (1961), 385–402.

Graham, Ian C. C. *Colonists from Scotland: Emigration to North America, 1707–1783.* Ithaca, N.Y., 1956.

Grandy, Moses. *Narrative of the Life of Moses Grandy.* Boston, 1844.

Green, Fletcher Melvin, ed. *The Lides Go South . . . And West, The Record of a Planter Migration in 1835.* Columbia, S.C., 1952.

Grimes, J. Bryan, ed. *North Carolina Wills and Inventories.* Raleigh, N.C., 1912.

Higginbotham, A. Leon, Jr. *In the Matter of Color: Race and the American Legal Process; The Colonial Period.* New York, 1978.

Hogan, William Ransom and Edwin Adams Davis, eds. *William Johnson's Natchez: The Ante-bellum Diary of a Free Negro.* Baton Rouge, La., 1951.

Hughes, Louis. *Thirty Years a Slave: From Bondage to Freedom.* Milwaukee, Wisc., 1897.

Hundley, Daniel R. *Social Relations in our Southern States.* New York, 1860.

Ingraham, Joseph Holt. *The Southwest. By a Yankee.* 2 vols. New York, 1835.

James, Newton Haskin. "Josiah Hinds: Versatile Pioneer of the Old Southwest." *Jour. Miss. Hist.,* II (1940), 22–33.

"James M. Torbert's Plantation Journal for 1856." *Ala. Hist. Quar.,* 18 (1956), 218–280.

"James M. Torbert's Journal for 1857–1874." *Ala. Hist. Quar.,* 22 (1960), 1–76.

Johnson, Michael P. *Toward a Patriarchal Republic: The Secession of Georgia.* Baton Rouge, La., 1977.

Jones, Hugh. *The Present State of Virginia.* London, 1724.

Jordan, Winthrop D. *White over Black: American Attitudes Toward the Negro, 1550–1812.* Chapel Hill, N.C., 1968.

Keckley, Elizabeth. *Behind the Scenes.* New York, 1868.

Kennedy, Joseph C. G. *Preliminary Report on the Eighth Census.* Washington, D.C., 1862.

Land, Aubrey. "Genesis of a Colonial Fortune: Daniel Dulany of Maryland." *WMQ,* 3rd Ser., VII (1950), 255–269.

Land, Aubrey, *et al.,* eds. *Law, Society and Politics in Early Maryland.* Baltimore and London, 1977.

The Lee Papers. N. Y. Hist. Soc., *Coll.* Vol. V. New York, 1873.

Lemmon, Sarah McCulloh, ed. *The Pettigrew Papers.* Vol. I. Raleigh, N. C., 1971.

The Letters of Honorable James Habersham, 1756–1775. Ga. Hist. Soc., *Coll.* Vol. VI. Savannah, Ga., 1904.

Levine, Lawrence W. *Black Culture and Black Consciousness: Afro-American Folk Thought from Slavery to Freedom.* New York, 1977.

Loewald, Klaus G., *et al.,* eds. and trans. "Johann Martin Bolzius Answers a questionnaire on Carolina and Georgia." *WMQ,* 3rd Ser., XIV (1957), 218–261.

Lyell, Charles. *A Second Visit to the United States.* 2 vols. New York, 1849.

———. *Travels in North America.* 2 vols. New York, 1845.

McLeod, Duncan J. *Slavery, Race and the American Revolution.* London, 1974.

Main, Jackson T. "The One Hundred." *WMQ,* 3rd Ser., XI (1954), 354–384.

Marshall, Thomas Maitland, ed. *The Life and Papers of Frederick Bates.* 2 vols. St. Louis, Mo., 1926.

Mason, Isaac. *Life of Isaac Mason as a Slave.* Worcester, Mass., 1893.

Mathews, Donald G. *Religion in the Old South.* Chicago, 1978.

Menn, Joseph Karl. *The Large Slaveholders of Louisiana—1860.* New Orleans, 1964.

Mississippi. *Proceedings of the Mississippi State Convention.* Jackson, Miss., 1861.

Mullin, Gerald. *Flight and Rebellion: Slave Resistance in Eighteenth-Century Virginia.* New York, 1972.

North, Douglass C. *The Economic Growth of the United States, 1790–1860.* Englewood Cliffs, N. J., 1961.

Northup, Solomon. *Twelve Years a Slave.* Ed. Sue Eakin and Joseph Logsdon. Auburn, N. Y., 1853, reprinted Baton Rouge, La., 1968.

Olmsted, Frederick Law. *A Journey in the Back Country.* New York, 1860.

————. *A Journey in the Seaboard Slave States.* New York, 1856.

————. *A Journey Through Texas.* London, 1859.

Owens, Leslie Howard. *This Species of Property: Slave Life and Culture in the Old South.* New York, 1976.

Owsley, Frank L. "The Clays in Early Alabama History." *Ala. Rev.,* II (1949), 243–268.

Pennington, James W. C. *The Fugitive Blacksmith.* London, 1849.

Perdue, Theda. *Slavery and the Evolution of Cherokee Society.* Knoxville, Tenn., 1979.

Phillips, Ulrich Bonnell, ed. *Plantation and Frontier, 1649–1873.* 2 vols. Cleveland, Ohio, 1910.

Phillips, Ulrich B. and James David Glunt, eds. *Florida Plantation Records from the Papers of George Noble Jones.* St. Louis, Mo., 1927.

Porter, Kenneth Wiggins. *The Negro on the American Frontier.* New York, 1971.

Potter, David M. *The Impending Crisis, 1848–1861.* Completed and ed. by Don E. Fehrenbacher. New York, 1976.

Price, Jacob M. *France and the Chesapeake.* 2 vols. Ann Arbor, Mich., 1973.

————. "The Rise of Glasgow in the Chesapeake Trade, 1707–1775." *WMQ,* 3rd Ser., XI (1954), 179–199.

Raboteau, Albert J. *Slave Religion: The "Invisible Institution" in the Antebellum South.* New York, 1978.

Rachal, William M. E., ed. " 'Secession Is Nothing but Revolution': A Letter of R. E. Lee to his son 'Rooney.' " *Va. Mag. Hist. Biog.,* 69 (1961), 3–6.

Reese, George H., ed. *Proceedings of the Virginia State Convention of 1861.* 4 vols. Richmond, Va., 1965.

Riley, Franklin L., ed. "Diary of a Mississippi Planter, January 1, 1840, to April, 1863." *Miss. Hist. Soc., Publ.,* X (1909), 305–481.

Rowland, Dunbar, comp. *Life, Letters and Papers of William Dunbar, 1749–1810.* Jackson, Miss., 1930.

Russell, John H. "Colored Freemen as Slave Owners in Virginia." *Jour. Negro Hist.,* I (1916), 233–242.

Scarborough, William Kauffman, ed., *Diary of Edmund Ruffin.* 2 vols. Baton Rouge, La., 1972.

Sitterson, J. Carlyle. "The William J. Minor Plantations: A Study in Ante-bellum Absentee Ownership." *JSH,* IX (1943), 59–74.

Smith, William R. *The History and Debates of the Convention of the People of Alabama.* Atlanta, Ga., 1861.

Soltow, Lee. "Economic Inequality in the United States in the Period from 1790 to 1860." *Jour. Econ. Hist.,* XXXI (1971), 822–839.

————. *Men and Wealth in the United States, 1850–1870.* New Haven, Conn., 1975.

Stampp, Kenneth M. *The Peculiar Institution: Slavery in the Antebellum South.* New York, 1956.

Steward, Austin. *Twenty-two Years a Slave and Forty Years a Freeman.* Rochester, N. Y., 1857.

Still, Bayrd, ed. "The Westward Migration of a Planter Pioneer in 1796." *WMQ,* 2d Ser., XXI (1941), 318–343.

Stroyer, Jacob. *My Life in the South.* Salem, Mass., 1898.

Sydnor, Charles S. *Slavery in Mississippi.* New York, 1933.

Takaki, Ronald T. *A Pro-Slavery Crusade: The Agitation to Reopen the African Slave Trade.* New York, 1971.

Taylor, Joe Gray. *Negro Slavery in Louisiana.* Baton Rouge, La., 1962.

Taylor, Orville W. "Baptists and Slavery in Arkansas: Relationships and Attitudes." *Ark. Hist. Quar.,* XXXVIII (1979), 199–226.

Texas. *Journal of the Secession Convention of Texas.* Austin, Tex., 1861, reprinted 1912.

Thornton, J. Mills, III. *Politics and Power in a Slave Society.* Baton Rouge, La., 1978.

Tise, Larry E. "Proslavery Ideology: A Social and Intellectual History of the Defense of Slavery in America, 1790–1840." Ph.D. dissertation, University of North Carolina at Chapel Hill, 1974.

von Briesen, Martha, ed., *The Letters of Elijah Fletcher.* Charlottesville, Va., 1965.

Wood, Peter. *Black Majority: Negroes in South Carolina from 1670 Through the Stono Rebellion.* New York, 1974.

Woodman, Harold D. *King Cotton and His Retainers.* Lexington, Ky., 1968.

Wooster, Ralph A. *The People in Power: Courthouse and Statehouse in the Lower South, 1850–1860.* Knoxville, Tenn., 1969.

————. *Politicians, Planters and Plain Folk: Courthouse and Statehouse in the Upper South, 1850–1860.* Knoxville, Tenn., 1975.

Wright, Gavin. " 'Economic Democracy' and the Concentration of Agricultural Wealth in the Cotton South, 1850–1860." *Agric. Hist.,* XLIV (1970), 63–85.

————. *The Political Economy of the Cotton South.* New York, 1978.

Wright, Louis B. and Marion Tinling, eds. *The Secret Diary of William Byrd of Westover, 1709–1712.* Richmond, Va., 1941.

Wust, Klaus. *The Virginia Germans.* Charlottesville, Va., 1969.

INDEX

abolitionism, 101–2, 130, 133, 136–7, 149, 150, 162–3, 208, 233–5
absentee ownership, 175, 219–20
"accommodation" or adaptation by slaves, 179–80
Acklen, Joseph, 155, 160
Adams, John, 140
age distribution of masters and slaves, 195–6
agricultural reform and reformers: critical of westward migration, 88–91, 204–5; in plantation management, 153–91
Alabama, 59, 73–86 passim, 139, 144
"Alabama Fever" (migration urge), 77
Alabama State Agricultural Association, 211
Allen, Alex, 64, 88
Allen, George, 81
Alsop, George, 5, 6
American Farmer (journal), 89
American Revolution, 28–33, 225–6; inspires secession, 239–42
Amis, Rufus, 75
Anderson, H. C., 80, 170, 222, 223
Anderson, Mary, 183
Anglican Church, 7, 193
anti-Catholicism, 130–1
anti-Semitism, 131
aristocracy: hostility toward, among

slaveholders, 137, 138, 143; slaveholders as, 37–41, 65–7, 256–7
Arkansas, 75, 79, 139, 144
Arkansas Gazette, 79
Arrington, Archibald, 66, 173, 175
Arrington, John, 66
artisans, 59–60

Bacon, Rev. Thomas, 5–6
Bailey, James, 183
Bailey, Mary, 78
Baker, Everard Green, 64, 103, 112, 113, 129, 164, 280
Baltimore, Md., 50
Baptists, 97; see also evangelical Protestantism
Barbour County Agricultural Society, 161
Barland, David, 48
Barland, William, 48
Barrett, James, 75
Barrow, Bennet, 148, 168, 170, 174–5, 180–2, 183, 189
Barrow, James, 114
Barry, James Buckner, 53–4
Bass, Samuel, 133
Bateman, Mary, 142–3
Bates, Frederick, 75, 118

A Note About the Author

James Oakes was born in New York City in 1953. He received a
B.A. from Baruch College, City University of New York, and an
M.A. and Ph.D. from the University of California, Berkeley. He is
currently teaching American history at Purdue University.